HILL, L.
Behind the screen
£5.50

Please renew/return this item by the last date shown.

So that your telephone call is charged at local rate, please call the numbers as set out below:

	From Area codes 01923 or 0208:	From the rest of Herts:
Renewals:	01923 471373	01438 737373
Enquiries:	01923 471333	01438 737333
Minicom:	01923 471599	01438 737599

L32b

Behind The Screen

The Broadcasting Memoirs of
LORD HILL OF LUTON

SIDGWICK & JACKSON
LONDON

First published in Great Britain in 1974
by Sidgwick and Jackson Limited

Copyright © 1974 by The Rt. Hon. Lord Hill of Luton

ISBN 0 283 98181 4

Printed in Great Britain by
The Anchor Press Limited, Tiptree, Essex
for Sidgwick and Jackson Limited
1 Tavistock Chambers, Bloomsbury Way
London, WC1A 2SG

To Marion

Contents

List of Illustrations

Preface

This book is not a treatise on the theory and practice of broadcasting or a scientific analysis of the role of the media in modern society. Rather is it a miscellany of personal recollection of the exciting years I spent with Independent Television and the British Broadcasting Corporation, prompted, in the case of the BBC years, by a diary in which I recorded not only events but my reactions to them, including the moods of delight and exasperation which they provoked. The labour involved was more an exercise in therapy than a contribution to history. Some of the diary entries are for my eye only. Even the entries I have chosen to include do not, I frankly recognize, stand up to the test of considered judgement or calm reflection. All that I can claim for them is that they faithfully recall my mood at the time.

I pondered for some time on the extent to which I could properly refer to the internal affairs of the BBC, balancing on the one hand the possible embarrassment to former colleagues and on the other the undoubted and justifiable public interest in the affairs of an important public body. I hope the balance is about right.

I have been greatly helped by many friends in both bodies, although none of them is in any way responsible for what I have written. I have reluctantly decided not to name them, lest this assurance should not prove enough to spare them embarrassment. But this need not apply to Mrs Hazel Fenton, my secretary for a quarter of a century, without whose persistent prodding and unfailing help this book would not have been written.

PART ONE

70 BROMPTON ROAD

1

ITA's New Boy

I was looking for a job. After ten years as a minister and five years in the Cabinet I had become redundant in July 1962.

I could not complain. Several months previously I had decided not to stand at the next general election and had expressed a wish to leave the Cabinet at the next re-shuffle. I ruled out returning to medicine as I had not practised for thirty years. My fame as a broadcaster had been a temporary wonder, unrepeatable.

In the autumn of 1962 – I was in Nigeria for a parliamentary conference – I read in the *Daily Express* that I was likely to become chairman of the Independent Television Authority. This was news to me. I had no reason to believe the story true. But I hoped it was. I had accepted an invitation to join the board of Laporte Industries, the chemical company, associated with my constituency, Luton. However, I needed more work to absorb my energies.

I heard no more of the *Daily Express* story until some months later when, on the infallible grapevine, I learned that Reg Bevins, the Postmaster General, was pressing my name on the Prime Minister for the ITA chairmanship. A difficulty was that my appointment to this job would mean a by-election in Luton, a marginal seat which the government might lose. Months passed and then in late May 1963 Mr Macmillan decided to risk the loss of a seat and to recommend me for a life peerage and the chairmanship of ITA. I was delighted to accept.

When I entered 70 Brompton Road, the headquarters of

Independant Television, on the first day of July 1963, my knowledge of broadcasting was slender. I had been Radio Doctor on the BBC during and after the war, rebuked by some and praised by others for my blunt indelicacy about bowels and prunes – 'black-coated workers' and 'the smallest room in the house' – and other embarrassing intimacies. But my broadcasting experience had given me little knowledge of its organization.

So I was virtually a new boy when I entered ITA headquarters on 1 July 1963. I was greeted by Sir Robert Fraser with his customary courtesy, and there began an association which matured into a firm friendship, despite some differences on the way. I never forgot, though he did not remind me, that this distinguished man was the architect of a service which, whatever its shortcomings, had become a national institution in less than seven years.

My first task was to assess the mood of Independent Television. It was still licking its wounds after the severe mauling it had suffered in the inquisition and report by the Pilkington Committee. Rather than answer the attack, it was standing in a corner and whimpering. Undeniably the Pilkington Committee had been brutal in its criticisms – so brutal, in fact, that the government, sensing that the BBC could not be so white nor ITV so black as Pilkington asserted, had rejected its main recommendations.

Independent Television had done well in the short period of its existence. A national service had been constructed from the ground in a few short years. At the outset it had had no alternative but to go all out for big audiences if it was to survive. Survival assured, now was the opportunity to improve the programmes and achieve the balance.

As the initial shock had worn off, some members of the Authority had come to recognize that the evidence given on its behalf to the committee had been, at least in some respects, an invitation to an adverse verdict. Put crudely, the Authority had asked for it. Quite early on, the Pilkington Committee had made clear the view eventually expressed in its report that television must be assumed to be a major factor in influencing the values and moral standards of our society, *unless and until there is unmistakable proof to the contrary.*

Yet in their evidence the spokesmen of the Authority, Sir Ivone Kirkpatrick and Sir Robert Fraser, had reservations about this doctrine of the social responsibility of television. Television was but one of the influences on society, they said. What had happened to society probably would have happened with or without television. On the other hand, Sir Hugh Greene, on behalf of the BBC, had virtually accepted the whole Pilkington doctrine. Who was right and who was wrong hardly counted : the ITA had begun its evidence on the wrong foot.

But this was not all. As I got around and listened to members of the Authority I found a feeling of something akin to guilt that they had exercised too little influence on the service. Robert Fraser was utterly devoted to this child of his creation, finding it difficult to see anything wrong in his growing offspring. If the companies erred they would realize their errors and in time correct them. They needed to be cossetted. Fraser saw ITV as one big happy and prosperous family. To the companies he was the Authority. So Authority members were not really in authority. They were observers, watching but not contributing – and certainly not controlling. The officials, dominated by the director-general, made the decisions; Authority members acquiesced.

*   *   *

Over the years I had been both a chief executive and a chairman. I had, for good or ill, developed my own style of chairmanship, based on discussion without undue repetition, and clear-cut decisions, succinctly worded. I disliked the raising of important matters under Any Other Business without warning or documentation – it is one of the oldest tricks of the bureaucratic world. Only in exceptional circumstances did I ever open a committee discussion from the chair with a statement of my own views, and I had little affection for the consensus type of committee discussion so beloved in Whitehall and not unknown in Cabinet which, after an exchange of views, leaves things floating in the air.

As a secretary I had learned, too, how indecision at board level left too much decision-making to the staff. What suited me as a secretary I discouraged as a chairman. While I preferred to reach conclusions without voting, I saw nothing wrong in majority decisions reached by show of hands where the consensus method would have enabled a minority of members to frustrate the wishes of the majority on an important isssue. Agreeing to differ is no substitute for decision in those cases where decisions are really needed. The consensus method is ideal where it is not intended (or desired) that a body should reach decisions. I was often told that my favourite phrase at the end of discussions was, 'Is the Authority now ready to reach a decision?'

My first impressions were these: there would have to be changes in the Authority's procedure; programme policy would have to be more positive; public relations needed a new approach.

But these would have to wait. I was faced with a more urgent problem.

2

The Authority and the Companies

At my first meeting of the Authority I immediately sensed a warm and friendly atmosphere. I remembered this with a wry smile four years later at my first BBC governors' meeting. Sir John Carmichael, the deputy chairman, used some pleasantly welcoming words. I responded by expressing the Authority's appreciation of his acting chairmanship over the past eight months, and we were speedily away on the business of the meeting.

The main issues for early decision were those relating to new contracts. Existing contracts would expire in little more than a year's time and the successful applicants, particularly if they were new to the job, would need adequate time to prepare. The fourth of December 1963 was the first of four exhausting days of interviewing applicants. With one or two exceptions the competition offered to existing companies was neither keen nor impressive.

Of the new applicants one made a strong impression. It was the so-called Morris Finer group, headed by a lawyer, Morris Finer, QC, and comprising Dennis Vance, John Burton, Wilfred Brown and C. R. McGregor. It set out to become a kind of United Artists, with the creative people in a dominant position. I liked the people and the project. It had often been said that in ITV there were too many hard-faced business men in control, concerned more with balance sheets than with programme quality; that writers and producers played too little part in policy. I and some of my colleagues probed this group about finance, to which they had given little attention in their application. Yet this was fundamental, for ideas are no good without resources. Their application foundered on this point. It was a pity. The Authority decided that none of the new applications justified the unseating of a sitting tenant.

I recall one minor incident which occurred during the hearing of a Scottish application. At the end of the row before us, I saw a great figure of a man I had not seen before. 'Who is that ugly one at the end of the row?' I asked Robert Fraser beneath my hand. 'That, chairman,' he whispered, 'is Arnold Goodman, the ablest man in the room.' I was to learn the truth of that statement before I left the ITA. Lord Goodman has become one of the great brains of our national life.

During my first six months in the chair at ITA we had frequent brushes with Granada. I was soon to learn that this was the most difficult and the most enterprising of companies. It did not take kindly to the exercise of authority from above.

I came to doubt whether Sidney (now Lord) Bernstein, its presiding genius, really accepted the constraints of the Television Act. Once committed to a cause or a campaign, he saw little virtue in balancing opposing views. That way, he held, lay programme death. He regarded the Authority as a body to be convinced of Granada's virtues after a plunge into dangerous waters, rather than one to be consulted in a programme's formative stages. Yet, despite the fact of living dangerously – or maybe because of it – Granada was live, vigorous and imaginative

Because of frequent brushes, the Authority decided at my second meeting to vet feature programmes, like *World in Action*, before transmission. When Miss Mandy Rice-Davies, who had been prominent in a famous sex scandal, visited her old school to talk to girls as they left, she was accompanied by a Granada camera team. The company was told by the Authority that in no circumstances would any such programme be transmitted. It never was. Later we had to require Granada to transmit the Queen's broadcast on Christmas Day.

In my first few months we set up four specialized committees, so that Authority members would be able to give more time to programme policy. First, a Programme Schedules Committee.

The new Television Act, in a toughly worded section 5, had compelled programme contractors to submit their programme schedules in advance for the Authority's approval. The Authority was thus put in a commanding position. It was a crucial change The Authority's approval could have been left to the staff acting on behalf of the Authority, but this was not what the Act said and not, I thought, what it intended. A committee of Authority members should study the schedules in detail.

Secondly, finance. I suggested, and the Authority agreed, that a few members versed in financial matters should form a Finance Committee under the deputy chairman (first Sir John Carmichael and subsequently Sir Sydney Caine) to advise the Authority. Thirdly, an Establishment Committee was formed, under the able and experienced chairmanship first of Lord Williamson and later of Sir Vincent Tewson, to report on staff matters and appointments. Fourthly, a Technical Committee was set up to consider technical problems. Later this gave way to the nomination of a technical member of the Authority.

The Authority, then meeting at three-weekly intervals, decided in future to meet monthly on Thursdays; another Thursday each month was set aside for committees. As every member of the Authority became a member of a committee, each then came to headquarters fortnightly instead of every third week.

These changes still seem to me sensible and desirable. A body confronted by a mass of varied and detailed material cannot concentrate on what matters most, general issues of policy. Weigh down a body with paper and detail, submit it to lengthy explanations by its officials, and before long it will find that it is not really involved in the decisions which it has in theory reached. This system makes for over-long meetings, far beyond the two and a half hours or so which I have come to regard as the limit of human fortitude in committee work.

One member of the Authority – as he has since told me – thought that my approach was that of a professional chairman, whose aim was not so much to reconcile differences as to reach decisions. This is a fair comment. The exchange of ideas can be valuable and stimulating. Sometimes it suffices. But often a decision is needed. I did knowingly and deliberately concentrate on the decision-making process. If opinion appeared to be fairly evenly divided, I preferred to adjourn the discussion to the next meeting rather than leave things in the air. Or perhaps decision would be possible on part of the problem, leaving the rest for future discussion. But I did always seek to get such decisions as were possible. I rarely pressed my own opinion. What I pressed for was decision and the implementation of decisions reached.

One inevitable result of the establishment of committees was the strengthening of the role of the members of the Authority and the weakening of that of the director-general. Now there would always be some members of the Authority who were fully informed of the details of the matters which came before it. A member of the Authority would present the report of the committee over which he presided.

I felt sure the Authority would never fully exercise the powers which Parliament had conferred on it unless it so organized itself as to enable it to concentrate on important policy issues, particularly programme policy. This did not mean intervention by the Authority in management matters properly belonging to the director-general; nor did it inhibit the director-general or his senior colleagues in saying exactly what they thought. But this structural change did mean a stronger role for the chairman. As he was an ex-officio member of all committees – though not chairman – he became much better informed as to what was going on.

Sir Robert Fraser concurred in this reorganization and in the shift of emphasis it brought. An extremely sensitive man, he had borne, in preceding months, a great deal of public criticism, much of it unfair. He may well have recognized that, with members of the Authority becoming more involved in the decision-making process, he would be less exposed to personal attack. It certainly turned out that way. Anyway, he loyally accepted the changes and with his customary efficiency saw to it that the new system worked. The Authority has since decided to meet fortnightly and to abolish its committees. Officials, I suspect, are on the way to restoring the power they lost in my day.

There was an important point on which Fraser and I did

differ. A closer link between the Authority and the programme companies was needed for the exchange of views on general questions of programme policy : each needed to understand better the role of the other. It was not enough for the Authority to meet the representatives of programme companies at contract time only. There should be more regular contact. Regular meetings already took place between the Authority's senior staff, led by Sir Robert, and company managing directors to deal with 'nuts and bolts' matters. What was now required was regular contact on major programme matters, in short a programme policy committee. So far we were agreed. But I thought that the chairman of the new committee should be the chairman of the Authority, while Sir Robert thought that he should preside over this committee, as he did over the 'nuts and bolts' committee. We reached a compromise, at least in words. He would be the chairman except when the chairman or the vice-chairman of the Authority was present, when one or other of them should preside. I was always present.

The Programme Policy Committee became a forum for frank, no-nonsense exchanges, as blunt as they were lively. Perhaps I may be forgiven for repeating the description by the managing director of one of the companies of the opening of the first meeting.

From the very beginning, from the moment Lord Hill walked into the conference room at the ITA's Brompton Road headquarters, it was clear that he intended to take Independent Television by the scruff of the neck and shake it hard. The sharp impact he made that morning must have stayed ever since in the minds of those present.

The occasion was the first meeting of a new committee – the Programme Policy Committee. It was also Lord Hill's first appearance in the chair. In attendance was a good cross-section of the industry's chiefs – the principals of the various ITV companies, including myself. In some ways, I suppose we resembled a bunch of pretty confident – perhaps even cocky – senior boys awaiting the entry of a new master!

We were prepared for practically anything, of course. Also, most of us were resigned to the inevitability of a lengthy piece from the new chairman, generously studded with the clichés and hackneyed phrases favoured by so many men of affairs. But what happened was refreshingly – almost startlingly – different.

Lord Hill entered the conference room and, looking neither right nor left, advanced briskly towards the chairman's seat. He walked with short, swift, urgent steps. He carried an aura of efficiency and steely determination. It was almost palpable. For me, Lord Hill's physical movements at that instant were uncannily reminiscent of the bustling motions of Harry S. Truman when he was dominating Washington. You half expected to glimpse the White House security guards just behind!

He reached the table and sat down. He flipped open the buff-coloured folder before him, looked once around the huge circular table and said: 'Gentlemen - this - is - the - first - meeting - of - the - Programme - Policy - Committee - and - the - first - item - on - the - agenda - is . . .' And, without any fuss or further preamble, we were on our way. Lord Hill conveyed with ice-cold clarity that this session, and all the others to follow, would be conducted on thoroughly business-like lines; and that this was to be his constant no-nonsense attitude to his task in Independent Television.

The Programme Policy Committee had no power of de-cision; it was a forum for argument. All the companies, large and small, were represented on it, and anyone could raise a point affecting programmes. Often the discussions were between companies, with the chairman the neutral figure: the smaller or regional companies would sometimes criticize the larger or central companies, or vice versa. Sometimes I would bring to the committee the view of the Authority on some point of pro-gramme policy; sometimes they would say what they thought of the Authority.

The companies soon took the point. The Authority would no longer, as one of them put it, 'reign benignly in the background, content to do little more than grace the industry with their pre-sence on formal occasions'. Naturally the companies were wary and vigilant. They wanted to be convinced that this was not

just an exercise in company-bashing, or yet another talking
shop of which the independent system had quite enough. They
needed encouragement as well as criticism, support as well as
stimulation. The discussions needed to be crisp and cogent as
well as relevant. I valued these meetings enormously. We
learned to insult each other without damage to good personal
relations.

An idea was put forward about this time – by Bernard Sendall, Sir Robert Fraser's deputy – for a series of consultations
so-called, at each of which the senior programme people from
all the companies would meet under Authority auspices to talk
about their problems. Religious broadcasting had already been
the subject of consultations, and it was now agreed that the
method should be extended to other programme areas. These
consultations helped to strengthen ITV as a single, coherent service, with a purpose and a philosophy. The plural nature of ITV
kept programme makers in closer touch with the communities
they served than was possible in a wholly centralized service.
But separation could go too far. Nothing but good could come
from pooling ideas.

Another necessary change was in the Authority's relations
with the public. Sir Robert Fraser, as a one-time journalist and
head of the Central Office of Information, was well equipped to
be the Authority 'voice', but after the Pilkington verdict he
agreed that too little had been done to present the Authority and
ITV to the public.

I had no doubt of the calibre of man needed to head the new
information and research division. When Chancellor of the
Duchy I had worked with such a man, Sir Harold Evans, who
had been public relations adviser to both the Prime Minister and
myself. Could he be persuaded to leave the government service
and fill the post? Authorized to 'cast a fly over him', I visited
him in hospital, where he was having a minor operation, in
November 1963. After much thought – he was never one to
jump at a new proposition – he took up the post of director of
information and research in the following February. As I knew
he would, he speedily created a new and efficient department
and began the work of explaining the Authority to the public.
His technique of giving the facts, fully and truthfully, and the

trust he inspired in his fellow journalists, yielded lasting dividends.

It soon became evident that he needed help and Barney Keelan, an old friend and colleague of us both in the Parliamentary lobby, was appointed as press and public relations officer in the following June. He brought wit and charm and life as well as skill to his job. No one who knows Barney will be surprised at this. Both appointments were immensely successful. Soon there was a marked change in the mood of the public and the press towards Independent Television. Harold Evans remained in the post for two years, when he was succeeded by Barney Keelan.

I sought to play my own role in increasing public esteem for the Authority by showing a constant willingness to listen to anyone who had views or criticisms to offer. Any letter addressed to me personally was answered by me personally. Often I put the Authority staff to a good deal of trouble in investigating complaints and collecting facts and figures to make possible reasoned answers to criticism. So, too, I felt it important to be prepared to meet and talk with people who were publicly critical of aspects of independent television. With Mrs Mary Whitehouse, for example, I maintained a postal dialogue which was helpful in providing an insight into the thinking that lay behind the considerable and important segment of opinion for which she spoke. I invited her to lunch with the Authority so that she could speak directly to its members.

The first eight months over, I was beginning to feel happy and comfortable in the saddle. The atmosphere of 70 Brompton Road was unusually friendly. The Authority's staff was small, between six and seven hundred in number, most of them engineers: there were about two hundred in Brompton Road. Shy and unassuming – even aloof, certainly not gregarious – Fraser was and he was known to be a kindly, gentle, understanding man. The staff had a deep affection for him.

Bernard Sendall and Tony Pragnell, his two lieutenants, were quite different in style. Bernard was thoughtful, unobtrusive and civilized, concealing a considerable strength behind a gentle manner; not least important, the companies trusted him. Tony was coolly and calmly efficient, with a passion for detail and a mastery of the facts; he never allowed emotion to colour his judgement. Tony Curbishley, head of finance, was a complete master of his subject, with an unusual capacity to expound it. A member of the Finance Committee – a business man with a financial head – once complained to me with mock sadness that he could never catch Curbishley out in anything, large or small. It was a very happy ship and I began to enjoy the day-to-day work enormously.

I went to the Authority's headquarters on four mornings a week, usually devoting the afternoons to my other commitments which included a directorship and, later, the chairmanship of Laporte Industries. I never went to Brompton Road on Fridays and I rarely attended the House of Lords.

Sometimes there was much to do, sometimes little. I met the director-general every morning for an informal chat on current points. I visited the headquarters of the companies to meet their boards and their staffs. I visited transmitting stations. I liked particularly to listen to the views of the entire staff, including their moans, often in the absence of their top management, though always with their consent. Sidney Bernstein suggested this practice on my first visit to Granada, and I adopted it for all my visits to companies. I sought to be approachable, particularly to those who made programmes. If there was a current Authority decision affecting them or their work, or a problem in the offing, I submitted myself to their questions on it, which were usually rigorous and sometimes indignant. What I heard, I reported to the director-general and to the Authority on my return.

Naturally, some visits were more successful than others. On one occasion I visited a company whose senior staff were noticeably cool to the grey-haired man from Brompton Road. They were mostly under thirty-five and I had heard that they believed that creativity in television was the preserve of the young : intervention from above meant interference by the stupidly senile. So I began by asking what they intended to do when they were forty, for by then the spark of genius would have died. Were the opportunities in administration adequate for such expired creators? We were soon involved in the problems of career development and the provisions for superannuation!

Sometimes the arrangements for my entertainment were distinctly formal. I am told by someone who was present that on one such occasion – I confess I do not remember it clearly – the chairman of the company presided at an expensive little dinner. At long last, the chairman invited me to open the post-prandial discussion. I am alleged to have opened up with the question 'What about those bloody awful programmes you have been producing?' The silence which followed was deafening. The chairman opened and closed his mouth like a carp seeking crumbs. It was not long before he drew attention to the fact that it was a quarter to ten and he had a train to catch. The evening was not successful.

There was the occasion of a visit to Westward's Plymouth station. I had yielded to the blandishments of the irrepressible and air-minded Peter Cadbury to travel with him in his private plane. The pilot was not quite sure where the landing ground was. Peter Cadbury, a wartime pilot, was so generous with his advice yelled to the fortunately serene and unconcerned commercial pilot that I was moved to ask him 'Who *is* flying the bloody plane?' There was the luncheon at ATV's luxurious headquarters after which Lew Grade was, with difficulty, persuaded to describe his life as a private in the army during the war. He had us in convulsions.

3

Battle for News at Ten

The nightly half-hour news bulletin, *News at Ten*, was one of the biggest steps forward during my years as chairman of ITA. To achieve it required a battle with the programme companies.

Independent Television News had been set up as a separate company in 1955 to provide a news service for all companies. It had been a considerable success, due in large part to Aidan Crawley, its first editor, and to the outstanding men it brought to the screen, including Robin Day, Ian Trethowan, Christopher Chataway, Ludovic Kennedy, George Ffitch, Brian Connell and, perhaps the ablest screen figure formed and developed by ITN, Alastair Burnet.

The new Television Act had required the strengthening of ITN and the widening of its membership from the six original companies to include all the companies, large and small. But the real problem of ITN, as seen by its second editor, Geoffrey Cox, was the amount of time allocated to news. More time on the air was needed. In 1964 the only guaranteed networked time which ITN had was twenty-three minutes forty seconds divided between the two daily news bulletins. In fact, ITN had less guaranteed time for news than it had had in 1955-6, though the amount of time allotted to news in depth and to current affairs had increased greatly.

I soon became convinced that Geoffrey Cox was right and that longer time was the key to ITN's future. But this was not a matter which I could influence directly. The ITN had its own board which was wholly responsible for its policy and practice.

B

The companies strongly resisted the granting of extra news time : they wanted to use any extra non-entertainment time for other programmes.

At the time, there was a late-night news-in-depth programme, *Dateline,* which ITN provided for Rediffusion. In the summer of 1964, the editor urged his board to press the companies either for a half-hour news or for the networking of *Dateline.* But his board could not agree and advised the editor just to press for longer time. This he did to the Network Planning Committee of the companies, asking for the national networking of *Dateline* and a weekly news programme. There was opposition.

At this point – and for the first time – this tangled problem was referred to the Programme Policy Committee under my chairmanship. It fell to me in effect to arbitrate on the issues. I ruled that :

1 *Dateline* should not be nationally networked but must be taken by all companies who did not produce their own late-night news-in-depth programmes.

2 *ITN Reports,* the weekly news programme, should be nationally networked at a reasonable hour within a twenty-four-hour period.

3 The main news at 8.55 p.m. should be extended by one minute.

This, I know, was modest and inadequate progress. I would have ruled for a three-minute extension of the 8.55 p.m. news if the editor had wanted it. But he believed that one minute was enough for the moment. If he could not get the national networking of *Dateline,* he preferred to switch his strategy away from trying to get a third late news programme like *Dateline* towards the lengthening of the main daily bulletin to half an hour. But he needed the staff capable of making and presenting a half-hour programme. Alastair Burnet had just become editor of the *Economist* and Nigel Ryan had not yet joined ITN. At the time I was puzzled by what seemed to be Geoffrey Cox's timidity. We were a little way forward but not much and, as I thought, not far enough.

The next step was to make *ITN Reports* a success. All went well in the early weeks when the news was dominated by Win-

ston Churchill's illness and death. Then it ran into a phase of
what one critic called 'pre-war Pathe Pictorial featurettes' with
items on beagling, the first night of a film in which the ex-
Queen of Persia starred, and mountain rescue teams in training.
Geoffrey Cox, sensing the danger to his whole strategy, set about
the task of making *ITN Reports* a success. He struck lucky because the next week's issue coincided with a dramatic ten-
minute recording of the first live pictures of the first American
moon probe reaching the moon. The programme began to improve.

Dateline, in the meantime, was running into difficulties. Rediffusion, the company for which the programme was made,
began to develop its own late-night news-in-depth programmes
and *Dateline* was pushed further and further back until it
was frequently broadcast after midnight. The BBC then began
24 Hours, thus further cutting the ground from under *Dateline*.

It was becoming clear that the only real solution lay in a
thirty-minute news, though Geoffrey Cox did not want to arouse
the companies. Again, I thought he was excessively timid but,
as he had to live with his board, I remained silent. Alastair
Burnet, editor of the *Economist,* had no such qualms. Invited
to give the 'Keynote' address at an ITV Consultation on News
and Current Affairs in January 1966, he came out strongly in
favour of the thirty-minute news. Geoffrey Cox had urged him
to hold back on the grounds that such public advocacy was
premature, but he was not to be deterred. The issue reopened in
this way, and discussion of it was resumed in the ITN board.
The arguments against it were repeated.

Anyway, in the course of 1966, ITN made a 'dry run' of a
half-hour bulletin which was liked by ITA officials, and another
which was seen and not liked by the ITN board. Later in the
year Robert Fraser argued that if there was to be half-hour
news, it should be placed early in the evening, as in the United
States. Cox wondered for a while whether to accept the argument and get his half-hour programme at the wrong time. But
the facts were against it. In America most of the news is in by
7 p.m.; in Britain the American news of the day is not in by
6 p.m. or 6.30 p.m., UK time. Much foreign film has not arrived
and Parliament is still sitting. By the autumn of 1966, the time

seemed ripe (I thought over-ripe) to face up to the main issue, a half-hour news programme at 10 p.m. The ITA was calling for a new look at peak-hour schedules in 1967. It was now or never – at least not for another year. I was determined that it should be 'now'. Fraser and Sendall made it clear to representatives of the companies that if they did not act the Authority would. They acted.

The new programme, *News at Ten,* which began in July 1967, was a resounding success from the outset, becoming an equal competitor for news with the BBC.

4

Improving the Programmes

A broadcasting service is judged by its programmes. ITV had been judged by Pilkington and, rightly or wrongly, found wanting. And so, during my spell with the ITA, we spent more and more time on programme problems.

The next phase of development, it seemed to me, as it did to many of the companies, should be one of better quality and wider range in programming. From the early days there had been a good deal of informal discussion on programme questions and programme schedules between the Authority staff and the programme heads of the companies and a good relationship had been built up. For the most part it was friendly and personal and none the worse for that. Now the Act required something more, namely the advance approval of programme plans and schedules.

The preoccupation of the Authority with programmes can be illustrated by the Authority interventions in the first eight months of the operation of the advance approval system. In October 1964 the companies were told that they should experiment with more intelligent and more genuine forms of quiz programmes, that more programmes made by the regional companies and stemming from local tastes and interests should be included in the national network, that the standard of children's programmes should be raised and that there should be more quality programmes from European countries. In December companies were asked to improve programmes between 8 and 9 p.m. and told that the Saturday schedules contained insufficient variety. At another meeting, companies were asked to increase the output of serious programmes between 7.30 and 10.30 p.m. In May 1965 concern was expressed at the absence of strong refereeing at wrestling matches and a company was told that an excess of 'give away' quiz programmes was not good for the image of Independent Television.

Later on, the interventions became more numerous and more detailed. The Authority's request to the companies the previous December to study ways of improving programmes between 8 and 9 p.m. had led nowhere. They still contained too much crime, adventure, western and American material. So all companies were asked to submit new programme schedules for the 8–9 p.m. weekday period which met the Authority's criticism.

To give further examples of intervention, the Authority required one company to find a place for *University Challenge* and another to put this programme on at an earlier hour. It instructed that the companies should be pressed to give a definite answer to the question whether wrestling bouts were genuinely competitive or whether the results were prearranged (a question which never received a really unambiguous reply!). Regional companies were required to take the currently networked arts programme unless they were providing alternative material on the arts, and all companies were told that the programmes proposed for the evening of Christmas Day were of a routine character unrelated to the special nature of the day and requested to do better when planning for Christmas 1966. One company was informed that its programme on the Aberfan disaster had totally failed to fulfil its aim. Another was bluntly told that one of its programmes was in formal breach of its contract.

One of our programme decisions relating to a play provided convincing proof – if proof were needed – that standards of taste change swiftly. In April 1964 the Authority, after viewing it in advance of transmission, deemed a programme obscene in two of its scenes and asked for their removal. Then, some nine months later, we viewed it again at the company's request. This time we passed it, one member of the Authority expressing satisfaction that the offending scenes had been cut out. In fact the play was unaltered : it was we who had changed.

This list of interventions, though far from complete, fairly illustrates the policy and practice of the Authority during my time in the chair. Yet, I suspect, the periodic two-day consultations at which the senior programme people of the companies met to exchange ideas on programme trends and problems were no less effective in raising standards. The first was held in March 1965 on television for children, a programme area then sadly in need of improvement. The second, in January 1966, was devoted to news and current affairs programmes. Subsequent lively consultations were on sport, light entertainment and comedy.

Some may think, as did some of the companies, that on interventions in programme matters the Authority was grandmotherly, even oppressive. But no one in Independent Television, as far as I am aware, doubted that our aim was to raise the esteem in which Independent Television was held in the community. All the time our eye was on our opposition, the BBC, then as now the finest broadcasting service in the world.

Some leaders of ITV, notably Sidney Bernstein, did not hesitate to say that their ambition was to create a service as good as, if not better than, the BBC. Indeed, one of the advantages to come from a system based on competition between a public service and a commercial service is that the commercial competitor is continually seeking, consciously or unconsciously, to emulate the standards of its opposition. Conversely, a public service is stirred to compete for audiences and to discard any propensity it may have to dwell overmuch on giving the public what it thinks it ought to want. Thus esteem is what ITV sought, once profitability had been achieved.

The companies came to realize that, however tiresome the interventions, the Authority was seeking energetically to do the job the Act had laid upon it and that this was in the long-term interest of the service and the system. Nor was a tough line by the Authority inconsistent with good relations between the Authority and the companies. Even in the roughest phases of the exchanges between the companies and the Authority, I was on the best of terms with the leaders of the companies. I liked them and I believe they trusted me. I did not expect them to be docile or dumb when I was presenting the Authority's criticisms. Nor, indeed, were they. But though the cosiness may have gone, it had not been replaced by cussedness.

5

Choosing New Companies

In the autumn of 1966 the Authority began to turn its mind to the selection of the programme companies who would fill the television screen after mid-1968, when existing contracts would end. Companies had to be selected by mid-1967 to have sufficient time in which to prepare themselves for broadcasting.

Under the original Television Act, contracts could be granted for the life of the Act, i.e. to end in 1964. They were so granted. The new Act was passed in 1963 – to operate from 1964. The second contracts to begin in 1964 *could* have been made for a period of up to six years. In fact (because of the possibility of a second ITV service) they were awarded for only three years, later extended to four years. This took them to 1968. In 1967 the third contracts were awarded for six years, the maximum permitted until the second Act.

The pattern had remained unchanged since the birth of the service. Enjoined by the Act to secure competition between the appointed companies, the Authority had accepted Robert Fraser's plan aimed, within the severe limitations of one channel, to ensure at least a semblance of competition. There were four main companies appointed : Rediffusion supplying five weekdays in London; ATV the weekend in London and the five weekdays in the Midlands; Granada five weekdays in the north, and ABC supplying weekends in the north and the Midlands. The rest of the country was served by seven-day, or regional, companies. The common element in the output of all the companies was the networked programmes (mostly supplied by the big four) which filled a large part of the broadcasting hours of all the companies.

The Authority decided that it was time for a change in the pattern. It approved in principle the introduction of a fifth major company covering Yorkshire. The London week would continue to be divided into two phases : one company to operate from Monday until a changeover time, probably between 6 p.m. and 7 p.m. on Friday, the other for the remainder of Friday evening and for Saturday and Sunday. For the Midlands, Yorkshire and Lancashire there would be a seven-day company for each area.

Conditions were attached to the award of a new contract. There were seven different journals of which one, the *TV Times,* was published in seven different regional editions. Some were good, some were bad. The Authority decided on the creation of a single national journal for Independent Television with regional editions, a single publishing company to be formed by the programme companies.

Some members of the Authority argued that ITV was doing far too little to support the arts and sciences on which so much of what is good in broadcasting depends. The companies were prosperous and should be persuaded to give generously. What were small amounts to them would be greatly welcomed by the arts and sciences, both centrally and locally. The Authority accepted the argument and decided in principle to create a fund under its aegis to which the companies would be required to contribute.

One other change was determined upon before contracts were awarded. The instrument for planning the national network had been the Network Planning Committee of the companies. It was a failure. In fact, most of the important decisions were taken by three major companies, Rediffusion, Granada and ATV, sometimes called the Star Chamber. It seemed to me that the first and crucial step was to create a central secretariat and planning executive. The committee agreed and Frank Copplestone, one of Bernard Sendall's staff on the programme side, was appointed to the newly created post of controller, network programme secretariat, at the Network Planning Committee of all the companies.

The Authority asked companies to make concrete proposals for centralizing their sports services. In response – and with a certain reluctance by some of them – some proposals were put up which were not thought to go far enough. They were sent back and the companies were asked to revise them so as to secure that the sports unit had a guaranteed budget and that it was given real power to negotiate sports contracts. Eventually the modified proposals of the companies were approved.

So much for the conditions attached to the award of contracts. The press began to scrutinize the candidates and to foretell the results. The *Guardian* opined that no new applicants (those for the new station, Yorkshire, apart) were likely to win a contract. The paper told the world that 'nobody faces annihilation and much of the lefty cultural barrage is designed to make it easier for Lord Hill to order the same again'. No newcomer, the paper argued later, could possibly prove his own competence as convincingly as the incumbent; to replace an existing incumbent would be a confession of failure on the part of the ITA; to take away any contract would be to remove the assets of a company. Peter Black in the *Daily Mail* agreed that it was highly unlikely that any one of the existing contractors who wanted to stay would be asked to go, adding that 'to change this set-up makes sense. But it will not be changed by shuffling contracts around.'

Bernard Hollowood, in *Punch,* wrote that I was 'presiding over' one of the most squalid operations ever to deface the fair name of private enterprise and that in all probability we would 'leave the existing contractors with their noses in the trough'. On the other hand, Joe Rogaly in the *Financial Times* said that all bids were open and 'no imaginable decision can be ruled out'.

Benedict Nightingale in *New Society,* in perhaps the most cogent and penetrating analysis, offered some advice. 'Throw out too many of the present contractors and you may create so much insecurity that no one will be willing to risk their money on ITA in the future. Throw out none and people will begin to think application pointless and your contractors will become smug and stale. Throw out just one and you will not only avoid both dangers but probably encourage everyone to see himself as the next victim.'

The game of spotting the winners began and went on throughout the interview phase. Scottish Television was dubbed as vulnerable, Granada was tipped for Lancashire, and the *Yorkshire Post*-Goodman consortium was thought a hot tip for Yorkshire, though Telefusion was thought by some 'a fancied outsider'. To my astonishment, a writer in *The Times* indulged in some pretty firm forecasting of the results on the day before they were announced.

I am fairly sure that no member of the Authority approached the task of selection with any preconceptions of what would happen. I certainly did not. No existing contractor had a prescriptive right to renewal, though unquestionably a tenant whose record was good stood a better chance than a new applicant of unknown potential. Performance was bound to carry more weight than promise. But this did not mean, and ought not to mean, that no new applicant would win. Nor would a decision to replace an existing contractor by a newcomer necessarily mean that the performance of the sitting tenant had been bad. Was a newcomer likely to do better than the holder of the franchise? That was the basic question.

I summarised the Authority's standpoint in a letter to Lord Derby on 19 June after the decisions had been announced :—

All Independent Television contracts are made for a fixed period of time. When a contract comes to an end, it comes to an end. There can be no presumption that the new contract will be offered to the same company.

I see no foundation for the view that fairness demands such a presumption. On the contrary, fairness demands that all applications are given an equal chance of success : were that not so, the whole process of inviting applications by public advertisement would be a farce. There must be a 'fair field for all', I said in 1963 when the present contracts were being discussed. I meant it.

All applications are entitled to an equal opportunity to be considered. It cannot be said that all applicants have equal advantages. When its old contract expires and it seeks a new one, an existing company can offer its performance but a new applicant only its constitution, its policy and its promise. But if promise is never to be preferred to performance, then every television company will go on for ever. No superiority in an applicant will suffice. He has not been in, and so he shall stay out. Is that the suggestion? If it is, I reject it.

As we studied the applications we were clear in our minds about the main criterion to be applied. Which applicant would, in our considered judgement, be most likely to produce the best programmes in range and quality, taking into account the talent available to it, the financial resources it commanded and the evidence there could be adduced of the prospect of a coherent and efficient team to manage it? Existing companies could produce performance as well as promise and in that respect they could have an advantage over those who had to rely on promise. We were selecting companies for the award of new contracts and not merely considering the renewal of contracts.

6

The Interviews

There was liveliness and sometimes drama at the ITA's head-quarters in Brompton Road as the companies competing for contracts were interviewed.

I began by asking our visitors to accept that we had studied with care the bulky documents which comprised their applications, as indeed we had. Was there anything new they wished to add? At the end of the questioning they would be free to say anything they wished in support of their application. This was the stage at which there were often given to us in complete confidence the names of a number of BBC staff who were willing to join the applicant if he were successful but who had not told the BBC of their intentions. In retrospect I find some of the names proffered very interesting, for they include one or two holding high office in the BBC today. Wild horses would not drag from me who they are.

After the preliminaries, I put two rather general opening questions intended to get the talk going. Then came the financial questions, usually put by the deputy chairman, Sir Sydney Caine, and questions from members of the Authority to which other members often put supplementaries. Finally the chairman of the applicant company would usually make a summing-up statement and the interview closed. The interviews were thorough and usually long. Only when all the applicants for a particular franchise had been seen did a general discussion of their merits and demerits begin.

The clearest-cut task before the Authority was the selection of a company for the Yorkshire franchise. Here was a new franchise, hived off from Granada-land, and the applicants were new companies.

As the interviews with the eight contenders for the Yorkshire franchise proceeded, it became obvious that two contenders had put up a stronger case than their rivals. One, Yorkshire Independent Television Ltd, was headed by Sir Kenneth Parkinson, chairman of the *Yorkshire Post,* Lord Goodman, Gordon Linacre, Lord Peddie, David Wilson (managing director of Southern TV), Tim Hewat and, though he was not present, Donald Baverstock. In confidence, two very prominent BBC men were mentioned as having promised to join the team if the application were successful.

It was a powerful and promising group. Indeed, it ran the risk of seeming too powerful in that a clash of personalities did not seem out of the question. The applicant before us had, until recently, been two applicants with two teams which had coalesced for the purpose of making the application. The combination was comprehensive but the stitching was visible. The spokesmen for the company were quite frank about their problems. But they were convinced that Tim Hewat, Donald Baverstock, David Wilson and the two BBC men would work well together. They would be blood brothers. Some Yorkshire universities would come in if the application was successful. All in all, this was an undeniably impressive application, with Lord Goodman as its most effective advocate and Tim Hewat its most candid and exciting speaker. Yet there could not be entirely eliminated the feeling that it had been contrived more with the purpose of impressing the Authority than with the confidence that a workable and amicable team had been assembled.

The other excellent application came from Telefusion Yorkshire Ltd, headed by Sir Richard Graham, Gwyn Ward Thomas, Sir Geoffrey Cox, Stuart Wilson and, as programme director, a senior BBC man – named in confidence – with whom they said they had agreed a contract and who had offered his resignation to the BBC only to be asked to continue with a major programme he had on hand. He was not present.

Almost as if they sensed the doubt we would entertain about their rivals, their spokesman laid great emphasis on the virtues

of the team they had collected. Sir Richard Graham and Sir
Geoffrey Cox were usually convincing in their answers to a
wide-ranging series of questions. The answers on programme
policy mainly given by Ward Thomas revealed clear thinking
and attractive ideas and a good deal of preparatory work.

When we came in due course to the final discussion there
was a general consensus of view in the Authority that this
application was marginally more impressive than the other and
Telefusion Yorkshire was eventually awarded the contract,
becoming the fifth network company. Incidentally, the named
BBC man did not, in fact, join the successful company and,
with the Authority's permission, Donald Baverstock from the
unsuccessful applicant took his place. He has now been
succeeded by Paul Fox, formerly controller of BBC 1.

The selection of the other four major companies – those for
London weekdays, for London weekend, for the Midlands and
for the north-west – all had elements of drama. The candidate
companies included the existing licence holders – Rediffusion,
ATV, ABC and Granada – and an impressive new applicant,
London Television Consortium.

Led by Aidan Crawley, David Frost, Michael Peacock,
Humphrey Burton, Cyril Bennett, with John Freeman and
Frank Muir in the wings, this consortium put in an unusually
strong case. It was rich in broadcasting talent. Crawley had
been the first editor of ITN as well as a sportsman of national
repute and junior minister; Frost had a unique reputation as a
broadcaster; Michael Peacock had had a meteoric career in
broadcasting, becoming the first controller of BBC 2 – a post
from which he had resigned in preparation for this application;
Humphrey Burton had won distinction in the broadcasting of
music and the arts with the BBC; Cyril Bennett was a competent programme controller of Rediffusion; John Freeman
had had a remarkable career as journalist, broadcaster and
diplomat, and Frank Muir had an unusually high reputation
as a script writer.

It looked a balanced team of unusual talent and experience.
Its programme policy, set out in its application and developed
at the interview, was as lively as it was imaginative, resting
mainly on the thesis that for some time there had been in broad-

casting in both services a too easy dependence on familiar and well-tried approaches in variety, popular drama and panel shows. It was urged that there was an unreadiness to recognize that good series, however well conceived initially, have a finite life, that there was a lack of forward momentum, of drive, of sense of purpose. In ITV neither the children's programmes nor the sporting side were as good as they should be. The documentary work was good, a lot of it done by ex-BBC producers who had become freelance. They said they had a new conception of what weekend broadcasting should be. They would offer something new in television. They had begun by assembling the talent and had then looked round for their backers. There was room at the weekends for deeper analysis of the week's events as well as light entertainment. Current affairs and plays had a place in weekend programming. It should not be assumed that people were less intelligent at the weekends. Serious Sunday newspapers succeeded, so should serious broadcasting.

It is an understatement to say that the Authority liked this application. The financial basis was sound. Even allowing for the fact that promising is so much easier than performing, it was difficult to resist the thought that here was a group which would bring new thinking, fresh ideas and a lively impetus to weekend broadcasting. It had to have its chance whatever the repercussions. This was the conclusion the Authority eventually reached.

Granada were virtually certain to be appointed to the part of the country they had made their own – Lancashire and the north-west – despite its reputation for cussedness, which they successfully maintained at some phases of the interview. They even had the cheek to say that they would like the Authority to send for them occasionally to say that their programmes were too dull, too ordinary, and to exercise more authority, not less. We had had some experience of sending for Granada! It was a lively session, with Sidney Bernstein as delightfully wayward as ever, his brother Cecil showing his usual sturdy common sense and Denis Forman demonstrating his comprehensive grasp of what broadcasting is really about. As a team they believed in broadcasting and in Granada.

The competition for this franchise came from Palatine Television Ltd, headed by Mr C. F. Carter, Vice-Chancellor of Lancaster University, and Professor George Wedell, Professor of Adult Education at Manchester University and former secretary of the Authority. This application, as its sponsors admitted, bore the signs of hasty preparation. No managing director could be named, even in confidence, and there were vague and scanty references to programme staff. On the other hand the strong merit of their case lay in their emphasis on local events and local talent as essential elements in regional broadcasting. Broadcasting should be brought back to the local level, they said. Overall it was a worthy application by serious-minded people who had left themselves insufficient time to prepare their case in range and depth. They could not succeed in competition with Granada and I suspect they knew it. The only question which remained was whether Granada should be awarded a London contract for which, somewhat late in the day, they had also asked to be considered. Perhaps their success in the north told against them in their bid for London. In any case, we could see ahead enough difficulty in London, and eventually Granada was reappointed to the north-west.

ATV had little competition in its application for the Midlands' franchise. Already a Midland company for five days a week (coupled with the London weekend company), ATV, with a shrewd assessment of the problem confronting the Authority and of their chances, had obviously decided that its best hope lay in the Midlands. The late Lord Renwick, Lew Grade and Robin Gill were the principal spokesmen, with Lew and Robin speaking alternately for most of the time.

The interview was an exhilarating experience and many of the answers were given with boisterous candour. More time was spent in this interview than in any other in lively exchanges on the successes and failures of the applicant's past programmes. It was an essay in superlatives. The successes were immense and the failures dismal. Lew was the life and soul of the application. Behind the exaggeration and the indiscretions, here was a born showman whose enormous energies were being wholly devoted to the job. His judgement might from time to time be faulty but his honesty and his dedication, to say nothing of his optimism, were unmistakable. ATV obtained the Midlands contract.

The representatives of ABC, hitherto a provincial weekend company covering the Midlands and the north, plumped for London, though they were obviously willing to take the Midlands. Led by Philip Warter, Howard Thomas and Brian Tesler, their case had been put with crisp efficiency, Howard Thomas dealing with questions with impressive professionalism. The company had wooed the audience as entertainers and had come more and more to provide information. ITV had grown more and more like the BBC, and the BBC had become more and more like ITV. Their ideas for developing Independent Television were clearly and cogently expressed. Here, undeniably, was a good balanced programme team with a good record and considerable potential, worthy of a place in the new pattern of things.

The following day, the representatives of Rediffusion, led by John Spencer-Wills and including Lord Tanley, Paul Adorian, John Macmillan and Cyril Bennett, came to see us. Rediffusion had been a sound company with a good reputation. Business men – and good business men – were in charge. For most of its life, there had been no programme man on the board. In some matters, such as schools broadcasting, it had been a pioneer. Its *This Week* current affairs programme was of a high standard, as were some of its children's programmes.

According to Peter Black in his absorbing book *The Mirror in the Corner* (published by Hutchinson in 1972), John Spencer-Wills later complained of the seating arrangements. 'We had all those people sitting about four feet above us on a three-sided dais, and we sat below in one long line so that I couldn't see my colleagues.' In fact, there was no dais. We all sat on the same level. Spencer-Wills must have imagined himself to be on a lower level than the Authority.

At the interview, the Authority's questions were answered in a competent if uninspiring manner, with Cyril Bennett as the most effective witness and Spencer-Wills as the most cautious. From time to time, Spencer-Wills was testy. And, in his final remarks, he repeated his oft-stated belief that in Independent Television, as in transport, licences should be automatically renewed save only when the contractor had fallen down badly on his job. Any flaws in the presentation of their case played no part in the final decision. We knew the company to have a record of competence and Spencer-Wills to be a sound and able business man.

We now had a difficult problem on our hands. The Crawley-Frost group had made out a strong case for their being appointed to the weekend franchise and ABC had put in a convincing application for a London franchise. Rediffusion had a good record of achievement. Once we had decided that the Crawley-Frost group should have the London weekend contract, the question remained of how could we accommodate ABC and Rediffusion, bearing in mind that the London five-day contract would be a very profitable one in terms of advertising income?

After a great deal of thought, and with some reluctance, we decided on a marriage of the two companies and the award of the contract to a new joint company. There would be an equal sharing of profits between them. But there remained the crucial question of which of the marriage partners should have the 51 per cent share in terms of voting shares, for we regarded a fifty-fifty as unworkable. Here the central consideration was the quality of the professionals. Howard Thomas and Brian Tesler had long impressed the Authority as a first-class team and we had learned by the time the decision had to be made that Cyril Bennett of Rediffusion was to go to the weekend company. Other members of the Rediffusion team had shown a wish to go to other companies if they were successful.

In the end we plumped for the Thomas-Tesler combination as the professional leaders of the new company most likely to bring new life and vigour to programmes. To give practical expression to this decision we decided that ABC should have 51 per cent of the voting shares of the new company. So we put professional talent above business competence.

There were two applications for the franchise covering Wales and the area centred on Bristol. It was an awkward area in that the broadcasters had to serve both Welsh and English viewers and broadcast in Welsh as well as English. A good deal of thought had been given to the creation of a purely Welsh franchise, one without an English 'rump'. A committee of Welsh MP's had urged this rearrangement upon me at the time that the whole pattern was being examined afresh, using the argument that Wales was a separate country, with its own culture and traditions, which could only be satisfactorily served by a company of its own serving it exclusively.

Incidentally, a prominent member of this same parliamentary group came to me a day or two later and pressed me privately to ignore what he and his colleagues had said. Wales needed the English 'rump', for without it and the advertising income derived from it a Welsh company would be too poor to put on an acceptable service. This, indeed, was the snag. The English part of the area supplied the larger share of the income, although its population was but a minority of the population of the whole area. Wales would have to pay for its nationalism and the price would be high. On balance we thought it wise to leave the mixed area untouched, even though it meant problems for the broadcasting company which were not easily soluble and which the BBC, which had a Welsh service, did not have to face.

Bearing in mind the fundamental difficulty of geography, TWW, the sitting tenant, had not done too badly, though there had been some grumbling in Wales that it was a London-based company too little involved in and too insensitive to the real life of Wales. Its managing director, its programme controller and others of its senior staff lived and worked in London. The deputation which came to see us did not include the programme controller, on the unconvincing grounds that to bring him as well as his juniors, the Welsh controller and his associate executive producer, was unnecessary.

Lord Derby had said at a recent annual general meeting of the company that too much was talked about Welsh interest and west of England interest programmes and that if the company was forced to be too parochial instead of regional, 'we would only succeed in annoying our Welsh viewers or west of England viewers and fail to meet our obligations to the viewers in our area as a whole'. This philosophy was unlikely to be sympathetically appreciated in Wales. The company had tried to meet Welsh dissatisfaction by establishing a Welsh board responsible for Welsh programmes and Welsh matters as well as a west of England board. It had recently appointed an executive of senior officers which met in London.

The interview, like the application as a whole, was uneven. In its application the company had suggested that it should enjoy a greater freedom in the production of its programmes but under questioning it had little to suggest apart from longer hours of broadcasting, and a vague reference to the inhibiting effect of the Act. They spoke, they said, from fear rather than actual experience. Its drama output came in for some vigorous scrutiny. Its record in religious broadcasting was good.

TWW were immediately followed by the Harlech deputation, led by Lord Harlech, Wynford Vaughan-Thomas, W. G. Poeton, the founder and chairman of the Bristol Art Centre, John Morgan and W. A. Hawkins of the *Bristol Evening Post*. Without mentioning their rival by name they stressed just those points on which TWW was weak. Emphasizing the rise of regional loyalty, they based their case on the need to foster and encourage it. Ownership and control should spring from the area and full use should be made of the talent available in the area. They would pursue a conservative dividend policy and would not diversify. They would establish an education trust which would be financed partly from the profits which would be earned by the special programmes initiated by a group of international stars such as the Burtons, Geraint Evans, Stanley Baker and others. From the trust, contributions would go to bodies concerned with the arts such as the Bristol Old Vic Company, the Bath Festival and the Welsh National Theatre. But it was their programme ideas, in the description of which John Morgan played a prominent part, which impressed most. I suspected the trust idea was an exercise, if unintentional, in gimmickry, and in my case it played little part in the view we eventually formed.

All this was, of course, promise and not performance, and no doubt much of it would be diluted by experience. But life and vigour and clear thinking were there, too. When the TWW representatives departed, I had no reason to suppose that they would not gain the contract. But when the Harlech interview was over it was clear that, whatever the consequences, we had

to concentrate our minds on the basic question of which applicant would be more likely to produce the better broadcasting
in the area. Where lay the greater talent, the fuller potential for
the next six years? TWW did not need to be bad to lose; Harlech had to hold out the prospects of something substantially
better to win. That it did hold out that prospect was the general
view of the members of the Authority, Harlech got the contract. That TWW had interviewed unevenly was not important; that Harlech had done well at the interview was not a
dominant factor.

Then came the applications for the main Scottish franchise
covering its thickly populated belt. First we saw the representatives of the existing tenants, Scottish Television, led by Lord
Thomson, Jim Coltart, Bill Brown and Mr Francis Essex. We
knew a good deal about the performance of this company mainly
because of our anxieties about it. The company tended to think
it was much better than its programmes indicated that it was.
On the occasion of one visit to meet the board in Glasgow I
had been shown, as a demonstration of its excellence, one of the
regular programmes of which it was particularly proud. I
thought it pretty poor and when the invitation came at the
luncheon table to comment on it I had expressed myself on it in
forthright terms. Some time later I saw Jim Coltart in London
and told him plainly that unless there was a speedy and substantial improvement in programme quality and range the chances
of gaining another contract seemed to me to be remote. He
acted immediately, almost within hours, making sweeping
changes in the top layers of the company and introducing some
new blood, including Francis Essex. Thereafter the combination
of Bill Brown and Francis Essex bought about a striking change
in the vigour and style of the company and its programmes. So
it was that when we interviewed the company we were aware
of its improved performance in the previous eighteen months
or so : it was on the upgrade, as it needed to be. At the interview,
which told us little we did not know, we could sense this new
leadership. But though new blood was circulating, there was a
good way to go yet.

The other contestant was Central Scotland Television, led
by Jo Grimond, Alasdair Milne, Alastair Burnet, Tom Taylor,

president of the Scottish Co-operative Wholesale Society (now Lord Taylor of Gryfe), and Professor Esmond Wright, then a Member of Parliament, accompanied by the editor of the *Observer* and the chairman of the *Economist*. They put up an excellent show with Alasdair Milne and Alastair Burnet outstanding and Tom Taylor and Professor Wright providing strong support. If their evidence had a weakness it was an overemphasis on the flaws in the performance of Scottish Television, particularly by a woman member of the deputation, Dame Jean Roberts. We knew STV's weaknesses and they were not as great as this lady would have had us believe. Even so, this was an excellent application supported by persuasive evidence and I was much impressed; more, as it turned out, than some of my colleagues. On the other side of the account, there was the substantial, if comparatively recent, improvement in the style and quality of the programmes of Scottish Television. Robert Fraser regarded this improvement as crucial and strongly advised its reappointment.

For some time I pondered over the choice to be made, inclining on balance to the view that the newcomer's case could not be resisted. But when the time for decision came, the balance of opinion in the Authority, greatly influenced by the recent and substantial improvement in Scottish Television, was that STV should be given the new contract. Jim Coltart, Bill Brown and Francis Essex had saved the day – but only just.

The rest of the decisions were not difficult. Some companies, such as Tyne-Tees, Anglia, Ulster, Border, Grampian and Channel had no competition. Others like Southern and Westward met their competition and won the day.

The main decisions were finally made on 9 June 1967 with, in some cases, a number of conditions being attached to the selection. At the time of the award of the previous contracts some three years before, a condition attached to the selection of Scottish Television was that the holding of the Thomson Organization should be reduced from about 80 per cent to about 55 per cent. This time a further reduction to 25 per cent was required on the grounds that no man should be in so commanding a position in a television company.

Incidentally, though we did not intend it, the timing as well as the fact of this requirement, as of the last, turned out to be particularly fortunate for Roy Thomson, who unloaded his shares at what was for him a convenient time – convenient that is in terms of their value. Some men are born lucky. We required that the non-voting shares to be disposed of should go to people and interests unconnected with the Thomson Organization, preference being given as far as possible to Scottish persons and companies. Additional directors not connected with the Thomson Organization should be appointed, voting shares going to them.

Harlech were required to offer to TWW at par 40 per cent of the equity and loan capital (an offer which TWW later rejected) and to buy at valuation as a 'going concern' the studio facilities which TWW wished to sell and to give prior consideration to TWW employees in filling their posts.

Telefusion, the winners of the Yorkshire contract, were required to give the newspapers associated with the losing applicant, headed by the *Yorkshire Post,* an opportunity to invest in the new company and to offer an investment opportunity to the Yorkshire universities. What lay behind the required invitation to newspapers was the feeling that the main newspaper interests not already enjoying it should be given an opportunity to join the club and share the profits – as some compensation for any loss of advertisement income. This was made possible, it seemed to me, by the almost universal decision of the press to allow their television correspondents complete freedom of expression, regardless of any investment the paper might have in a programme company. Milton Shulman clearly enjoyed that freedom in his articles in the *Evening Standard!* A similar step was taken to require the new London weekend company to admit to investment the *Observer,* the *Daily Telegraph* and the *Economist.*

ATV were required to strengthen their Midlands structure, adding not less than two directors associated with the life of the Midlands and appointing a full-time member of the board to manage the Midlands operation. Similarly Granada were required to add two directors from within its area.

Also, certain general conditions attached to all companies were spelt out. No one should continue on a board after the age of seventy without the Authority's approval, which would not be given beyond the age of seventy-five. It was also considered undesirable that an individual should be, at the same time, chairman of a programme company and a member of the House of Commons.

The decisions made, they had to be speedily announced. None of them had leaked, which is more than can be said of most important decisions nowadays. There would be Stock Exchange repercussions from some of the changes and we therefore settled for Sunday 1 June as the day for announcing the decisions, two days after the Authority's decisive meeting.

A press conference was called for the afternoon and in the morning I asked the representatives of the applicants most affected by the decisions to come to see me at Brompton Road. As I write these words, some six years later, my recollections of some of those morning interviews are somewhat patchy. They were, to say the least of it, tense. Not unexpectedly those who represented Telefusion, the winners of the Yorkshire contract and Harlech were delighted and, I thought, astonished. Spencer-Wills was deeply shocked, if not flabbergasted, but courteous throughout.

I shall never forget the reaction of Lord Derby who, the staff had told me, had been difficult to persuade to come; he had planned to go to Paris that day. He was furious to learn that Harlech had won the contract. His subsequent statement that I, on being asked the reasons for the decision, had muttered 'Because you are a London-based company', is roughly true. Confronted by his anger, I was not at my articulate best.

Lord Thomson was quietly composed, as he had every reason to be, taking it in good part when I said that he owed the decision to reappoint his company to Bill Brown, who accompanied him, and his colleagues. When I told him of the decision to require him to reduce the holding of the Thomson Organization from 55 to 25 per cent (in 1964 the Authority had required a reduction of the Thomson holding from 80 per cent to 55 per cent) he asked for a change of words. Would I make it 'to not more than 25 per cent'? He had swiftly calculated, I surmised, that this was the time to unload even more than the 30 per cent we had required. And events proved him right.

In the afternoon, the representatives of the press were plainly surprised, not to say astounded. Early in my opening statement, I gave a clue to the decisions when I defined the principles which had guided the Authority in making the decisions:

First, and all the time, we have borne in mind the quality of the programme service which Independent Television will offer in the new contract period. We have scrutinized the applications from this point of view because the Authority can have no more important consideration in awarding contracts.

The second principle may be put in the form of an answer to a question. Must the doors of Independent Television remain for ever closed to new applicants, however good they are? If the answer is 'yes', then those companies already appointed are there for all time. But the Authority's answer must, of course, be 'no'. It follows that the choice may well not be between a good applicant and a bad applicant, but between a good application and one which, after full consideration, the Authority believes will be a better one.

I cast a careful eye on the representative of the press who, the day before, had chanced his arm on a forecast of some of the decisions, beginning his piece in *The Times* with the announcement that T. Dan Smith's Trans-York television company had 'won the fight for the lucrative Yorkshire area ITV contract'. He was wrong and I looked for pallor on his face as I announced the real winner. But, alas, it was so covered with beard that I could detct no signs of remorse. But then, with the long experience I had had of the press, I was foolish to expect them.

The next day the press gave the decisions a welcoming reception. The facts told their story and were fully and objectively reported in the national press. The *Guardian* said that 'Lord Hill and his colleagues had given the whole of Independent Television the sort of jolt which every established industry requires from time to time'. The *Daily Express* criticized the decision not to reappoint TWW. The *Financial Times* approved, though it felt that the ITA should be made to justify its decisions in public. The *Daily Telegraph* thought it seemed odd

that TWW should have had so little intimation beforehand
when it was about to be closed down. The television correspondents were, for the most part, cautiously approving.

The exchanges with Lord Derby were not over. In public and
private, by letter and telegram, he protested with vigour. He
argued that the Authority might have come to a different conclusion had it known of some changes in the composition of the
Welsh board of TWW he was contemplating. Why did not the
Authority, which knew of such contemplated changes, ask
about them? The Authority should reconsider and receive further representations from TWW, something which the
Authority declined to do. He informed all TWW shareholders
that the company had had no warning of any kind that the contract was in danger, that at the interview one member of the
Authority had implied that the contract would be renewed and
that, if the Authority had complaints against the company, it
was not necessary to penalize the shareholders. 'They could have
directed changes in the Board and other matters as they pleased
without any change of capitalisation, and without the gratuitous
loss inflicted upon you.' Lord Derby went on to say that the
company did not accept the decision and were making the strongest possible representations against it.

In reply, I felt bound to elaborate the Authority's position:

There was a time when TWW understood the Authority's
duties better. In 1963 TWW was offered its second contract.
At your Annual General Meeting in April 1964, you said to
your shareholders that this was a 'gratifying vote of confidence' because, you explained, 'the procedure of renewal was
anything but a formality, and the claims of every other new
applicant for an ITA area were most meticulously considered'. You continued: 'Our new licence will operate for
three years, and is subject to renewal at the option of the ITA
for a second period of three years.'

Well, the time came for a new contract period. Again, all
claims were 'meticulously considered'. And the claim of the
Harlech Consortium was judged unanimously by the Authority to be the better claim.

They made their case in writing, as you did. They made

their case in interview, as you did. You found the consideration 'meticulous' in 1963, 'routine' in 1967. The outcome was different: but nothing else was different, either in principle or procedure. The Authority chose the applicant judged the better. Is there something else it was supposed to do?

You complain that you were given no warning. How could we warn you? Until we had studied both applications and interviewed both groups, we could not know whether the new contract would be offered you or not. Had you not encountered a superior application, it would have been offered you. It was, of course, quite impossible between the interview and the announcement to give you any warning because of the need to avoid premature reaction on the Stock Exchange. Our security was deliberate, not accidental.

When our procedures were over and the decision reached, we could not come to you and say: 'You have lost. You had better amend your application in this and that respect, and then we will appoint you.' We could no more do that than go to Harlech Consortium and say: 'You have not succeeded, but if you make this change and that you will win.'

I now come to the position of TWW shareholders as you describe it to them. I cannot accept the implication that, when contracts are being considered, the Authority's freedom to choose the best applicant is fettered in the case of companies the shares of which are quoted on the Stock Exchange. This again would be to say that, in every such case, the programme company originally chosen has a permanent right over newcomers.

I refer also to the suggestion that the Authority owes a duty to the shareholders of TWW since their money has financed the operation over the last years. Let me refer first of all to the founders. On our estimate, anybody who made and retained an original investment of £1000 in TWW has an investment worth, at Friday's price, about £10,000. He will also have received a further £10,000 in dividends after tax.

I recognize that not all present shareholders have enjoyed such profits and capital appreciation, and that some may not have heeded the notice you gave in 1964 that the company's contract was for a limited period. If, with these shareholders in mind, TWW wish to make proposals for some preferential allocation of shares to be made directly to them out of the 40 per cent which we have required the Harlech Consortium to offer to the company, this is something which we would certainly consider. I find it strange that you did not describe to your shareholders either this offer of 40 per cent of the non-voting shares and loan capital at par in the new company or the requirement on the Harlech Consortium to offer a fair price for your studios in Cardiff and Bristol.

You have referred elsewhere to the brevity of our meeting on Sunday, 11 June, and said I gave you no reason except that you were 'London-based'. It was not I, you will recall, who brought our meeting to an abrupt end.

You also said that you formed the impression from questions put to you by one of the Authority's members that you had succeeded. I and others were left with no such impression. The commanding fact is that the Authority unanimously decided in favour of your competitor.

Let me say this. It is no pleasure to the Authority to be parting in due course from a company with which it has worked for ten years. It would be easier in so many ways to leave things alone. But that is not what the Television Act says we should do. However adequate its programmes, a company always lives with the risk that it will encounter a better competitor. In the nature of things, it may not happen often. This time it did.

Lord Goodman, in his capacity as legal adviser to the company, pursued another line at meetings between himself and Fraser, in one of which I participated. Control of the policy of the company was vested in the small number of voting shares. What the Authority was seeking to do was to transfer this control to another group of persons. All that was necessary, therefore, was to transfer the voting shares to Harlech, leaving the non-voting shares in their present ownership. This was the nub of his argument presented at first with sweetness and smiles and later, when we appeared to be unimpressed by his argument, with growing toughness and hints of trouble to come. It was all so beautifully done. The trouble with this argument was that its acceptance would leave the great bulk of existing shareholders with their lush profits, while those who did the work and bore the responsibility would have precious little share in the equity. It made no appeal to me.

From time to time and certainly after the 1967 contract phase doubts have been expressed as to the method of selecting companies. Vast sums of money go with the decisions, as they do in, say, planning decisions. As the *Economist* put it on 3 June 1967, 'A statutory body is in process of deciding which limited companies should be granted the monopoly right for six years to share a total annual income now running at over £80 millions.' Put in another way, the Authority has to decide not only which applicant is most likely to put up the best programme performance but which group of financiers should be given the opportunity to earn profits substantially higher than they would get in any other enterprise, to say nothing of substantial capital profits. Was it right and fair that such decisions should be made in private by a bunch of amateurs? – as one critic put it. It was the Star Chamber technique, said another. Again, as the *Economist* said, 'this statutory body is being allowed to reach its decisions without any serious public discussion whatever.'

In retrospect, I think that there is one change of method which could sensibly and safely be made. That part of the application which describes the programme policy statement of the applicant could be made public before the application is considered. It is, in effect, its promise to the public against which, in the case of the successful applicant, its performance can be judged. In fact most of the policy statements of the applicants in 1967 were published in dribs and drabs after the hearings. On the other hand there is some information the Authority needs, including the references to possible recruitment from the BBC, which can be made available only if confidence is preserved. The interviews of the applicants would, in my view, lose in value if they were conducted in public, with or without lawyers in attendance.

On the point of whether the Authority, composed as it is of non-professionals from a variety of occupations appointed as trustees for the public, is the right body to make decisions of such importance and cash value, I find it difficult to think of any other procedure which would not be open to similar or stronger objections, whether the decision was made by a government department, a select committee of Parliament, or a court or commission or committee appointed for the purpose. Some body of persons has to undertake the unenviable task of selection and it seems sensible that it should be undertaken by the body appointed by the government to run the service.

Were the Authority's 1967 decisions wise? Did they stand the test of time? One member of the Authority, Sir Sydney Caine, has made public that, in retrospect, he regrets the decisions and that he did not oppose them with more vigour at the time.

Patently one decision did not stand the test of time: that to appoint the Crawley-Frost group, afterwards London Weekend. As Peter Black put it, the Authority believed the promises of the applicant because the company had the talent to fulfil them. Yet the company was torn apart by clashing personalities. Out went Michael Peacock, and a number of those whose talents had impressed us resigned in sympathy. Should the Authority have foreseen it? Should it not have spotted the weaknesses of the structure and the team? The plain fact is that it did not. Nor can I pretend that I had doubts about the wisdom of appointing this company as I did about one other, Scottish Television. At least, it is yet another reminder of the fallibility of human judgement when applied to the assessment and selection of human beings for responsible appointments and their capacity to work together.

The education and cultural trust envisaged in the Harlech application was not in fact set up. The expected income from 'star' programmes did not materialize and Harlech chose to contribute to the central fund for aiding the arts and sciences. In the year ending 31 July 1973 it contributed nearly £30,000 to the support of local cultural and educational activities. A close observer has told me that both Yorkshire and Harlech had uneasy starts, particularly Harlech, but that they are both now very successful, doing distinguished work and employing some talented people.

The marriage between ABC and Rediffusion to form Thames

was such a shot-gun affair that early difficulties were inevitable. Nowadays I do not see many of its programmes, but from those I do see I agree with the verdict of a close observer that it is having very real success, due in no small part to marriage-broker Howard Thomas who has done, as I expected, a first-class job. It is good to know that he is now chairman.

7

A Grand Team

I enjoyed my four years at Brompton Road immensely. The
staff team was small and close-knit. From top to bottom – from
the director-general to the hall porters – the mood was easy and
friendly.

The smallness of the organization made co-operation between
colleagues physically easy. Yet there was more to it than pro-
pinquity. The atmosphere stemmed from the personality and
the kindness of one man, Robert Fraser, for whom I developed
an admiration generously tinged with affection. Admittedly he
often used two words when one would have done : true, there
were often terrifying pauses in our conversations while he lit
one of his favourite cheroots. If he had a weakness it was to
apply intellectual processes equally to things which mattered
little and things which mattered much. Subtlety seldom yielded
ground to simplicity in his mental process, which was odd in
so essentially simple and sympathetic a man. But these were
minutiae when set against his essential greatness.

Not least of his qualities was that, although he recognized
before anyone else that I was determined to strengthen the role
of the Authority at the expense of himself as well as the companies, he suffered me without too obvious or too frequent signs
of exasperation. Nor did he at any time seek to thwart me, whatever misgivings he may have had. He was the deeper thinker; I
was perhaps swifter in action. Two quite different men, we
learned to work together in tandem and my affection for him
grew.

I have written of Bernard Sendall, calm and civilized, and

Tony Pragnell, practical and competent, and of Tony Curbishley, the master of finance who said 'no' with such an innocent grin and really comprehended the incomprehensible. There
was Archie Graham, in charge of advertising control, whose
confidence in his own judgement was matched by his grasp of
his difficult field; Howard Steele, as technically adventurous as
he was sun-tanned; the secretaries who managed us all anony-
mously but inexorably (including Hazel Fenton, my supremely
competent manager since BMA days); and the regional officers
and engineers at the stations. They and others were part of a
lively and efficient team, devoted to Robert Fraser. This may
seem too good to be true, but true it was.

Then there were the company chiefs. I had had little experience of this species of tycoon and not unnaturally I wondered
whether I would succeed in establishing good personal relations
with them, bearing in mind my intention to emphasize the
separate role of the Authority and the abrasiveness which might
from time to time be inescapable. I need not have doubted, even
though I argued fiercely with most of them at one time or
another.

There was also Lew Grade, an articulate impresario of enormous enthusiasm to whom everything was as black as ink or as
white as snow : explosive, temperamental, as lovable as he was
irrepressible, as generous with his mild cigars as with his not-
so-mild outbursts, as straight as they come with every one of his
many words his bond. I shall never forget the small drinking
party to celebrate his knighthood : we did the drinking, for Lew
never touches the hard stuff. There was none of that bogus
business about the honour having been intended not for him
but for those with whom he worked. He was pale with a pride
which was as childlike as it was complete. A child of a Polish
immigrant family, a former dancing champion, he had been
honoured in the country of his adoption. He had arrived.

Lew never minded admitting his errors. Towards the end of
my time at the ITA, I was visited by a distinguished stage per-
former who complained bitterly that the show in which he was
appearing in London had been filmed by a programme company for a television showing without any consultation whatever
with the actors. Although Lew had known nothing of the film-

ing, the responsibility for the slip-up fell on him as the managing director of ATV. I asked Lew to come and see me and meet the complainant, and subsequently told him that in my view there was only one thing to do, to apologize to the cast of the show for the discourtesy shown to them. Either Lew or his deputy should, I suggested, address the cast after an evening performance and express regret for what had happened. Lew exploded. 'Not on your life' was the substance of his reply, although his words were quite different. Eventually he calmed down and said he would arrange it. His deputy did what I had asked and the cast, perhaps as astonished as his deputy, clapped vigorously. 'You were right and I was wrong,' said Lew when next I saw him.

On another occasion the late Norman Dodds, an aggressive back-bencher, wrote to me bitterly criticizing Lew personally as well as professionally. I arranged for him to visit Lew for a talk. I heard no more criticisms from Norman Dodds.

Sidney Bernstein was quite a different character. He combined an innocent air of omniscience with a delightful self-delusion that he was merely one among equals in the controlling team of Granada. He really believed this, though no one else did. A passionate believer in minority programmes for the cultivated, he had the showman's art of appealing to the largest numbers in much of what Granada did. A generous giver to the arts, he saw to it that Granada produced some of the cheapest programmes in the network. He pleaded with the Authority to intervene more and vigorously resisted the interventions we did make. Yet this complicated character really understood the producer's problems and genuinely grasped the role of television in our modern society. His brother, Cecil, was the solid, reliable, practical man of affairs while Sidney was the visionary. It was a strong combination. Granada may not have been quite as good, quite as noble as Sidney asserted, but it was good all the same.

John Spencer-Wills looked and was the man who had risen to the top of his business by unusual ability and sheer hard work. He preferred fact to fantasy. Essentially a cautious man, he had in fact taken some nerve-racking risks in the very early and anxious days of television.

Inevitably, my relations were happy with those who it seemed to me were making an outstanding contribution to Independent Television, as with those who were congenial and candid friends. Norman Collins of ATV (to whom more than anyone else the creation of Independent Television is due), Howard Thomas of ABC, Aubrey Buxton of Anglia, John Burgess and James Bredin of Border, Tony Jelly of Tyne-Tees, Jim Coltart and Bill Brown of Scottish TV, and John Davis, David Wilson and Berkeley Smith of Southern fall in the first category, and the irrepressible Peter Cadbury of Westward and Tim Hewat of Granada in the second. John Macmillan of Rediffusion, a wise and helpful friend to the Authority, was an innocent victim of the contract decisions, despite the new post which was invented for him. Oddly enough, one of the ablest chairmen presided over the tiniest company of all, Wilfred Krichefski of Channel.

I run the risk of boring my readers, I know, by praising the men with whom I worked : good conduct, like happy matrimony, is not newsworthy. Yet the truth must be told even in a world in which so often malice is preferred to goodwill and misconduct to good conduct.

My four years with the Authority were among the happiest years of my working life, before and since. That is the simple unvarnished truth, due not least to my colleagues on the Authority. Sir John Carmichael, my first deputy chairman, who had been acting chairman for some months, and Sir Sydney Caine, who succeeded him in that office, were two quite different men, yet with some things in common, including an aptitude for finance. Both became efficient chairmen of the Finance Committee. Both had been distinguished government servants, John Carmichael in the Sudan, and Sydney Caine at home and abroad. Both were modest and unassuming men who, quite unlike me, made their points with under-emphasis, even diffidence.

John Carmichael, with his extensive experience of practical business gained after his official career, preferred to weigh the pros and cons of a particular proposal for a time before making up his mind. Sagacity was his strength – and once convinced he was as tough as he was courteous. Sydney Caine, with his tolerant liberal philosophy, preferred never to intervene unless the case for intervention was overwhelming. People should be free to decide for themselves, however wise or foolish their decisions might seem to him. He had no use for change for change's sake. Although John Carmichael and I found that a mutual understanding came more readily, both men were immensely helpful to me during my tenure of the chair.

When appointments to the Authority were being considered I consistently pressed upon the Postmaster General of the day that the number of women members should be raised and when I left it had reached four, out of a total of thirteen. The proportion has now slipped back. This is a pity. In my experience – and this applies to both broadcasting services – women are especially effective in many of the problems which arise in broadcasting, especially those relating to programme standards.

The contributions of the women on the Authority varied just as the women varied. Isabel Graham-Bryce and Dame Anne Bryans, who were already members when I arrived, contemplated the new boy, I thought, quizzically if not suspiciously. Later came Lady Burton, Mrs Mary Adams, Lady Plummer and Lady Sharp. Elaine Burton, formerly the charming and sometimes ferocious critic of the Ministry of Food in the days when we were both in the other place and I was parliamentary secretary of the ministry, was a first-class member – breezy, optimistic, thorough, and always in the vicinity of the kitchen when the heat was greatest. Mary Adams, after so many years at the BBC, saw ITV through BBC spectacles, no bad thing for ITV. The late Beattie Plummer was unusually kind and friendly, though her real interests were farming and politics. Evelyn Sharp, forthright as ever, the ablest woman of her generation, could turn her mind to any problem, however difficult.

The men I remember best are Lord Williamson, as sturdily sensible and wise as he had been throughout his long years in trade unionism; Sir Vincent Tewson, deliberate – even prosy – and as sound as a bell. Then there were Sir Ben Bowen Thomas, Sir Patrick Hamilton, Sir Owen Saunders, Bill McFarlane Gray and Professor Hugh Hunt, from quite different stables with quite different approaches to television but all bringing their own brand of wisdom and experience. It was a grand team.

PART TWO

PORTLAND PLACE

8

Shock at the BBC

About nine o'clock on the evening of 25 July 1967 my wife
and I were dozing peacefully in front of our television set at
home in Hertfordshire when the telephone rang.

The caller was Philip Phillips, the television correspondent of
the *Sun*, who began by apologizing for disturbing our domestic
peace, and went on to say that he had just heard a story, which
he realized must be a load of nonsense, that I was to be appointed
director-general of the BBC and that someone named Bowden
would succeed me at the ITA. Would I comment? I promptly
agreed that any story that I was to be director-general of the
BBC was a load of nonsense. Later that night there were three
or four more calls from the press which my wife answered with
the standard reply that I was not available.

I rang the Postmaster General to find that he was at a public
dinner. Eventually I tracked him down on the telephone and,
when I told him what had happened, he said that he had heard
a similar story from a *Daily Mirror* executive an hour or two
before. Subsequently he rang to ask me to call on the Prime
Minister at the House of Commons at half-past two the next
day.

I duly presented myself at that time in the Prime Minister's
room at the House of Commons. Harold Davis, Mr Wilson's
parliamentary private secretary, who was in the outer office,
looked astonished to see me. Punctually at 2.30 pm I was called
in to find the Prime Minister in a relaxed mood and smoking a
big cigar. Accompanied by Edward Short, the Postmaster

General, he opened by saying that I had done a good job at Independent Television. The post of chairman of the BBC was, as I knew, vacant following Lord Normanbrook's death. Would I go to the BBC in the office of chairman of the governors? The press had got wind of what was in his mind and it would be convenient if I could give my answer forthwith with a view to an announcement at midnight.

I was, to say the least, surprised. It is true that some two years or so before the Prime Minister, at that time involved in a fierce argument with the BBC, had said to me in light-hearted fashion at a lobby lunch that he would have to get me to take on the chairmanship of the BBC. I attached no importance to this sally and, in any case, the job was not vacant. One or two lobby men, standing nearby, took the remark more seriously than I did. Before the interview with the Prime Minister I had had an occasional hint that such an invitation was on the cards, as had one or two members of the press, but I could not really believe that it would happen.

A number of stories appeared in the press in the next few days suggesting that Harold Wilson had attached some strings to his invitation, that he had asked me to do a hatchet job on the BBC, that the whole thing was an anti-Greene move, and so on. In fact, nothing of the kind took place. What happened was that I received a straightforward invitation to take on a new job. I told the Prime Minister that in some quarters the reaction to my appointment would be explosive, only to be told by him that over the years we had both been used to that sort of thing and that we would just have to put up with it : the prospect of criticism did not worry him. The Prime Minister added that three additional governors would soon be appointed.

My immediate reaction was to ask for a little time to consider the invitation, although I appreciated from past experience the embarrassment to a government when the press has wind of an impending announcement. It is good sense in such circumstances to expedite the announcement. This kind of leakage happens with increasing frequency nowadays. So I was not surprised when the Prime Minister said that the circumstances demanded that there should be an early announcement; indeed, some time that evening. I decided to accept, suspecting that my

decision would have been the same after a period of consideration. The invitation was irresistible. A Conservative Prime
Minister had appointed me to the chair of the ITA, a Labour
Prime Minister was proposing to recommend my appointment
to the chair of the BBC. Flattery works with me as with most
people. I had had a long association with the BBC as a broadcaster and I hoped that in the inevitable controversy to come
this would stand me in good stead, an assumption that was
proved in the event to be unfounded.

The Prime Minister had not given me a choice between an
extension of my job at the ITA or the acceptance of the BBC
chairmanship. If he had, I suspect that I might well have
accepted an extension of the ITA chairmanship. When he
asked me to take up my duties at the BBC at an early date, I
replied that Robert Fraser had been under great pressure and
was due for a holiday he badly needed in August, and that
1 September was the first practicable date. He agreed, adding
that the announcement would be embargoed until a minute
after midnight.

The interview over, I returned to 70 Brompton Road, and,
after binding him to secrecy, told Fraser what had happened.
His reaction was a mixture of surprise and excitement. We had
worked well together, we had become good friends, we had
come to understand each other. The talents, if that is the right
word, of one had complemented those of the other. But undoubtedly his powers had been restricted for he had lost some
of the virtually complete independence of action and authority
which he had enjoyed since Independent Television began.

Our immediate problem was how best to tell the Authority
so that the first intimation did not come to them from the press
next morning. Fortunately, there was to be a farewell dinner
that night to the retiring deputy chairman, Sir Sydney Caine.
I said that I did not want to complicate the dinner to Sydney
and I thought it best to keep silent until the dinner and speeches
were over. Incidentally, I was called to the telephone during
the dinner by the Prime Minister's private secretary who asked
me to agree that the story be released earlier, at 10 pm, or even
earlier (I believe, in fact, it was released about eight o'clock).

The dinner in honour of Sydney Caine followed the usual

course. About ten-thirty, just as the fidgeting began, I got up and said that there was something that members of the Authority should know before reading tomorrow's press. Tomorrow would be the last occasion on which I would be presiding over an Authority meeting, as I had that day accepted another appointment which was inconsistent with continuance in the chair of the Authority. I paused a moment and then added that I had that day accepted an invitation to become chairman of the governors of the BBC.

At first it was thought it was one of Hill's little jokes. Then, following some confirmatory head-nodding by Robert Fraser, there went round the room a buzz of astonishment. Patrick Duncan exclaimed 'no, no'. Lady Sharp looked as if she could murder me. According to my wife, Tony Pragnell, one of the deputy director-generals, was physically shaking with surprise. It had been quite a day. My last meeting of the Authority on the following day, however, proceeded as if nothing had happened. I made no further reference to my departure apart from agreeing that 31 August would be convenient for my farewell dinner.

Kenneth Adam, at that time director of television at the BBC, writing twenty months later in the *Sunday Times*, reported that an emergency meeting of the Board of Management was called in the director-general's room as soon as Sir Robert Lusty, the BBC's acting chairman, returned from the Post Office with the news. According to Adam, Greene, sitting 'behind his desk with a dark baffled face', told his colleagues the dread news – and asked them if he should resign. Somebody said that 'that would be playing "their" game', another 'if you go, we all go'. I have heard another and quite different account of what happened. Again according to Adam, at a dinner which Greene and his colleagues were giving that night to Tony Barber 'even those the most abstemious drank more than usual so that a kind of frenzied gaiety took hold'. When the governors gathered for their meeting next morning, according to the same source, 'several Governors were furious and made no bones about it'.

Next morning the press reaction was better than I had expected. The press headlines varied from 'Lord Hill switches to the BBC', in the *Mail*, to 'Anger at the BBC over Lord Hill

takeover' in the *Sketch*. The *Daily Telegraph* put it soberly as
'Hill leaves ITA to run BBC' while the *Mirror* announced 'The
BBC gets the Radio Doctor's medicine'. 'I doubt if even the
BBC can digest Lord Hill', wrote Nancy Banks-Smith, while
'Just how tough will Lord Hill get with Alf Garnett?' was an-
other headline. 'Consultant or Sawbones', 'Is this the politi-
cians' revenge?', 'Sensible Choice', and 'No room for a strong
man at the BBC' were other samples.

Then came the press speculation. Was this a preamble to a
proposal which Edward Short had been floating in speeches
that there should be an amalgamation of the BBC and Independent Television? Was this intended to crush the freedom of
expression in the BBC, something which Harold Wilson was
believed increasingly to dislike? Did it mean that the BBC was
to go commercial? As far as I knew it was just speculation with
no foundation in fact.

Soon it became clear that the reactions of the hierarchy of the
BBC were seeping through to the press, for Robert Lusty and
Hugh Greene had not been silent. According to the *Times*
Diary, the governors at their meeting the following day shared
the strong sense of outrage which ran from top to bottom of
the BBC at the news of Lord Hill's switch of channel. It was a
slap in the face for Sir Hugh Greene. With a touch of irony it
was recalled that at the Labour Party Scarborough Conference
in 1963, the year of my appointment to the ITA, Mr Wilson,
'who was working himself in as the new Leader, pitched into
the Tories for appointing Lord Hill as Chairman of the
ITA'.

There then followed the usual congratulatory letters, many
of them from within Independent Television at all levels. There
were none whatever from the BBC hierarchy, governors or
management.

Two or three days later, I was telephoned by a senior official
of the Post Office whom I knew and who said that he had been
lunching with a senior executive of the BBC who had prompted
him to suggest that I should offer 'an olive branch' by phoning
Greene at his home in Suffolk and inviting him to meet me. At
first I bridled a little, retorting that the olive branch should be
proffered by others. I had not spoken to the press or to anyone

else : the bitterness had come from the BBC, not me. But I soon subsided and said I would think it over.

I rang Sir Francis Maclean, BBC director of engineering, thinking he was the BBC executive the Post Office man had met. I later discovered it was Frank Gillard, director of radio. Maclean strongly urged that I should invite Greene, who was stunned by my appointment, to meet me for a talk, and I agreed. As soon as this conversation ended I rang Greene at his Suffolk home and suggested that we should meet halfway between his home and London. He did not drive, he said, and he suggested a meeting in London, to which I agreed, suggesting tea at my club, the Reform, a day or two later.

Our talk there was calm and frank, and not unfriendly. Whether he liked it or not – and clearly he did not – I had become a fact in his working life. We could, I believed, work out a way of living together in a civilized way, once the hubbub had died down. As far as I knew, there was no anti-Greene motive in the appointment : certainly there was none in my mind. He appeared to accept what I said and we parted on good terms, with Greene introducing me to my BBC chauffeur who, I thought, was in urgent need of a haircut.

About this time I received a letter from Robert Lusty suggesting that we should lunch together at the BBC and I accepted for Tuesday 8 August. In the meantime I arranged for two senior officials at the ITA to get in touch with senior officials of the Corporation to discuss certain mundane matters. For example, I already had a car supplied by the chemical company of which I was chairman. I did not need a BBC car, I told them. The reply was that it was unthinkable that a BBC chairman should move around on his duties in a car not belonging to the BBC : the present one was worn out and a new one would be bought.

Secondly, I already had a colour television set for the ITA had had one installed in my home only a few weeks previously. It was a hired set and a year's rent had been paid in advance and therefore I should not need a BBC one for almost a year. The BBC was not impressed. It was their job to install their television set in their chairman's home.

Thirdly, the BBC reacted violently to my intention to bring

my own secretary. As I had already found out, it was customary at the BBC for the chairman to share the secretariat of the
director-general. There was no room in Broadcasting House for
an additional secretary, I was told. I thought this attitude un-
reasonable. Any man in a responsible position, even a non-
executive one, needs to be served by his own secretary. Had the
BBC offered to supply a personal secretary serving me and me
alone, I should have accepted unhesitatingly. As they did not,
I resolved that the remarkably efficient secretary who had
worked for me for twenty years, and was my secretary at the
ITA, should be asked to come with me to the BBC.

Then came the lunch with Robert Lusty. He spoke of the
shock which the BBC governors had sustained at the news of
my appointment. They had not been consulted. Indeed he, as
the acting chairman, had been told only a few hours before the
public announcement. He foresaw great difficulties ahead and
he offered to mediate between me and Greene.

He launched into a comparison between a public service and
commercial television, to the latter's great disadvantage, asserting that only the former could really satisfy the public interest.
To say he was patronizing would hardly be fair; to say he was
sadly contemptuous would be nearer the mark. He suggested
that at my first meeting he, not I, should take the chair; that I
should come as an observer to see how the BBC did things. Although up to this point I had listened in silence, this last suggestion was more 'than I could take. I then told Lusty that I
needed a secretary who was responsible to me and to no one
else, that I could not accept the sharing of a secretary with the
director-general or anyone else, and that I was not prepared to
argue this point.

Between lunching with Lusty and my first day at Broadcasting House there was much to do. I cleared up what I could at
Brompton Road, although I was clearly leaving a number of
ends untied following the programme contracts decisions. I
lunched as the guest of Sidney Bernstein, at the Ritz. He thanked
me for teaching him how to engage in controversy without ran-
cour; it was a very pleasant meeting with a remarkable man
whom I much admired. I talked with my successor, Herbert
Bowden, so clearly relieved to be departing from politics. I had

at his suggestion with Harman Grisewood, formerly Hugh Greene's chief assistant.

A little later Robert Lusty wrote to suggest that I should withdraw from an engagement into which I had entered for November, that of presiding over a Granada lecture at the Guildhall to be given by Fred Friendly of the United States. It would, he thought, be inappropriate for me to continue with an engagement under the auspices of a commercial company which I had accepted while chairman of the ITA. I declined to withdraw, thinking it would be discourteous to Granada as well as to Fred Friendly, whom I regarded as an important and powerful figure in broadcasting, engaged as he was on a campaign to promote public service television in his own country.

On the morning of 1 September I arrived at Broadcasting House to be received with a theatrical salute by the commissionaire. Greene was away on holiday in Suffolk. Amongst the engagements in the next few weeks were lunch at Television Centre to meet Kenneth Adam, Huw Wheldon, Paul Fox and others and a call on the Postmaster General who described to me Lusty's reaction on being told of my appointment: dumb astonishment.

Incidentally, it did not help matters that the Postmaster General should have made a slip in referring to the new chairman of the governors as Charles Smith instead of Charles Hill. No doubt Charles Smith, then general secretary of the Post Office Engineers, was on his mind! Short told me that after Lusty had returned to the BBC to tell the news, Hugh Greene had rung the Postmaster General to demand an immediate interview, adding that he could not undertake not to issue a statement if the interview were not granted. The Postmaster General agreed to see him, but not until late the following day. Next day Greene withdrew his request.

During this time I saw Lord Fulton, who would become vice-chairman from 31 January in succession to Lusty, and he promised his support in the difficult months ahead, a promise that he fully kept. He urged upon me a policy of gradualism. I visited the main London broadcasting centres. At the television news headquarters at Alexandra Palace I was received by the editor of television news, Desmond Taylor, and others. My first impression was that my reception by Desmond Taylor was cool; only when I got to know him better did I realize that this was his normal demeanour : I was seeing hostility where none was intended. I also toured Bush House and was very impressed with the director of external broadcasting, Charles Curran. I attended ITV functions at which I received gifts from ITA companies and managing directors. I went back to Brompton Road for drinks with regional officers. My first job as chairman of the BBC was to open an international broadcasting conference. I plunged into my job with energy and enthusiasm.

Then, three weeks later, came the first meeting of the governors over which I would preside. I behaved as if I had been the chairman for years. I welcomed another new member, Lord Dunleath. No one welcomed me; in fact, no one referred to my arrival. Before the meeting I had cast a careful eye over the minutes of the previous meeting held on the day of the announcement of my appointment to see what report it included of the indignation meeting which had taken place. Alas, the minutes were silent on this subject.

Early on I sensed that the members of the board most likely to oppose me would be Robert Lusty, Dame Anne Godwin and Lady Baird, though in this I was not wholly right. After an uneasy phase, Lady Baird, as I believe she would agree, accepted my chairmanship without demur if not with enthusiasm. The Welsh National governor, Professor Glanmor Williams, often opposed me although he did it with great charm and courtesy.

It soon became clear that governors' meetings were friendly, Christian-name affairs. It also became obvious that they decided very little and that a common form of so-called decision was what the governors agreed with the director-general. In my first two or three months in the chair I gained some impressions of people, not all of which were justified on closer acquaintance. The hostility I found was mainly at governor level and it was not unanimous at that level. John Fulton, who had expressed his loyalty to me, was unfailing in his friendly support; we did not always agree but his attitude to me was loyal, generous and understanding. Peter Trower also made it plain to me at the outset that he was not unfriendly : unfortunately he died within a few months.

Of Greene my first impression was that he was aloof, cautious, telling me very little. But throughout our period together our relations were uniformly civilized and adult. He came to see me weekly and we discussed things in an easy, friendly way.

Oliver Whitley, who had succeeded Harman Grisewood as Greene's chief assistant, was the perfect gentleman. Kenneth Lamb, the secretary, was charming, if long-winded, and Kenneth Adam, the director of television, greeted me on my visit to Television Centre with great bonhomie, as if we were old friends. He had lived in Harpenden as we did during the war and I had sometimes met him on the station platform. 'I will call you Charles,' he said, 'when no one else is present.'

Huw Wheldon, frank, friendly, argumentative, remarkably fluent, with the ideas tumbling out in an eloquent torrent, I liked from the outset and I usually forgave him for taking so long to reach his conclusion. He always came to the point in the end. David Attenborough, youthful, charming and astonishingly talented, told me that the reaction to the news of my appointment had been just as if Rommel had been appointed to command the Eighth Army. When I asked him whether he meant that the staff doubted whether I was a good general, he replied 'No. They know that you are : but they need convincing that you are fighting for the same things as the previous one.' Frank Gillard was the same Frank Gillard I had known years ago, open, straightforward and reliable. I suspected that they all hoped to tame me but did not yet know where my weaknesses and wickedness lay.

October was a busy month inside and outside the office. I had resolved that if I were to do the job properly as a trustee for the public I should do what I had done at the ITA and read and reply to those incoming letters which were addressed personally to me. The number varied according to the liveliness of the controversy of the time, between fifteen and thirty a day, not all, of course, on different subjects. To a few of them I dictated the answers; in replying to the remainder I sought drafts from the highly efficient secretariat, scrutinizing and if necessary modifying the drafts. It seemed to me that one of the best ways of performing the trustee function which fell on governors, and of learning how the machine worked, and how its people 'ticked', was to answer my own letters. Indeed, this practice gave me a card of entry to the programme-making machine and over the years it was to be the largest single element in my daily work.

For the rest there were engagements of one kind or another. I made a speech at the Radio and TV Retailers' dinner, an occasion which I was told in the BBC was not quite up to chairman's level. I went all the same. I also made my first speech on television problems to the Westminster Chamber of Commerce.

Then, on 18 October, there was the first meeting of the General Advisory Council at Television Centre. It was a set piece, with the chairman and director-general sitting beside the chairman of the council and other governors sitting at a side table. The council was a high-powered body consisting mostly of well-known figures and, as one would expect, there was highly intelligent talk on general broadcasting topics. The director-general answered the questions and replied to points of criticism, yielding nothing in the process. My first impression of the General Advisory Council was of a decorative and distinguished body which was allowed little influence.

I lunched with the then Government Chief Whip, John Silkin, on 23 October. We discussed ways and means of handling problems between Westminster and the BBC. He spoke very well of Oliver Whitley who dealt with these exchanges. When I told him that I hoped that party political broadcasts could be abolished, he did not object. In early November I also lunched with Willie Whitelaw, Opposition Chief Whip, who spoke well of his relations with the BBC and particularly Oliver Whitley. He, too, was not opposed to the abolition of party political broadcasts.

On 26 October came my first press conference on the subject of the BBC's accounts. The press was naturally lively and inquisitive but I kept the answers to finance, though one man asked a leading question about my appointment. I told him that part of the trouble with the press was that they believed what they wrote.

Then on 9 November I received a deputation consisting of Mrs Whitehouse and two others. Apparently my predecessor, Lord Normanbrook, had resisted a suggestion that the Viewers and Listeners' Association should have a special position in an advisory capacity to the BBC on the grounds that it was an undemocratic body. She said that changes had now been made and it was now a democratic body. She took it from Lord Normanbrook's letter that it would now be accorded special advisory status. I rejected the argument, as I did the interpretation which she put on my predecessor's letter, making it plain that no organization would have a special position in relation to the BBC, though her organization was entitled to have its views considered as well as any others. At the BBC, as at the ITA, I treated Mrs Whitehouse and her colleagues with courtesy and their representations with care, recognizing that the central theme of her campaign could not be contemptuously dismissed, even though I was rarely able to agree with her.

It was not long after my arrival that I raised the matter of my office. The office traditionally used by the chairman was on the third floor separated from the director-general's office by the room occupied by his secretaries. My secretary was a flight of stairs away on the fourth floor on the grounds that there was no room for her on the third floor. My office, I thought, resembled an oak-lined coffin, airless and sunless, and after an hour or so the atmosphere became heavy and stuffy. I asked for another and more cheerful office, preferably one with an adjacent room for my secretary. I did not ask for an office on another floor, for I did not mind where it was, provided it was light and airy, with my secretary's room close at hand. Nothing happened for some time, as is the way in big organizations, and I asked that the search for a new office should be intensified. Once it was clear that I was serious, the Central Services Department got cracking and eventually I was offered two small offices, adjacent to my secretary's office on the fourth floor, which could be knocked into one. This plan had the further advantage that there could be provided close at hand a bathroom and a bedroom for changing and for sleeping on those nights when BBC work kept me late in London. I approved the plan and the work was quickly done.

Those who have visited me at Broadcasting House know the modest but adequate office that resulted, but this did not prevent the press describing it as a penthouse on the top floor. I read, too, that I had deliberately moved to another floor to set up a chairman's establishment in competition with that of the director-general. This was not my last experience of a pastime indulged in by some BBC staff of feeding the press with malicious tit-bits. The fact is that I would have stayed on the third floor if someone had been willing to move to give me house-room.

All this seems very petty, I know. But petty it was.

It is not easy for me to analyse the initial hostility with which I was received at Portland Place. Obviously the appointment of a new chairman of governors was a matter of some importance, for the advent of a new head of any organization is likely to disturb expectations, to awaken ambitions and to arouse fears. Maybe it happened at a particularly vulnerable time for the BBC. Possibly there was a personal element, although I was unknown personally to most of the governors. I was from a professional stable – no disadvantage I would have thought. I had been a minister, and it might have been feared that I would be on the side of politicians, whatever their colour, and encourage inroads into the independence of the BBC. As a former Tory minister, maybe I was suspect to the Left. The government of which I had been a member had created the rival service from which I had come. My head and heart might still be with Independent Television. Worse still, I might regard advertising as the right basis for both broadcasting services. My earlier career might have suggested that I would be unsympathetic with the professional's distaste for management. And it could have been that the object of my appointment was the correction of the so-called anarchy of the BBC, that I was an instrument to put the BBC in its place.

Whether these fears – or others – existed I do not know. Did I yield to lobbies, political, libertarian or others? Did I turn over the BBC professional to the mercies of the layman? Did I argue for advertising on the BBC? The answers are to be found in the record. But whether such fears and apprehensions were justified or not, what was not justified or sensible or defensible was the pettiness, the childishness, of some people at the top of the BBC before and after my arrival.

9

BBC Money Problems

Soon after my first meeting of the Board of Governors I had a telephone call from the Postmaster General who told me that ministers had been considering the BBC's finances. There were ministers, he said, who felt that the BBC was extravagant, that there was surplus fat in its finances, and who, in any case, were unfavourable to any suggestion that the licence fee should be increased. Some ministers favoured reference of the licence fee to the Prices and Incomes Board. No decision had been reached and the Prime Minister had asked that I should immediately begin a personal and comprehensive study of the BBC's finances, including the possibility of further economies and alternative ways of raising any money needed, reporting within a month. No decision on the licence fee would be reached until this report had been considered.

I told the Board of Governors of this invitation at its next meeting, adding that I had agreed to comply with the request. At the next meeting of the board I would indicate the general lines of what I proposed to say. Insofar as any of the proposals differed in any significant way from the policies hitherto followed by the board, I would draw the attention of governors to such points. Should the views of governors differ from my own on these points, I would include these views as well as my own in the report that I submitted to the Postmaster General.

This was not universally popular amongst the governors. Dame Anne Godwin saw it as a departure from the principle of the board's collective responsibility. I had put the board, she thought, into an extremely awkward position. Robert Lusty thought that the government's action had placed every governor, including the chairman, in an invidious position. I said that I could go no further than to repeat the undertaking to keep governors fully informed and closed the discussion by saying that the board would have a full opportunity to consider the whole matter at their next meeting.

These doubts were natural enough. Not surprisingly, some governors were suspicious of their new chairman. I understood their misgivings but, bearing in mind the antipathy towards the BBC amongst some members of the government, it seemed to me that I had no choice but to accept the invitation in the BBC's own interest. Anyway, I did accept and, at a subsequent meeting of the governors, produced my report.

This time the tone was quite different. Lusty, the vice-chairman, said it was a magnificent paper and that coming from the chairman its impact might perhaps be decisive. He thanked me for having given governors the opportunity to read it in advance of the meeting. The one thing he doubted was the wisdom of inviting outside consultants to study the Corporation's financial organization. Dame Anne was silent on this occasion.

The report was an exhaustive one which began by reciting the background of government promise and action and went on to a detailed analysis of the financial position. The general conclusions were that an increase in the licence fee was essential, that advertising was wholly undesirable and that a firm of management consultants would be called in 'to ensure that the possibilities of further economies, if they exist, are exposed'. In the event, the combined licence fee was increased from £5 to £6 from 1 January 1969.

The suggestion of an external scrutiny by management consultants came up as it seemed to me that the kind of general criticism of extravagance which was being made could only be met, and critical voices subdued, if we brought in from outside a firm of management consultants with particular emphasis on the financial side. From such experience as I had had of management consultants in another organization, I was not particularly impressed. Despite this, I felt that it was important to take this step in the case of the BBC, lest the vague assertions which had been made about extravagance should stick, without any attempt being made to disprove them.

Some people within the BBC thought that such external experts could *never*, in the relatively short time at their disposal, understand what the BBC was and how it worked and consequently they tended at first to resent their suggestion which they saw as an invitation to outside interference. Nevertheless the governors agreed, and Hugh Greene and I called on a number of leaders of industry who had had their organizations subjected to such study by outside experts, seeking to know their experience and from that to judge which body was likely to prove the most appropriate for the BBC. Eventually we settled for McKinseys, who began a most detailed study of the whole BBC structure. They impressed me greatly – as they did most, if not all, the people they met within the Corporation. The man in charge, Roger Morrison, was an unusually intelligent and pleasant man who soon learned far more about the BBC than most of those working within it had grasped in years.

10

Sir Hugh Greene

Just before Christmas 1967 there arose a matter which was to have important repercussions. Greene told me that his wife proposed to divorce him and that he feared that a Sunday newspaper would publish something to that effect very soon, for a reporter had been hanging around his country home. Though nothing had yet appeared in the press he thought that it would soon.

I told Greene that I thought a divorce was a matter for himself rather than for me and the governors : a man's private life was his own. Those who were happily married, as I was, should hesitate to pronounce on the actions of those who were not, for they were unlikely to understand their problems. I said that I hoped to be able to sustain this position among the governors, believing that a public man should be judged by his successes or failures in his public life and that it was not for others to judge his private life unless one overlapped with the other. There the matter rested for, in the event, nothing appeared in the press at the time.

A few months later, in April 1968, I received a remarkable letter from Hugh Greene asking that the governors should publish forthwith that he would stay until the age of sixty and possibly thereafter and that his successor should come from inside the Corporation. I told him that I doubted the wisdom of putting his suggested draft announcement to the governors. How could they make what was the equivalent of an announcement that whatever happened he would be safe until the age of sixty?

I suggested that at the next governors' meeting but one I should open the whole question of future senior appointments. He was then fifty-eight and it *might*, I said, be convenient that he went either earlier or later than sixty so as to facilitate the best and most timely appointments to senior posts. He agreed. His demeanour, I thought at the time, seemed to be changing. Though solemn in manner he was co-operative, and clearly concerned about his future.

In early May 1968 Greene and I were talking in general terms about future senior appointments and the question of the succession to him arose. We spoke of potential director-generals – Curran, Wheldon and Attenborough among them. Naturally we got round to his own future. When would the question of the succession to him arise? Had he in mind to go on after sixty, the normal retiring age? Had he considered retiring before sixty. I expressed the view that a man holding a senior post ought to have the chance to retire before sixty while there is still time and he is of an age to be considered for other posts. He might think that he had given all he could to broadcasting and that, without reflecting in any way on that contribution, the time had come for a change. On the other hand, if he did not retire before sixty there was a good case for him staying on a few years after that age.

He was not in any way taken aback by the course of this discussion, though he said he had no other plans apart from the chairmanship of the family brewery. He seemed to want to go early, though he did not say so explicitly. It occurred to me that, although he wanted to retire, there was a nagging doubt in his mind and I believed I knew what it was. If it should happen that he retired from the BBC at or about the time of the announcement of a second divorce, the two things would be connected. There had been from time to time cries from Mrs Whitehouse and others that Greene should go. Would it be said that, whatever the nature of the public announcement, he had been made to go because of his second divorce? I felt instinctively that this was his worry.

I then had an idea. If he really wanted to go could anything be done to minimize the danger of an association between his departure and his divorce? He had rendered immense service to the Corporation and to broadcasting. The thought occurred to me that if he were appointed a governor of the BBC after his retirement from the director-generalship there could be no basis whatever for any suggestion that he had been required to depart because of the divorce. He could go with honour. I put the idea to him although I had no power to put it into effect.

The idea attracted him and we agreed to talk further some two days later.

Then it was that Greene told me that he was interested in an early retirement with a governorship. He recognized that he had probably given all he had to give and to end with a BBC governorship would be something he had never expected. If his five years as a governor began in 1969 he would be a member of the board and so able to advise his colleagues when the next enquiry began. He would prefer mid-1969 as the time of his retirement, when the news of his divorce would have died down. He expected publicity by June and the completion of the proceedings by the summer or the autumn. He regarded retirement plus a governorship as a package to be considered as a whole.

With some diffidence he suggested that a life peerage would enable him to be 'active on the fringe of politics'. I told him that I would consult the Prime Minister on the possibility of a governorship; that I hoped that the arrangements could be completed and announced before the news of the divorce though that might prove to be impossible; that I had in mind a somewhat earlier retirement than mid-1969; that I would mention the life peerage to the Prime Minister but that was as far as I could go; and that I would not raise the matter with the governors until after I had sounded the Prime Minister.

Subsequently I saw the Prime Minister and told him what had happened. In effect I asked him to recommend Hugh Greene for a BBC governorship following his retirement from the post of director-general. He agreed. To my surprise the Prime Minister knew of the impending divorce and agreed that announcement of both the retirement and the governorship should be made early, even though the date of operation could be early next year. I mentioned Greene's hope of a life peerage and then went on to press for a speedy decision on the outstanding matter of an increase in the licence fee which he said the Cabinet would consider the following week.

Greene was delighted when I told him of the outcome. Clearly he saw this in the context of his impending divorce, the honour of being the first director-general to be made a governor and possibly the prospect of less contact with me. I asked him to write to me asking for release on 1 April 1969, so that I could discuss the proposed package with the governors. Next day I received a letter from Greene which I thought was too tentative, too vague. I told him this and he agreed to make it clearer and stronger.

At the outset of their meeting the following week the governors met without Greene (it was not until May 1972 that it was first suggested that the governors should meet alone at dinner). I read to them Greene's letter and described my talk with the Prime Minister, stressing that the suggestion that Greene should be a governor was my own, that the impending divorce proceedings were irrelevant except as to timing, that if approved the package would be announced within the month. The governors were surprised, to say the least, and at first there was no comment. One governor doubted whether an ex-director-general could be a satisfactory governor and manage to avoid breathing down the neck of his successor. At first other governors remained silent but eventually all agreed to accept the position as conveyed in Greene's letter. Greene then joined us and I told him of the governors' reluctant acceptance and said that the only misgiving was the possible effect of his presence on the board on his successor.

In mid-July Greene and I met the press to announce his retirement in the following April and his appointment as governor in the following July. In a prior meeting with colleagues to discuss the mode of presentation of the announcement, what was most feared was a 'Hill sacks Greene' headline. Would Greene have retired without the governorship – would that be asked? And, if so, what should the answer be? It was agreed that it should be 'no'. Should I reveal that I had recommended the governorship? We agreed that the answer should be 'yes'.

At the press conference itself things went reasonably well. After the bald announcements, Greene talked about his own satisfaction, even delight, at the change of role. He gave a broad hint that in his view his successor should come from inside and not outside. He said that our relationship had been pleasant and enjoyable and that he was walking upstairs, not being kicked upstairs; in fact, he was walking upstairs with pleasure.

In their reports the next morning the press, on the whole, accepted our explanation. Some were tempted to read into the announcement that there had been a blinding row between Greene and myself, that we found it impossible to work together or even that it was part of some nefarious plot on my part. On the whole, the press praised Greene, and rightly so, for his remarkable leadership over the previous eight years.

There were some predictable reactions, Mrs Whitehouse and one or two others thought that the permissiveness associated with his name had gone too far. But, on the whole, there was widespread recognition of the fundamental nature of the changes he had wrought in broadcasting. T. C. Worsley in the *Financial Times* put it well. He 'carried the BBC struggling and kicking out of its auntie image into something more relevant to the decade. Instead of reflecting the respectable old-fashioned middle class values of the past that were over and done with, the BBC began to mirror at least equally the aspirations and attitudes of the generation of the newly enfranchised young who had come up via the grammar schools and the red-brick universities . . . Sir Hugh gave them their chance. It might be said that what George Devine did for the theatre in the fifties . . . Sir Hugh did for television in the sixties'. Only one correspondent was indecently brutal. He called the whole business a 'politicians' wangle.'

I had dropped a brick at the press conference, however. I announced that Frank Gillard would reach the strict retirement age at the end of the year, and that Kenneth Adam would be retiring at the end of the year. What I had not been told was that, although the decision that Adam should retire – or, to be exact, that his extension beyond the retirement age should finish – had been made, and although he had been told, there had not strictly speaking been an official promulgation. In fact, Adam had not told anybody, not even his secretary, and naturally he found the announcement embarrassing.

Incidentally, at about the time I was preoccupied with Sir Hugh Greene's future and successor, I dined with his illustrious predecessor as director-general, Lord Reith. Reith was just out of hospital after having had a pace-maker attached to his heart and he was really rather proud of his operation and his little gadget.

At first he was cautious and uncommunicative. And I made a bad start by reminding him that the previous occasion on which we had met had been at the luncheon table of ATV, with Prince Littler presiding. Bearing in mind his powerful attacks on commercial television I soon realized that this was, to say the least of it, a little tactless : it was as if he had been caught scrumping apples.

Eventually the great man warmed up, taking no trouble to conceal his contempt for television generally and for Hugh Greene in particular. Things had gone to hell since his day. The governors should do something about it. When I chided him that it was his strong director-generalship which had laid the pattern for the future, based on a powerful director-general and a weak Board of Governors, he made the retort, which he has since made on other occasions, 'I took what I was given, nothing more. I always addressed the Governors as "sir", never by their Christian names.' The unbending rigidity of this man was really remarkable. Everything was black or white but never grey.

There was a curious side effect of this social occasion. A few weeks later there was to be a memorial service to Admiral Carpendale who in pre-war days had been Reith's right-hand man. Reith said that if Greene was going to the memorial service he was not. I told him that this really was extraordinary. Carpendale was the man to whom he had owed most of all during his years with the BBC : he should go to the memorial service whether Greene went or not. I then, having thought of it for the first time, said that I was going. He wrote to me two or three days later to tell me that, although he would go to the service, he must make a protest and that he would therefore decline the invitation he had received to read the Lesson. In the event I read it in his stead.

I found John Reith not so much frightening as exciting. He loved praise, warming to a regular dose. He spoke at the dinner table as if he had created not only the BBC but (as chairman of Imperial Airways) BOAC as well. He spoke in high praise of no one. He repeated again and again that he was wrong to leave the BBC and that he had only just learned to live, and so on. It was material similar to that he used in the famous Muggeridge interviews.

11

Feeling My Way

Early in 1968, the BBC's current affairs programmes, *24 Hours* in particular, came in for a good deal of public criticism, and found their way to the governors' agenda quite frequently. It was at one such discussion in early February that there emerged a suggestion from a governor that there should be a paper on broadcasting and the public mood. The essence of the public criticism echoed by some governors was that the underlying purpose of *24 Hours* seemed to some people to be 'discover anything that was good or anything which had existed for some time and then seek to destroy it' There was a negative spirit. There seemed to be little control over the producers by anyone. Why was everything knocked? This was the sort of public criticism which came in in hundreds of letters. Then the governor who had raised the matter suggested that there should be a policy paper from the director-general, bringing into focus the issues that had been raised.

I thought that it might be a timely intellectual exercise to consider a paper on what should be the relationship between the mood of the country and the BBC. Greene, who was leaving for New Zealand the next day, said that he would ask Oliver Whitley to prepare such a paper while he was away and then to pass it to the board through the Board of Management.

I have read in the press that while Greene and his colleagues were away in New Zealand at the Commonwealth Broadcasting Conference I consolidated my position, and this document was given as an example of the mischief I got up to in their absence. It is true that the director-general and the directors of television, radio and engineering all left this country for five weeks some five months after the arrival of a new chairman. It is also true that in that time I added considerably to my knowledge of what was going on in the BBC. What is not true is the suggestion often made in print that the document was devised and issued behind the back of the director-general while he and his colleagues were abroad.

In due course a beautifully written draft appeared before the board; indeed some thought it more literary than cogent, with more style than substance. There were criticisms of it and back it went to the Board of Management. When it came back to the Board of Governors in modified form there were still doubts about its cogency; so I said I would myself revise the document and a few days later got down to the task. The revised document came to the governors via the Board of Management and it was eventually printed for discussion within the staff, being published at the same time.

'Broadcasting and the Public Mood' was not a good document, too many pens had contributed to it. It was never effectively discussed within the BBC. I came to realize that my fatal mistake was in redrafting the paper myself: this made it a governors' document and sealed its fate within the organization. As Adam put it, it was 'unlikely that an encyclical from the governors would carry any real weight' even though, according to him, 'it was rewritten in a way which satisfied the Board of Management'. I ought to have realized that a document stemming from the Board of Management, however imperfect, stood a much better chance of acceptance within the organization than one which came from the boardroom table.

After six months in the chair I set down some early reflections on the conduct of business. I found the work of the Board of Governors extremely well organized with plenty of opportunity for governors to express their views on most topics, particularly during a regular agenda item 'Governors' questions' when there were some quite fascinating contributions at the board table. But these discussions, however exciting, however valuable, seemed to lead nowhere. A point was made, the

D

director-general replied and that was that. Sometimes we came back to it at a subsequent meeting but not often.

On one occasion a governor raised the matter of reports of the party conferences. Why had it been decided, as he had read in the press, that there would be less reporting of the next conferences than in the previous year? That, said Greene, is an editorial matter. I intervened to point out that governors could raise any question that they liked, although I would always advise them not to raise questions of management.

The range of subjects discussed at the board was wide. There was the usual emphasis on current affairs, their balance, the observance of the requirement that there should be no editorializing, the methods of interviewers, and so on. The *Wednesday Play* came up again and again for scrutiny, for both praise and criticism. Bad language, emphasis on sex, all these matters came up frequently in one form or another. But there the matter seemed to end. We could talk but that was all. Policy was made by management.

I put a document to my colleagues proposing changes in procedure. My main proposal concerned finance. The Corporation was spending more than £80 million a year. The board's responsibility for finance was clear-cut and inescapable; yet the spending proposals were dealt with quite superficially and speedily. It could hardly be otherwise, for governors knew too little about their background to comment effectively. It seemed to me that two or three members of the board should constitute a finance committee which would scrutinize financial proposals with considerable care before they came to the board, and maintain a continuous watch on spending generally. For years past the annual income of the Corporation had risen steadily and quite steeply as the number of viewers and listeners increased. But virtual saturation point was approaching and henceforth the Corporation would have to learn to live within an income which was rising but modestly, except when the licence fee was increased. I had been asked as chairman to agree between meetings to a proposal to spend some £1¾ million on films, which involved a responsibility that I was loath to accept as an individual. It was this sort of consideration which led me to propose that there should be a finance committee of the board, which, while in no way removing from the board or modifying the full responsibility it bore for money matters, would make a particular study of the Corporation's finances and any proposals for substantial spending, reporting to the board through its chairman.

Some governers had said they were not entirely happy about the way the board was carrying out its financial stewardship. But rather to my surprise there was considerable opposition to this proposal. Dame Anne Godwin said that the existence of sub-committees could destroy something of the vitality of the board. She doubted whether standing committees would be able to deal in much greater detail with matters in their areas of concern than the whole board. Lady Baird said that her experience on the board had convinced her that the present system was much better than one which might have the effect of constricting the Corporation's 'clever and dedicated top officials'. Glanmor Williams said that his three years as a governor had convinced him that the board already dealt with its responsibilities carefully and thoroughly : governors could not become professionals nor should they take up the time of directors by intervening in committees between the Board of Management and the board. I listened, astonished but silent.

Then I emphasized that this proposal was not intended in any way to limit the scope or authority or responsibility of the board itself, but designed rather to free the board to concentrate on major matters of programme policy which should be their prime concern. The director-general thought that the appointment of a finance committee meeting monthly might lead to the slowing down of the despatch of urgent financial business. He queried whether there would be sufficient work for such a committee to justify a monthly meeting; his concern was that whatever change was instituted should not have the effect of grit in the machine. Eventually I decided to put the matter to the vote and the proposal to establish a finance committee was approved by five votes to three. I am sure that no one would suggest today that we should return to the old system – or lack of it.

One suggestion which subsequently proved to be of considerable significance was that the director-general's report of the work of the Board of Management should be fuller, and this was agreed. The reason for this was that I found from its minutes that much of interest to the Board of Governors was discussed at the Board of Management. Another proposal was that the board should be supplied with a monthly summary of the public's reactions to the BBC and, although the director-general said that an additional member of staff would be needed to compile it, this too was approved.

After six months or so I was feeling fairly comfortable in the chair. The Corporation fascinated me. Bulging with talent, it had a life of unbounded vigour : new ideas were freely accepted for argument and knocked about in meeting after meeting within the organization. The management seemed to me to be highly efficient. The governors seemed to be just beginning to feel their way to the assumption of some responsibility for overall policy, though there were still those who thought that the governors should remain an advisory committee to the director-general. Some of the new members were feeling that a good deal needed to be done to place the governors in a position of real responsibility for overall policy matters, while transmitting to management the views and feelings of the outside world. Personal relationships were less chilly. I had had a few indications that the hostility to me was mainly concentrated at the top and was not so evident in middle and programme-making levels of the Corporation.

I continued with my programme of visits to the non-metropolitan centres. I attended a meeting of the Broadcasting Council for Scotland in London and heard a complaint that there had been no real consultation with the council about the recent appointment of Alasdair Milne to the controllership of Scotland. I promised to remedy things in future, adding that, although technically there was no formal obligation to consult, courtesy and good sense required that there should be consultation. With my wife, I visited Lime Grove. Derek Amoore, then deputy editor of *Panorama,* seemed, I thought, mildly hostile, though the atmosphere improved with whisky. With him, as with Desmond Taylor, I was quite wrong. I visited the Newcastle Centre, on the day I attended Peter Trower's funeral. I went to Bristol, following what became my normal practice : dinner and talk with senior staff on the evening of my arrival and visits to the studios and an informal meeting of the whole staff the next day. I went to Glasgow, Manchester, Leeds and Cardiff.

Looking back, my diary entry on the Glasgow visit is especially interesting :

> Alasdair Milne, the controller, clearly eyes me cautiously. He was, after all, the proposed programme chief of the Jo Grimond group which did *not* get the Scottish ITV contract. He became controller, Scotland, designate about the time I arrived at the BBC.
>
> Dinner of local worthies. Not a great success. Mrs Alasdair Milne tried to pump me about the BBC and my intentions. Lord Bannerman great fun.
>
> Spent next day at BBC, coffee with senior staff, lunch with 20 or so senior staff. Addressed meeting of whole staff, some 200. I answered their questions freely and frankly. They seemed astonished that a chairman of governors should visit them.
>
> Gradually Milne lost his reserve. I found him impressive. His professionalism is commanding the loyalty of his staff.

In London, I was equally active. I visited the Maida Vale Studios, Aeolian Hall and the Camden Theatre. I lunched with regional controllers and my diary reminds me that I agreed that 'more decentralization to the regions' was necessary.

My wife and I dined with the Wheldons, an occasion which my diary records : 'Wheldon was immensely eloquent. He still regards me with some suspicion. Yet he faces the fact that I am here to stay and is clearly seeking good personal relations.' I also met the senior staff of Television Centre at a tea party arranged and presided over by Huw Wheldon.

I attended my second meeting of the General Advisory Council and, in my diary, described it thus : 'Members make their points, Greene and his colleagues reply, nothing really happens. And no one would think that the governors exist. The BBC regards the GAC as a protective screen, not a source of advice.'

I went to a cocktail party given by the ITA to delegates attending a conference on colour; the BBC gave a similar party to the same delegates to which I was not invited. I lunched with old friends in Fleet Street, like Denis Hamilton, Hugh Massingham and Derek Marks. Derek told me that at the time of my appointment Greene had said to him he would soon have me tamed. I occupied a room adjacent to him and all my visitors had to pass through his outer office. I told Derek, with the straightest face I could muster, that I was shortly to move to another office.

In the first half of the year I spoke at many conferences, lunches and dinners including those of the Guild of Newspaper Editors, a Welsh adult education conference, the Song Writers' Guild, and the Newspaper Society. I presided at a dinner to Alistair Cooke to mark his thousandth letter from America. I became president of the Radio Industries Club.

Usually accompanied by the director-general, I called on the Postmaster General of the day to discuss broadcasting matters, normally at his invitation. Edward Short was the first of six Postmaster Generals I was to meet during my span of office, although two of them were called Ministers of Posts and Telecommunications: of them he was the most sharply critical of the BBC. I also called on the Attorney General to be told that our action in putting Dr Savundra on the air while he was awaiting trial might be held to be contempt of court.

Those early months of 1968 were busy and interesting. They set the pattern for the years to follow.

12

Mr Wilson's Suspicions

A number of breezes blew up with Prime Minister Harold
Wilson during my spell at the BBC. The first was in April 1968.
A comedian on one of our programmes had used a phrase once
used about Lyndon Johnson about Harold Wilson. It was 'if his
lips are moving he's lying'. A few days later the same jibe was
repeated on another programme. After the first occasion an
apology was promptly sent by Oliver Whitley to John Silkin,
the Chief Whip. Subsequently I received a letter from Silkin
to say that the Prime Minister was very upset by these incidents
and had sought legal advice. He seemed to want a direct apology
accompanied by some publication of it.

This seemed to me absurd. Politicians, including Prime
Ministers, have to take a great deal of abuse. To broadcast an
apology for such admittedly insulting remarks would give the
insults a circulation they would not otherwise have had. We
would be accused of kow-towing to the Prime Minister and he
would be dubbed thin-skinned. I thought I had best see Harold
Wilson and I asked Oliver Whitley to arrange it with John
Silkin.

The meeting was arranged for the next evening. The next
morning, however, a private secretary at No. 10 telephoned to
say that on advice from Lord Goodman, his solicitor, the Prime
Minister had decided that my proposed visit was unnecessary.
Suspecting this was a lawyer's device to underline the threat of
legal action, I replied somewhat sniffily to the private secretary
that I had asked to see the Prime Minister, and later in the day

he rang to say that Harold Wilson would be glad to see me later in the week. To my mind it would be ridiculous for the Prime Minister to bring an action for libel against the BBC. I felt too I should try to improve the background mood, particularly as the licence fee was still unsettled. Indeed the director-general had told me that he had heard from the Post Office that ministerial enthusiasm for an increased licence fee was noticeably lacking and that there was no sign of any desire to reach a decision.

I reported these exchanges with No. 10 to the governors, who were meeting on the day of my appointment at No. 10. I told them that we had heard through the Post Office that the atmosphere in relation to the licence fee had never been worse, or the prospects of a favourable decision dimmer.

Eventually I saw the Prime Minister in his room at the House of Commons. He was courteous and friendly as he was to be in almost all our meetings. We talked for an hour and a quarter, despite the fact that a ministerial reshuffle was going on at the time. Barbara Castle left the Prime Minister immediately before I entered and Peter Shore was waiting to go in when I left.

I spoke plainly, for I had learned that Harold Wilson prefers plain speaking. I spoke of the jibes and our apology. I said it would be a nonsense for the Prime Minister to bring an action against the BBC; indeed, he would have to sue me, virtually his appointee. He could sack the governors but he could not sensibly take them to court. In any case it would be he and not the BBC who would suffer from such a course of action. He seemed to accept this, though he added that he would consult his solicitor.

As we talked on, it became perfectly clear that he was intensely suspicious of the BBC, even regarding it as a conspiracy against him and his government. He embellished this charge with an astonishing wealth of detail. He mentioned, too, the employment by the BBC of Ian Trethowan who, as well as working for us as an objective commentator, wrote political articles in *The Times* (Trethowan is now managing director of BBC radio). He gave other examples of the Corporation's wickedness, many of which went back long before my time.

Throughout these illustrations of an astonishing memory

Harold Wilson was amiable and cheerful. We consumed two decent-sized Scotches. At the time the political pressures on him were heavy and the going was rough – yet he was cheerful and relaxed. He spoke more of his performance at golf than of the heavy seas around him. He was obviously confident that he could win through all his current worries. What he resented most of all in public criticism was the theme of the credibility gap.

I told him that his detailed recital of events and their interpretation astonished me. Did he ever forget anything? Clearly he disliked the BBC. I do not doubt that his belief that the BBC was continuously unfair was genuine.

After these exchanges, I felt sure that the libel action would be dropped, though he did not say so. He would have to consult his solicitor, Lord Goodman, he said. I then raised the question of increasing the licence fee. To my relief and to his credit he did not relate the two things.

A day or two later I called on Roy Mason, the new Postmaster General. Youthful, bright-eyed, confident, plainly delighted to have the Post Office, he immediately referred to an attack on the Post Office in *The World This Weekend*. Unfortunately for the BBC it contained inaccuracies, not the least of which was a statement that the Postmaster General was a junior Minister of State. This was, to say the least of it, an untimely inaccuracy. We soon got on to the licence fee on which he was glad to hear my views. He seemed friendly and frank but, as I reflected in my diary, we would have to wait. New department ministers naturally want popular success, and from the available evidence it did not seem that the road to ministerial popularity lay in pressing an increase in the licence fee on his colleagues.

Towards the end of April, Hugh Greene produced proposals for the strengthening of the public relations activities of the Corporation. The publicity work under George Campey was being magnificently done, and still is today. But what were needed were better contacts at Westminster and in Whitehall. Greene knew that I had undertaken to prepare a note on this subject for the next governors' meeting, and maybe he suspected that I would advocate a new appointment. He was seeking to meet me halfway and I appreciated it. He suggested that the secretary of the Corporation, Kenneth Lamb, give half his time to this work and that Harman Grisewood should be invited to come back on a part-time basis to assist. I agreed to this, as a first step and a useful experiment.

Towards the end of 1968, there was yet another instance of Mr Wilson's displeasure with the BBC. In two live and unscripted radio programmes there had been some disparaging references to him. In an *Any Questions* programme Dominic le Foe had launched without warning into some derogatory remarks about Mr Wilson's facial appearance and general image on television. The Labour Chief Whip had asked for an assurance that nothing of the kind would happen again and the director-general had refused to give any such undertakings, regarding such things as among the accepted hazards of broadcasting. In any case Mr le Foe's remarks had been strongly contested on the same programme by Lord Soper.

The second incident complained of occurred in *Night Ride*, a late-night pop music chat programme. The director-general reported to the board that in a discussion on the Nigerian situation John Wells had bitterly impugned the Prime Minister's motives and personal probity. The BBC, in Greene's view, had no alternative but to offer a public apology to Mr Wilson and to balance the biassed comments about the government's Nigerian policy by including an interview with Lord Hunt, who had recently returned from that country, in a subsequent edition of the programme. One governor said that the BBC should rephrase Anthony Wedgwood Benn's notorious dictum that 'Broadcasting is too important to be left to the broadcasters' to read 'Broadcasting is too important to be left to producers'.

These complaints followed on the heels of a speech by the Prime Minister to the Labour Party Conference in which he introduced a derogatory reference to the BBC, implying bias in its political reporting. He gave no evidence or illustration of such bias and my first reaction was to ask him to produce evidence in support of his allegations, but having slept on it I decided that the remark should be ignored. The words were not in the advance text which had been issued, so presumably it was an after-thought intended to relieve the tedium of his speech.

Governers wondered what the BBC's offence was. Was the Prime Minister referring to the inclusion in the *Todays Papers* of the previous morning of a quotation from the *Daily Telegraph* that Mr Roy Jenkins's speech at the conference had been received with only modest applause? This was thought unlikely. Another governor thought that a recent unflattering profile of Mr Wilson in *The World This Weekend* might have rankled. We shall never know. The governors shared my view that the BBC had little to gain from over-reaction to such criticism. We allowed sleeping dogs to lie.

Entries in my diary a few weeks later tell their own story :

29 January 1969

Governors entertained Prime Minister to lunch. After lunch, when I invited Harold Wilson to speak, he asked that discussion should proceed by question and answer. He was friendly, confident and chatty. Clearly he wanted to bury the hatchet (leaving himself free to dig it up). As a senior colleague put it afterwards, 'he has buried the hatchet but marked the spot'. On this occasion the PM did not recite old complaints. He said he wanted less politics on the air, not more. He had never complained of rough usage by interviewers. But if he had a complaint, it was about *The World This Weekend*. He knew so much more about radio than television. Bland, uncomplaining – apart from a few asides – skilful, resourceful, articulate. But, in reality, he said nothing, gave nothing away.

5 February

Complaint from Harold Wilson about a reference to him in *The World This Weekend* last Sunday.

13

Candidates for Top Posts

Interesting and difficult problems for the BBC Board of
Governors in the middle of 1968 were the appointment of a
director-general to succeed Sir Hugh Greene and the filling of
other top posts.

Hugh Greene and I discussed the matter at the end of June,
before the announcement of his retirement. His ideas were clear-
cut: he favoured Curran for director-general, Wheldon for
director of television, Whitley for director of overseas services
and Lamb for chief assistant to the director-general. I did not
venture a view at this stage, except to urge that somehow or
other Attenborough should find a place on the Board of Management. He was, in my view, the man of the future.

For some weeks, private discussion went on. I discussed the
subject on a number of occasions with Lord Fulton, the vice-
chairman. Wherever governors met the discussion continued.
One governor thought highly of Curran but doubted whether
he was big enough, another wanted to look outside the Corporation for a director-general. Attenborough, it was generally
agreed, was a man of unusual brilliance. Oliver Whitley,
approaching retirement, was no longer regarded as in the
running. There was no enthusiasm for Huw Wheldon as
director-general (except from me). It really is astonishing how
his loquacity, which I find as fascinating as it is skilful, arouses
real antagonism in some people. Many a first-class man is
unfairly condemned merely because 'he talks too much'. Maybe
the reason I do not share this attitude is that I talk too much
myself.

Then, on 27 June, the governors had their first preliminary discussion of the appointment. Overall Curran was generally regarded as the best insider, though there were some doubts expressed about his capacity for decision. I suggested that Attenborough might become chief assistant to the new director-general, whoever he was, with a better title. Once Wheldon had been shot down, my mind was turning to Attenborough, despite his relative inexperience. When one governor was divided between Curran and Attenborough, another governor pointed out that this admitted a doubt about Curran. To my surprise, one governor said that a less well-known director-general might be an advantage now that we had a strong chairman.

As the discussion proceeded it became clear that at a first look over the field Curran for director-general, Whitley for overseas services, Lamb to remain secretary, Wheldon for director of television and Attenborough for chief assistant were beginning to emerge in a number of minds as a possible pattern, though not at this stage in my own. Greene did not like the proposal that Attenborough should be chief assistant to the director-general. He suggested Curran for director-general and Wheldon for director of television for five years with Attenborough first as his deputy and then as his successor.

Again and again in the weeks which followed this initial discussion the question was raised as to whether Curran was strong enough. Of his remarkable talents, there was no doubt, as those who had been governors while he was secretary of the Corporation could and did testify. But the majority of governors, including those who thought he was the best man, still had doubts about his toughness and capacity to reach decisions.

On 9 July, while we were engaged in these informal discussions, Oliver Whitley came to tell me that he had something momentous to say and that having said it he proposed immediately to withdraw, saving him and me embarrassment. The preface over, he said that he had been at Nuffield College, Oxford, the previous weekend at an informal conference on broadcasting. Robert MacKenzie had told him that at dinner the previous night Dick Crossman had said that on 15 July Greene's retirement would be announced. The story was out and as usual from someone near the top. I pondered a while and then under a pledge of secrecy told Whitley the whole story. He began to relax, even to smile. He thanked me for telling him and left it at that.

Between meetings, I sought ways and means of reconciling the conflicting views which had been expressed by the governors. I was looking for a consensus. I put it to those who were doubtful about Curran that we should appoint a deputy director-general who would be likely to supply the strength which the minority believed Curran to be lacking. Would the appointment of Wheldon as deputy director-general make sense? Judging from Greene's absence abroad the director-general would be absent for at least three months a year. I knew that this was not a perfect solution, though it had the incidental advantage that Attenborough, in whom I had great faith, could take charge of television. I asked my colleagues to turn this suggestion over in their minds before the decisive meeting a few days hence. I also sounded Roger Morrison of McKinseys who, in a preliminary report, had advised against a deputy director-general. He later admitted, as I had suspected, that he had accepted without much discussion Greene's view that a deputy was unnecessary.

A day or two later Harman Grisewood came to see me. He talked about anxieties within the BBC since my appointment. Was I really a dedicated BBC man? Was I assuming a new and strengthened chairman's role at the expense of management? Was this not creating tension? I told him that those who assumed that I sought to strengthen the governors' role in overall policy were right in their assumption. I did. But this did not involve taking over the proper role of management. This would be as undesirable as it would be difficult. Since Reith's days, the governors had for the most part been ciphers. Incidentally, as a former chief assistant to the director-general he was strongly in favour of creating the post of deputy director-general.

During July, at the governors' request, I saw the senior executives in confidence and I asked for their views on the filling of the top post. There were some interesting responses!

The decisive day for the appointment of the director-general was 31 July, two weeks after the announcement of Greene's retirement. Hitherto I had expressed no firm view. Curran I thought the best insider in terms of intellect. His grasp of ideas, his command of facts and his mental agility were really remarkable. Yet I, like others, had a niggling doubt. Would he, at times of difficulty, discuss rather than decide? Had he that streak of ruthlessness which the proper exercise of authority occasionally demands? Or was he too nice a man to exercise authority? And would he, blessed as he was with so many talents, rise to the role and grow to fill the director-general's chair?

Man for man, Attenborough seemed to me to have almost all the post demanded, though his inexperience in management pointed to next time instead of this. Would a gamble with Wheldon, 'the last great actor-manager' as someone had called him, come off! I would have chanced it had there been some signs of support. In view of the doubts about Curran did a caretaker appointment of Frank Gillard for two years or so make sense? These were the thoughts moving around in my mind. On the other hand, the one candidate who had a clear, if modest, majority (and Greene's full support) was Charles Curran.

At our invitation Curran, Whitley, Lamb, Wheldon and Attenborough came to talk to the board in turn. Whitley was pale, buttoned-up and wholly excellent in his replies to questions. He really did answer the questions put to him, instead of using them as a peg for prepared answers to questions which had not been put. No one could have failed to be impressed by his honesty and integrity; five years earlier he would certainly have been appointed director-general.

Curran was his usual charming, mercurial self. Lamb was skilful, intelligent and slightly pompous. He wore the air of an archdeacon if not an archbishop. He irritated slightly by generously punctuating his answers with 'you know'. Although rather wordy he could not be faulted for the substance of his replies.

Wheldon was beautifully loquacious. Ideas, convictions, prejudices poured out unceasingly and I was fascinated by the man and the performance. Imaginative, eloquent, at times arrogant, at others modest, he could not resist a parenthesis though he invariably came back to his main theme and his central point in the end. He left us somewhat exhausted. Again and again as he was talking, I wondered whether he was not really our man. I should have loved working with such a man. But, alas, I proved to be alone in this reaction to him.

David Attenborough was not at his best that day. He was not helped by the serving of tea while he was with us. The cups rattled a bit. Yet, despite a poor showing – poor for him – he left the general impression that, although not yet sufficiently experienced for appointment now, he was the best bet in the long run. Next time, as City aldermen say to an unsuccessful candidate for the lord mayoralty. Incidentally, as he once made plain to me, he would never have agreed to supersede Wheldon.

Eventually, after yet another exchange of views, the time came for a decision. By now the minority of doubtfuls had resolved their doubts, although of two governors a truer statement would be that they were less doubtful. Charles Curran was unanimously appointed, his duties to begin on 1 April the following year, although from 1 January he would be freed from other duties to prepare himself for the job. He was appointed for eight years in the first instance. This would take him to the age of fifty-five. It was agreed that the board of eight years hence would be told of our hope that, if his appointment was not extended, he should be permitted to retire on the pension he would have received had his appointment continued until the age of sixty.

At the same meeting Lamb was appointed to a new post of director of public affairs. He would be responsible to the director-general for the evaluation of communications between the public and the BBC, 'with special responsibility for, among other things, ensuring that the BBC's advisory machinery is fully effective'. The title of the existing heads of output, Wheldon, Gillard and Whitley, was changed to managing director.

We then passed to the matter of a deputy director-general. In the director-general's absence, someone had to deputize for him. What I would have preferred was the creation of a permanent deputy director-general to assist the director-general in all the work the latter cared to designate as well as to assume the full responsibilities of the director-general in his absence. I suspect that most governors approached this question with Huw Wheldon in mind. But could Curran live with so lively, force-

The author placing a ring on Lady Hill's finger. The ring was part
of the presentation made in 1963 by the people of Luton following
Lord Hill's retirement from the House of Commons.

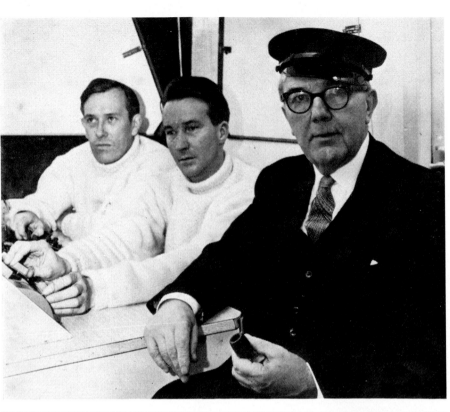

Lord Bernstein, chairman of the Granada Group.

Opposite:

Lord Hill aboard *Southerner*, Southern Television's outside broadcast launch.

Lord Hill with Sir John Carmichael, deputy chairman of the ITA from June 1960 until his retirement in July 1964.

"I CAN'T TEAR HIM AWAY -- HE'S TERRIFIED LEST HE
SHOULD MISS A PRACTICAL DEMONSTRATION BY LORD HILL".

7. xi. 69.

ful and eloquent a character? Or would he be submerged? I was asked to consult Curran.

After the meeting, I told Curran in secrecy of the decision to appoint him and went on to consult him on other senior appointments, emphasizing that it was his view I was seeking and that if he found himself in disagreement with Greene on appointments he should demonstrate his independence of view from the outset. It was his staff, not Greene's, we were shortly to consider.

The next day I lunched with Attenborough. I asked him whether he wished to be considered for the post of managing director of radio, which would soon be vacant, with the number two post in television as the alternative. He unhesitatingly chose the latter. I asked him to think it over but a day or two later he reached the same conclusion. Sensing his reluctance to become an administrator I urged upon him that a creative man turned administrator is well equipped to ensure the creative freedom of his staff and that, in any case, administration is the route to the top. He did not seem impressed and, as I was to learn nearly five years later, he was not.

The following day, Curran came to my house to lunch. We went over the draft announcement of his appointment and passed on to the yet undecided appointments, the deputy director-general and the managing director of radio. His attitude to an all-the-year-round deputy clearly stemmed from the assumption that if the post were created Huw Wheldon would be appointed – an assumption of which I could not honestly disabuse him. What we could not do to a new director-general, I then felt, was to appoint to such a post a man he did not want. Curran plainly feared that he would be overshadowed by the voluble Welshman. He said he strongly preferred the deputy-in-absence alternative, with Whitley as the choice. Clearly his wishes would have to prevail and in any case Whitley was a man whose character I admired and whose judgement I had come to trust.

We passed to the top post in radio. One possible successor to Gillard was Gerry Mansell, but we agreed that outsiders need not be excluded and I mentioned as a 'possible' for consideration a man for whose talents I had considerable admiration, Ian

Trethowan. He liked the idea, as did Gillard, and said he would 'cast a fly' over him.

In the general talk which followed, he surprised me by the vehemence with which he condemned the more festive aspects of the behaviour of BBC delegations to overseas broadcasting conferences, saying that this was a matter he would swiftly put right. On this occasion, as on so many others, he demonstrated a remarkably agile mind. A note in my diary that evening reads, 'Whether his capacity for decision is of the same order we shall soon find out', adding that I liked him better every time I met him.

At the next meeting of the governors on 7 August, we discussed the appointment to the post of managing director of radio. We saw Gerry Mansell and Paul Fox, controller of BBC 1. Mansell seemed able, diplomatic, shrewd and articulate : our doubts were about his decisiveness. In many ways he was remarkably like Curran. Paul Fox on the other hand seemed determined not to ingratiate himself with anyone. The impression he left on me was that of the supremely competent professional, clear-headed and determined. But he was not particularly attracted by radio : television was his love.

We decided to continue discussions about the appointment and the possible extension of Gillard's appointment in the Autumn. Passing to the deputy director-general question, we agreed to accept Curran's idea of an 'absence only' deputy. In the circumstances this was inevitable, though in retrospect I think it was unwise. We set aside the other appointments until the autumn and got on with our other business, including some recommendations from McKinsey.

On 8 August Curran's appointment was announced and he handled press and radio with assurance. Indeed, in some of his phrases, he seemed mildly contemptuous of governors, trying in the process, it seemed, to prove his fitness for the post. He would stand up to them. I came in for the usual stick from the press – autocratic and interfering and the rest. It really is remarkable how the BBC feeds the press with its legends! How some BBC people loathe any suggestion of exercise of authority by the governors. Only one public reference annoyed me. In *The World at One* Curran was asked whether he would be 'Hill's tame poodle' and, quite rightly, he vehemently rejected the suggestion.

At the end of July – before any appointments were decided upon – McKinseys had made an interim report to the governors intended, as Roger Morrison put it, 'merely to provide Governors with a preview of conclusions insofar as they had relevance to the Board's current consideration of top management appointments'. I had already had some indication of McKinseys' early reactions. The programme cost economies of recent years were not, they thought, real economies, for they had been made by increasing the proportion of normally cheap programmes and not by lowering the average cost of normally expensive ones. There were long delays between the making of a proposal for action and the action itself – the atmosphere of the BBC was not conducive to cost efficiency and so on.

Then we were given the 'preview of conclusions'. McKinseys recommended that the three output directors of radio, television and external services should be, and be seen to be, fully responsible managers of *all* the production and engineering activities of their services. They should be renamed managing directors. As they would be assuming increased managerial responsibilities, the director-general would not have to undertake management duties on a day-to-day basis and operational responsibility would be carried by the managing directors. The intention was, according to Morrison, 'to build into the BBC a positive system of management which did not depend on the spending of money handed down from above but which would demand the active participation of those spending the money in the setting and achieving of objectives related to the more effective and economic use of available resources'. The current budgeting procedure would be turned upside down. It would take three years for the full benefits of the new system to accrue.

When asked whether creative people could be expected to be efficient managers, Morrison said that he had found among many heads of programme departments a real and imaginative interest in such matters which was there for the harnessing. Greene endorsed the general proposals for the organization of top management and governors generally approved them. I found the arguments behind these McKinsey proposals irresistible, and a valuable preliminary to our decisions on top appointments.

Some months later, McKinseys followed this preliminary report with their main recommendations and a wealth of detail to support them. In true American style, they gave to the governors a presentation as they had previously done to the Board of Management. If the status quo were maintained, radio would be in the red to the tune of £8 million by 1972. Music in one form or another accounted for about two-thirds of the BBC's total radio output. The live and recorded element of the output cost much more than pre-recorded music. The limit on the latter, the result of the BBC's agreements with Phonographic Performance Ltd, restricted by the attitude of the Musicians' Union, was costing the Corporation large sums of money. The BBC should try to save money by acquiring the rights to more 'needle time'. It should take advantage of the right under the existing agreement to repeat every live performance once instead of repeating only a quarter of them.

McKinseys went on to recommend that in the long term the BBC should reduce its commitment to its own house orchestras, particularly in the regions. The regions, McKinseys pointed out, accounted for a significant proportion of total BBC expenditure yet their productivity compared unfavourably with the London-based operation. They recommended a thorough examination of the role of the regions.

Their report went on to redefine responsibility for the management of resources, to emphasize the need for new and better management of information, to recommend the strengthening of the role of managing director in relation to engineering services and to the news, which they thought should be responsible managerially to the managing directors. They recommended the establishment of productivity targets, the strengthening of planning and control of information, the streamlining of administrative procedures.

Greene told us that broadly speaking the McKinsey proposals, except the one dealing with the managerial control over news, were acceptable to him. As a journalist by profession, he had no doubt but that to separate the managerial from the editorial control of news would be wrong: the two were inextricably related. He disagreed with the suggestion that the managing directors should exercise discretion and judgement over the content of news programmes. News was not a controllable commodity; news bulletins depended on events, and staff and resources had to be deployed as the events dictated. It was essentially a unity, with its own philosophy, its own methods of recruitment and training, and its own professional union. It was the rock on which the BBC's reputation was founded. I and the majority of my colleagues found Greene's arguments convincing and the McKinsey recommendation on this subject was rejected while the report as a whole received general approval, as did a plan for further work by them.

To come back to outstanding appointments. In August a group of governors, John Fulton, Tom Jackson and I, with the director-general and director-general designate, began the work of interviewing possible candidates for the top radio post, some of them more than once. We saw Arthur Clifford (from Independent Television), the late Tom Sloan, Lance Thirkell, Gerry Mansell, Ian Trethowan and Peter Dimmock. We decided to put three names to the Board of Governors in the autumn, those of Mansell, Dimmock and Trethowan, and in October they were interviewed by the whole board.

Gerry Mansell was not at his best, and may even have talked his way out of the job. Dimmock was clearly a remarkably competent manager, though he did not do as well as at the first interview : and more than managerial competence was needed. Trethowan was quietly impressive though there were doubts about the sufficiency of his managerial experience and about his toughness. Eventually the choice fell on Trethowan, with Greene murmuring in my ear that the decision was a mistake.

A factor in the failure of Mansell's candidature which was widely entertained by the board was the doubt about his capacity for decisiveness. Yet two years later, during the controversy on 'Broadcasting in the Seventies', he proved to be as decisive as he was unflappable. We had been quite wrong in our assessment of him. Fortunately the third managing directorship, that of the overseas services, became vacant soon after the controversy and Mansell was unanimously appointed to it. And the

doubts about Trethowan's administrative capacity and toughness of mind turned out to be completely misplaced too; indeed,
these proved to be areas of strength. What a difficult and uncertain business is the assessment of people for appointment or
promotion, even of those long known within the organization!

In the assessment of a candidate for the controllership of
Radio 1 and 2, later in the year, I was in a stronger position. In
the autumn of 1967, I was in Hong Kong on my way to Australia on non-broadcasting business. The director of the island's
official broadcasting services, Donald Brooks, gave a dinner to
my wife and myself which was attended by the Financial Secretary of the island government, his wife, and others, including
a young man whose name I had not taken in at our introduction. After the meal, there was the usual spate of talk with three
or four conversations competing with each other. While I was
trying to keep up with the Financial Secretary's wife, I gradual-
ly became aware of a much more vigorous exchange which was
going on across the table between the Financial Secretary and
the young man I could not identify. The Financial Secretary
was laying into the BBC with blimpish vigour and wholesale
condemnation. Eventually I realized that the unknown young
man was more than holding his own. Calmly, courteously but
devastatingly, he was dissecting the exaggerated assertions of
his loquacious neighbour. The Financial Secretary was destroyed but not disturbed, for his wounds were as cleanly as they
were respectfully administered. I was as delighted with the technique as I was with the theme; it was a perfect demolition job.

I asked Donald Brooks who this young man was. I was told
he was a Douglas Muggeridge from BBC overseas services in
Bush House in London. I did not see Muggeridge again until
he appeared before the governors as a candidate for the controllership of Radio 1 and 2. At least I felt I knew something of
this man. He got the job.

14

Lapses of Taste

Some critics of the BBC say that its producers have too much freedom. The opening of the windows during Greene's director-generalship was healthy and effective. Inevitably this new freedom was occasionally abused, with lapses of taste and language.

I recall the Board of Governors having a very full discussion of the problem in May 1968. Kenneth Adam, Huw Wheldon, David Attenborough and Paul Fox joined the governors for the purpose. It arose because one of the governors, at an earlier meeting, had drawn his colleagues' attention to two examples of what, to his mind, had been regrettable and unnecessary lapses of taste. The example quoted was of a *Wednesday Play*. He criticized the excessive use of the word 'bloody' in one case and the over-explicit bedroom scene in the other.

Huw Wheldon expressed the view that both the 'bloodies' and the bedroom scene had not been lapses but fully justified in their context, pointing out that the *Wednesday Play* had accounted for only 5 per cent of the television service's total output of drama. It was within this small sector that most of the offences took place and if one was going to have a policy of presenting contemporary plays it was difficult to see how a policy of no offence could be operated.

I said that one had sometimes to look at these things through the eyes of the ordinary viewer and I quoted from some of the complaints I had received in recent months. The burden of these complaints was, in their reference to one play, that it was transmitted at 8 pm, had been full of sods, bastards and other swear words and had contained a scene in which a young man had undressed a girl before having intercourse with her and had then been shown in bed with her discussing the sexual act which they had just performed. In the words of one correspondent, 'it was intolerable that stuff of this kind should be able to come without warning at such an hour into homes where it was not the accepted thing'.

How, I asked, should I reply to such a complaint? What was our defence? It was surely not enough just to say 'if you don't like this sort of thing you shouldn't watch it'. And how had it come about that a play of that nature had been transmitted at the early hour of 8 pm? David Attenborough said that the answer was 'a lapse of vigilance on the part of those responsible' – a matter which he had already taken up.

One governor was less worried by the permissiveness in contemporary plays than by what appeared to be a growing tendency towards smut and sexual innuendo in comedy programmes. Wheldon regarded this as a much more difficult problem, springing partly from the fact that coarse humour and blue jokes were very much part of the vaudeville tradition to which modern comedians were heirs. The jokes heard on television were mild indeed compared to what one could hear in the clubs and the variety theatres.

I asked whether Wheldon would justify the gross sexual innuendo which had occurred in another programme. Wheldon said that when a programme was successful and caught the public fancy, people were willing to forgive it a great deal which they might otherwise have complained of. Bellinger said that he did not think the BBC was right to take refuge behind the comparison with novels, films and theatres and to make it an excuse for permissiveness. Permissiveness was a slippery slope with few or no footholds. He thought it was not a bad idea when a particularly difficult play was to be transmitted for it to be prefaced by some kind of explanatory introduction. This was a discussion typical of many that we were to have over the years, interesting, relevant, but leading nowhere.

About this time a quite different controversy blew up in Parliament and the press. Danny Cohn-Bendit and other Continental student rebels had been invited to come to London to take part in a programme in which Robert McKenzie would question them. There was some bother with immigration officials at Heathrow and the press was alerted to their visit. The BBC was bitterly criticized for inviting them to the air and paying their expenses to London. We were giving a platform to anarchy and a pat on the back to student rebels – and so on. The governors unhesitatingly endorsed the decision to invite them and their only criticism was that the management might have anticipated the rumpus and told me, if not the governors, instead of leaving them to read about it for the first time in the press. In the event McKenzie was devastating in his cross-examination and the rebel students looked a pretty poor lot.

I was coming to realize that one of my main concerns was the preservation of the BBC's independence, which involved resistance to external pressures, which I sensed were becoming stronger and more frequent as our society became more open. In my early months, I had not often taken an initiative in programme matters, although they were fully and intelligently discussed at most governors' meetings. I participated but I did not lead.

I did raise one major programme point, and not very successfully, a year or so after my arrival. I give it in some detail because it is typical of so many discussions on programmes and reveals the usual range of expressed opinions. I raised the question of a *Wednesday Play, On the Eve of Publication.* I said I found it most powerful and absorbing. Yet there were certain scenes in it, for example a man relieving himself, and certain coarse words, for which I could not see justification on grounds of dramatic necessity. Their inclusion seemed to be a kind of self-indulgence by the writer and the producer or both. I would firmly defend such scenes and such words if I genuinely believed they were essential to the play. In this case I did not think they were. They were a gift to the ever ready critics of the BBC.

One governor supported this criticism; another, who had not seen the play, spoke generally of what he called 'such lapses'. Another governor said that the BBC had a very difficult problem. Playwrights of the calibre of David Mercer would not go on writing for the BBC if the hand of editorial control was too heavily and frequently applied. One should respect the views of such writers. This discussion ended with my saying that I still felt there were occasions when self-indulgence got the upper hand : as well as respecting the artist-creator we must also have respect for the public.

The discussion was resumed at the next governors' meeting when I drew attention to a minute of the Board of Management in which it was said that it would be difficult to put the points made by governors at their previous meeting to David Mercer, who would be unlikely to agree that these words and scenes were 'unnecessary'. These words implied, I said, that it was the playwright and not the BBC who had the last word in these matters. The director-general thought the words used at the Board of Management were not intended to bear this interpretation.

This discussion, like so many others, illustrates the dilemma of the BBC. A proper, indeed crucial, part of the role of public service broadcasting is to provide a platform for the younger generation of writers. Often their approach to morals and manners is not that of their elders. Indeed, they are often hostile to traditional standards. They demand the right to experiment and where they see fit the right to shock. Should the older generation expect of them obedient adherence to its own standards, acquired in other days and in another society? At first, I was doubtful. I did not see the necessity of some of the explicitness of modern drama. It seemed to me that the goodwill of the older generation was being needlessly thrown away at a time when the support of this section of the listening community was increasingly necessary to a BBC under fire.

Looking back, I think I was possibly too preoccupied at this time with the image of the BBC. I came to appreciate that the intellectual and creative freedom of the artist – with all the risks it involved – was an essential element in an imaginative broadcasting service. As I was to hear Huw Wheldon say so often, excellence was a prime consideration in good broadcasting. A real enemy was mediocrity. In any case, this kind of experimental drama was but a small part of the whole output, set in a recognizable 'slot'. Viewers knew what to expect and the switch was there on every set. Those who preferred traditional drama with an obvious plot, a beginning and an ending – preferably a happy one – were generously catered for.

My generation cannot escape from its own upbringing. But that does not necessarily mean that my generation was invariably right and the younger generation always wrong, or vice versa. Nor was it reasonable that I should react with horror at the use of language which I often used myself. Unless broadcasting portrayed the world as it really was, it would lose its credibility and lapse into a world of unreality. Certainly this is what some people want of broadcasting all the time – and most people some of the time – an escape from the drabness and dreariness of everyday life. The answer to them is that they can get it from much that is broadcast on both services.

A policy of genuine creative freedom for the artist had risks. The producer referred a programme in the making to his superiors only when he judged it to be necessary. He might fail to refer upwards scenes or words which were dramatically unnecessary and so unnecessarily offensive. He might even intend to attract criticism and its attendant publicity. He might be 'trying it on'. He might be thinking more of the reactions of his professional colleagues than of those of the public. Naturally the risk is greater where the producer is not on the BBC staff and comes on contract for one or two plays.

Throughout all such discussions I had in mind the replies which could honestly and reasonably be given to criticism made in letters to the BBC or in the press. Indeed my practice of replying personally to all the letters which came to me by name compelled me to form a view and express it in my replies.

During 1968 the board acquired three new governors, all of them excellent though in different ways : Sir Robert Bellinger, Mr Tom Jackson and Dame Mary Green. Bellinger, who was to prove an admirable chairman of the Finance Committee, candid and cogent, did a very great deal in adapting the Corporation's financial methods to the realities of the seventies. Tom Jackson proved a shrewd and discerning critic of programmes and one of the best governors I have worked with. Molly Green, as charming as she was clear-headed, did more than anyone else in visiting BBC stations. I greeted their arrival with great relief : at least they were neither pro-Hill nor anti-

Hill and could examine our problems with a new and uncontaminated eye. They wanted to be active governors, not ciphers, and such they proved to be. The balance was changing.

Towards the end of 1968 the Board of Governors discussed a paper in which Hugh Greene urged that the political parties be given notice that party political broadcasts would end after the next general election. The BBC had the power to do this because the broadcasts stemmed from an offer which it had made to the parties years before political controversy was permitted on the air. The BBC could withdraw the offer and Greene urged that notice of this withdrawal should now be given. Only shock tactics would be effective with the political parties.

I supported this view and suggested that the first move should be made in April 1969 with a letter to the parties. Every public issue of importance was ventilated in one or other of the many current affairs programmes. Party politicals were usually badly done and but for the simultaneity of appearance on all three television channels few people would view them. In any case, I doubted whether they had any impact, at least any favourable impact. In private almost all party leaders had said at one time or another that they would like to see them go, with the spokesmen of the government of the day more emphatic than those of the opposition.

The majority of the governors were doubtful of the wisdom of withdrawing facilities. One of them saw much in the contention that this was the only opportunity the parties had on the air of speaking directly to the public : in the usual public affairs programmes their views were filtered through an interviewer, who might or might not allow the party spokesmen to deliver themselves of what they really wanted to say. It would be untimely, thought another governor, to raise the matter until such politics-in-depth programmes as *Gallery* had been restored to the air. Another view expressed was that the BBC stood greatly in need of the goodwill and understanding of the parties. What was proposed would surely prejudice its chances of obtaining them.

It soon became clear that the proposition stood no chance of acceptance. Eventually I withdrew the issue and undertook to put a draft letter to the parties to my colleagues for further discussion. At the back of my mind was the thought that, as a first step, a proposal to end simultaneity of party broadcasts on all three TV channels could stand a better chance with my colleagues. Later this proposal to end simultaneity was put to the political parties and rejected by them.

Another question which arose about this time was the publication of cigarette advertisements in the *Radio Times*. Lady Baird, a doctor, felt strongly that it was our public duty to reject such advertisements. She had raised the matter, though unsuccessfully, six months before. The director-general and the Board of Management were strongly opposed to such discontinuance, asserting that it would cost the *Radio Times*, and so the Corporation, about a quarter of a million pounds a year. The chief medical officer of the Corporation was present at the governors' meeting at my invitation. I had never met him and did not know for sure what line he would take, bearing in mind the strong line the Board of Management had taken. In the event, he spoke powerfully for discontinuance of the advertisements.

The usual arguments were used against discontinuance. Alcohol was damaging to health, so why not ban advertisements for that? Advertising was to promote competing brands and did not itself increase consumption – this was another line of argument. I decided that, as on the previous occasion when the proposal was rejected, it should be put to the vote. Lady Baird's motion was carried by five votes to four, with myself voting in favour.

Then the fun began. The senior staff, headed by Greene (not including the chief medical officer), were visibly appalled – possibly by the decision and certainly by the effrontery of the governing body in rejecting the advice of the management. 'The worst day's work for a long time,' said Greene. 'Democratic but wrong,' said Curran. Whitley, who sat next to me at lunch subsequently, said he could not bear to discuss the subject. Later Kenneth Lamb said that I had not allowed time for alternative ways of handling the matter to be considered.

A few days later Greene raised the matter again in my room, 'more in sorrow than in anger'. Surely, he said, such a decision should be reached by a consensus between management and the board and within the board, and not by a small majority. How can you expect a consensus on such a clear-cut issue I asked him? Would he have been satisfied if the Baird proposal had been rejected by a small majority? Yes, he replied. Then, I argued, what was really disturbing him was the character of the decision and not the size of the majority for it. My usual method was to seek a consensus or a compromise. Again and again when differences of view arose I suggested deferment of discussion in the hope of a consensus. But some issues have to be decided by counting heads, otherwise the consensus method would enable the minority unreasonably to obstruct the view of the majority.

Life at the BBC is never dull for very long. With its vast output in sound and vision, at home and abroad, it is a winnable bet that from time to time someone, however gingerly he walks, will tread on a landmine when he least expects an explosion. Everything the BBC does is exposed to public view or public hearing. And the world is full of experts on the broadcasting art who, in a love-hate relationship with the medium, burst into print or speech on the slightest provocation – and sometimes with no provocation at all.

All this is as it should be. The BBC is a public service and no one should demur if the public reacts with vigour and candour. The difficulty is that there are many publics and many generations : what pleases one appals another and the BBC is caught in the cross-fire. Sometimes the BBC is in the wrong and when it is it should say so, if only because it is the swiftest way of ending the criticism. Despite this, great corporations, including the BBC, dislike intensely any public admission of error, as I was reminded early in 1969.

David Dimbleby had been given the job of reporting President Nixon's arrival at Heathrow for a one-day visit to meet Mr Wilson. According to newspapers, when reporting the President's arrival he had said that both Mr Wilson and Mr Nixon had 'expensively hired press secretaries whose job is to disguise the truth' and that President Nixon was 'wearing his face for all seasons'. When reporting the departure he had said, 'Well, the road show is on the way', and described the American press accompanying the President as 'These dancing girls of the President who go strewing words before him and behind him . . .'

These words were thought to be inappropriate to the occasion and could conceivably have soured the atmosphere of the visit.

Greene and I, to avoid the possibility of such repercussions, decided to apologize, sending a copy to the Prime Minister and to the American Ambassador. There followed a minor storm in the press and inside the BBC, not because of Dimbleby's words but because of our decision to apologize.

*   *   *

There was another event early in 1969 which was much more important to the future of the BBC. It concerned the BBC's finances and their handling. In February 1969 the Finance Committee which, under Sir Robert Bellinger's efficient chairmanship had been steadily developing a closer acquaintance with the Corporation's finances, brought the Board of Governors face to face with some hard realities of its financial position, particularly its budgetary methods. Since the introduction of television the number of television licences had increased quite steeply year after year and, enjoying an annually increasing income, there had been little need for the BBC to keep an unduly tight control of expenditure. Now the position was changing. Saturation point in terms of numbers of licence-payers was approaching and, this reached, the only source of substantial increases in income would be an increased licence fee which, while it was reasonable to expect one every few years, certainly could not be counted on as an annual event. What had been a steep ascent would soon become a plateau or, more accurately, a series of plateaux.

It was against this background that the Bellinger exercise was conducted, and superbly well. Hitherto, he pointed out, there had been an automatic uplift to the budget of some 8 per cent a year, each increase becoming a permanent part of the base of the next year's expenditure to which another 8 per cent was automatically added. Of this 8 per cent, 5 per cent was to meet rising costs and 3 per cent for maintenance and development of television output. If this formula were continued in the future, television expenditure would rise from £53 million in 1968-9 to £78 million in 1973-4 and radio expenditure from £20 million to £25 million in the same period. We should be seriously in the red. Income from licence fees was divided between television and radio in the ratio of 4 : 1 while expenditure was divided approximately 3 : 1 so that radio, not surprisingly, showed a deficit.

Bellinger concentrated his attention on the automatic annual increase of £1 million a year for 'development and maintenance', bearing in mind that the main implication of the estimates was a deficit of £4½ million by 1973-4. He argued that the provision for television development and maintenance should be reduced from £1 million to £600,000 in 1969-70 for the simple reason that on our own calculations we would not have the money. He was against budgeting for a deficit even though the Corporation was permitted to incur a deficit of £10 million on current account and, with the permission of the Treasury, £20 million on capital account. And we should start the process of adjustment forthwith to avoid deficit budgeting in the financial year immediately ahead, 1969-70.

Not surprisingly, this proposal was vigorously resisted by Curran and Wheldon. Rising costs had already appropriated £600,000 of the proposed £1 million for 1969-70. The renewal of sports contracts would eat up £146,000. In light entertainment and drama, artists and writers were demanding more money. These items are the raw material of maintenance which Wheldon defines as 'the ability to repeat next year the successes of this year'. Without money for development, Kenneth Clark's *Civilisation* could never have grown from the standard six-part series first planned to a *magnum opus* costing £250,000.

Eventually Bellinger won his point and the board decided, by five votes to four (I voted in favour), that the six-year projection should be adjusted so that it did not forecast a deficit. As for the year immediately ahead, with all the commitments already entered into, Wheldon was asked to submit a paper at the next meeting. This paper convinced the board that the increase of £1 million should stand in the year immediately ahead, largely on the ground that the bulk of this money was already committed.

Bellinger, as tenacious as ever, did not fail to point out that, despite the decision not to budget for a deficit, that was precisely what we were doing for the year ahead. For the longer future, however, crucial changes in procedure were decided upon. Each year, sufficiently early for changes to be made, there would be put to the board an estimate for the following year, accompanied by a five-year fiscal forecast, the estimate not to exceed the provision in such forecast. The principle of no budgeting for a deficit would be applied after 1969-70. Although, as will subsequently emerge, we did not succeed in maintaining this principle in all its purity, its adoption had a salutary effect on future financial control, thanks to the insistence of Robert Bellinger.

A significant side issue arose, at least in my mind, during these debates. It seemed to be assumed by management that the income for radio should still be arithmetically determined by the number of radio licences (and the radio slice of combined licences). I objected to this, arguing that the income from all licences should be divided between radio and television on policy, not historic, grounds. I wanted nothing to prejudice any future decision to give more to sound on merit, for I was beginning to sense a revival of interest in radio and the possible need to spend more on it, despite the strong competitive force of television in peak hours.

Indeed, interest in radio had become so great that when, in July 1969, the BBC published its plan for reorganizing radio, there was a great outcry. In the next chapter I shall explain why.

E

15

'Broadcasting in the Seventies'

The BBC's plan for changes in radio, 'Broadcasting in the Seventies', caused heated controversy when it was published in July 1969.

The role and structure of radio, in a world in which television had largely supplanted it in the evening, had been under expert scrutiny for some years. Frank Gillard, Richard Marriott and Gerry Mansell had led the probes and presided over a series of studies. These had already led to big changes – for instance, the music programme, Radio 1, and local radio.

On 30 September 1967 Home, Light and Third had become Radios 1, 2, 3 and 4. Previously, Radio 3 had been called the Third Network and included the Music Programme, Study Session and the Third Programme, which Radio 3 continued to embrace until April 1970 when it became simply Radio 3. Radio 1 had been invented as part of the policy of defeating the pirates.

Eight pilot local radio stations were on the air and the experiment was judged a success, at least by those who had heard its broadcasts. The BBC had asked the Postmaster General to empower it to provide forty local stations. Local radio had succeeded at a moment when there was growing resistance to the dominance of London. We needed non-metropolitan broadcasting in which local feeling and interests could be expressed. If the Postmaster General approved the forty local radio stations, nearly 90 per cent of the population would be covered. The existing regional and area radio programmes would be super-seded. Regional opt-outs – periods when a region opts out of the Radio 4 service from London to put out its own programmes – would eventually go. The four cumbersome regions of England and Wales would be replaced by eight smaller regions as the main units for localized television and about forty local radio stations. But it would not be enough merely to graft a county-wide local radio service on to unchanged existing services. Radio needed to be considered as a whole.

Some preliminary ideas for reorganizing radio were expounded to the governors in May 1969 by Gerry Mansell. There were three main questions. What radio networks should be provided in the seventies? Should these remain on their present scale or had the time come for a substantial reduction now that television had become the main medium for entertainment and information in the evening? And what level could the BBC provide on its existing income?

The public was certainly not turning away from radio, despite the advent of television. Just over half the total public made some use of radio every day, slightly more than the number of people who watched BBC television : they listened on average for nearly two and a half hours a day. Though evening audiences were falling, the audience for day-time radio was growing. In 1964, 4 million radio sets were bought compared with nearly $1\frac{1}{2}$ million televisions.

On the other hand, there were signs of change in the public's listening habits. The success of the music programme and Radio 1 suggested that the public wanted specialized rather than all-purpose channels. The old 'brow level' concept of Home, Light and Third was outmoded. The public wanted to know where it could easily find the kind of programme which fitted its mood or its age, pop, sweet or light music, serious music or speech.

The broad theme was accepted by the board and included the separation of Radio 1 and Radio 2, the concentration of serious music in Radio 3 (this designation to replace the old one of Third Programme) and the provision of a new speech network on Radio 4 for news and current affairs, serials, documentaries, discussions, popular drama and light entertainment.

There were difficulties. Fully to separate Radio 1 and Radio 2 would be too costly. The Third Programme had highbrow avant garde items which could not sensibly be transferred to Radio 4. To discard them because of their small audience and high cost would deprive an intelligent section of listeners and be a blow to the BBC's reputation. On the other hand, there was a good case for a change from the then current average of 50 per cent music and 50 per cent spoken word to roughly 75 per cent music and 25 per cent spoken word. From this change a saving of between £100,000 and £200,000 per annum would result.

Radio 4 presented problems too. Schools programmes occupied the mornings and afternoons for much of the year. This prevented the transfer of Woman's Hour from Radio 2 to Radio 4, while the Open University at various times used both Radio 3 and Radio 4. A possible solution would have been to transmit educational programmes on Radio 4 on VHF only, but this would have involved considerably increased expenditure and poorer coverage of Radio 4 after dark due to bad reception on Medium Wave. Radio 3, on the other hand, would be better served on VHF bearing in mind that VHF would provide a coverage of virtually 100 per cent in first-class quality for a predominantly music programme : it was only on VHF that stereo transmissions were technically possible.

Then there were financial considerations. On present form radio would be in deficit of nearly £12 million by March 1974, not counting the cost of local radio. McKinseys had identified a number of potential savings, but they could not be achieved without staff reductions.

One area of very high spending was music. The agreements with the Musicians' Union, with its wholly understandable desire to maintain musical employment, meant that the BBC employed musicians in orchestras it did not need. Indeed, the number of musicians employed by the BBC could, from the broadcasting angle, and that only, be reduced by about 50 per cent. This reduction went far beyond what was likely to be acceptable to the Musicians' Union. For broadcasting needs we needed the BBC Symphony, the Northern Symphony, the BBC Radio, the Midland Light and the Scottish Radio. By the yardstick of broadcasting needs, we should disband four orchestras, the Scottish Symphony, the Northern Dance, the London Studio Players and the Training Orchestra. The BBC could remain a patron of music only if it had money for the purpose.

I found Gerry Mansell's analysis and proposals convincing. Whenever he was challenged he was persuasive and well-informed. The board decided to study them in greater detail at a special meeting a week later. At this meeting, McKinseys made a 'presentation', Mansell repeated his main arguments and proposals and Sir William Glock, controller of music, made his contribution – and a very impressive one it was. Incidentally, I argued on this occasion that network radio should not have to find savings to finance local radio and that new money would have to be found for this.

Up to now discussions about radio's future had been internal and no public announcement had been made. Our advisory bodies had to be consulted before the policy statement could be finalized. It was only courteous and fair that the views of the General Advisory Council and the Regional Advisory Councils should be considered. Besides, we really wanted their views.

In the meantime, there was little chance that the proposals would not leak from that leakiest of all organizations, the BBC. Some of its staff never hesitate to use the press to assert their own views and even to castigate their superiors. We did not have to wait long for, on the following Sunday, the press was lively :

Diary 2 June
Sunday Times running a campaign to protect music programme (which is not in danger).

Sunday Telegraph says why not urge increases in licence fee (and would oppose it, if we did).

The fact is that the press wants to run our affairs and resents what it calls 'secrecy'. All we are doing is to consult our advisory bodies before reaching final decisions and publishing them for public discussion. What's wrong with this? Incidentally, it is apparent that some BBC staff are fanning the flames.

3 pm
We decide to issue a statement to explain the position, promising statement by early July, after which BBC will wel-
come public discussion.

Charles Curran, George Campey drafted a letter to the
press; Curran to consult Post Office as they were concerned
with the local radio aspect.

3 June
Curran told me that PMG [Postmaster General] would
resent it if we were to issue our proposed letter to the press.

I rang the PMG who changed his tune. He merely wanted
to see draft. We sent it along and apart from trivial altera-
tion, he agrees. We issue.

4 June
Times does not publish our letter, although it is a reply to an
attack (on BBC) in its leader columns. The *Guardian* mixes
it with interpretative comment.

In parallel with the consultations with advisory bodies, Ian
Trethowan, who was working with Frank Gillard before taking
over wholly at the end of the year, was busy drafting the policy
statement for public issue in July. A top-class journalist, he
would be more likely to produce a readable document than any
committee! From time to time, the draft came to the governors
via the Board of Management, although, as it turned out, it
needed little amendment from either body.

The consultations with advisory bodies began on 6 June with
meetings of the National Broadcasting Councils of Scotland and
Wales. A week later there was a joint meeting of the Regional
Advisory Councils, the Northern Ireland Advisory Council and
the chairmen of Local Radio Advisory Councils.

My diary entry on this meeting reads:

12 June
Mansell was superb. Curran excellent. The reaction of many
was to feel stunned. Mansell proceeded from the facts to the
conclusions. Devastingly effective. I sense that some who had
come to scorn felt disappointed – even, to use Curran's word

– 'conned'. It was evident that the main issue is London v the Rest. 'Save the regions' is to be the cry. Local radio cannot take its place (especially from those who have never heard it). Anyway, a good morning.

Invited chairmen of Regional Advisory Councils to attend governors' meeting next week.

Then came the meeting of the main advisory body, the General Advisory Council. At its outset, I explained why the proposals had been kept secret : so that advisory bodies could be consulted first. I described, too, the governors' attitude to advertising as a source of finance for the BBC. I was strongly 'agin' it and said so.

Diary 18 June
Then a Mansell presentation, long but very good. Charles Curran spoke. Then questions and discussion. Following speech by Alfred Morris MP, Charles Curran gave a remarkable outburst answering points Morris had not made. 'I was born in Yorkshire' etc. His point was the sound one that the North Region was varied but I was so embarrassed I scarcely heard what he was saying.

Lord Harewood, speaking on the generic principle, and doubting its wisdom, was very effective. Frank Gillard replied that television has taught people to switch, looking for what they wanted. This was happening more and more on radio. Frank, with his open, honest manner, was very persuasive. Regional chairmen revealed that governing their attitude was a suspicion of London. I think they are right in this and I am determined to protect, indeed foster, nonmetropolitan broadcasting.

The day after the meeting of the General Advisory Council, the chairmen of the various advisory bodies came to the governors' meeting led by Niel Pearson of the north. Pearson, an able advocate, somewhat overstated his case, arguing that the cumbersome North Region, less Lincolnshire, should be retained in order to have a louder voice in London. Of our visitors Dr Harper of the south-west was the best. It seemed to us, when, our visitors having departed, we discussed what we had heard, that their most telling point was that, with the disappearance of the large regions and their replacement by a larger number of small ones, there was a danger that the regional voice in London discussions would be muted. There was something in Niel Pearson's argument. To meet it we decided to create a new post of controller of English regions to bring to bear on London the viewpoint of the provinces.

We were impressed, too, by a fear our visitors expressed that less money would be available for locally produced non-London programmes. We decided to make clear in the final draft that more money, not less, would be needed for these programmes. My diary continues the story.

20 June
Lunch with PMG. Stonehouse exhibits grand manner, part tycoon, part statesman. He agrees date of publication. He dislikes removal of medium wave from Radio 3. The permanent secretary gave us the impression, without saying so, that government would approve local radio proposals and raise licence fee by 5s. He spoke as if the rest of the BBC proposals involved government approval. I spoke firmly against this.

3 July Governors' meeting.
My worst meeting yet. We had to decide final policy statement. Under guise of drafting alterations, some governors and staff were wobbling. Greene excellent at his first governors' meeting. Curran did not wobble. Anyway we got through.

4 July
Group of Members of Parliament has demanded to see me before we publish next Thursday. Why not know what the policy is before protesting about it?

The press conference on 10 July at which we issued the new policy statement was a subdued affair. Flanked by Curran, Gillard, Wheldon and Trethowan, I made a short opening statement, thereafter passing most of the questions to the team. 'Frank Gillard was the best by far [I wrote in my diary of 10 July]. I was not in good form. Nothing sparked me off. I got the meaning of one question wrong. The main subjects of questions were advertising, orchestras and money.'

The next day the press was mixed but not violent. By some, the proposal to establish forty local radio stations was seen as a blocking device to discourage the establishment of commercial radio. Not all saw this as a good thing. The BBC's role as a patron of culture is one of the few solid justifications for financing it out of the public's pocket, said one newspaper. With an eye on Radio 1, it added that 'one kind of patronage which is obnoxious is that which is dedicated to disseminating sheer drivel which could as easily be financed by ordinary commercial means'. Some said that serious cuts in serious music were to be made to make way for the extension of local radio. We should have gone for an increase in the licence fee instead of devising a plan which assumed financial restraint and a condemnation of advertising as a source of income. We were accused of dropping the Third Programme and cutting serious music while manufacturing an extra output of pop. The most serious criticisms were about the proposal to cut orchestras and limit Radio 3 to VHF. This latter criticism grew in intensity as the weeks passed. It was asserted that the Third Programme was being destroyed by its conversion into Radio 3. On the other hand, the generic principle of specialized networks was not disputed.

The proposals in 'Broadcasting in the Seventies' were now launched on the public for discussion. Rather unexpectedly there was little public or published discussion, once the initial publicity was over. Frank Gillard and William Glock corrected some of the more obvious mis-statements in letters to *The Times*. Curran and Mansell took part in an hour-long discussion on Radio 3.

In a House of Commons debate on broadcasting the Postmaster General dropped a hint that the licence fee would be raised in due course, adding that the Corporation should look again at its proposals to disband orchestras. But it was two or three months before the pace began to quicken and new critics were to find their voices, mostly in the unwarranted belief that the Third Programme was doomed.

We were now ready to discuss the licence fee and on 18 July the Postmaster General invited Curran and myself to meet him.

He said he had in mind a composite licence fee of £6 10s, a 10s increase on the current fee, and the abolition of the sound-only licence. Naturally we asked for details of his arithmetic, only to be told that 'More than £6 10s was not on'. I replied that facts were facts and we must know whether the proposed amount was enough : eventually we agreed that our finance people should meet his that afternoon, when our people told the Post Office staff that they calculated that a £6 10s licence fee would mean in five years a deficit of £10-13 million.

Later that evening Stonehouse sent a message asking that we should clinch the deal at £6 10s, adding that, on his figures, it was enough. My diary goes on :

I asked Curran to see Fred Peart who had earlier advised him not to clinch a deal with Stonehouse.

19 July
Charles saw Fred this evening and phoned me. Government decision not imminent. Stonehouse has no business to make an offer. I advised Curran to remain quiet – a ministerial row is no business of ours. But it does look as if we are to do local radio and be paid for it.

20 July
Stonehouse rang me at home at 10 pm. He was annoyed. We were lobbying ministers : we had given information to Dick Taverne. (So we had; he had asked for it as a Treasury minister.) We were being difficult in financial calculations so as to defeat him on extra hours. Some of his colleagues wanted us to advertise.

21 July
Curran and Mansell and I spoke to both Tory and Labour Broadcasting Committees. Labour committee clearly on our side, except for orchestras and wavelength of Radio 3. Tories seemed rather ashamed of their commercial radio ideas. Following the Stonehouse conversation, I sent him a paper on our financial calculations.

22 July
Debate on broadcasting in the House of Commons. Bryan bad; Stonehouse fairly good. All that now remains is 'how

much?' Stonehouse hinted at higher licence fee. It was widely said that our plan is really a crafty ploy to get higher licence fee. In fact, it is not. But what matters if we get it? Like Liberace, we can cry all the way to the bank.

29 July
Stonehouse rang to complain that our figures for increased licence fee had been sent to Peart and Taverne and so they have.

31 July
Stonehouse rang at breakfast time. Government had turned his proposals down, though Broadcasting Committee (of Cabinet) was with him. No additional hours. Talk in Cabinet about advertising by BBC. Cabinet against increase of licence fee, though hoping that a start might be made with local broadcasting and that orchestras would be saved. I grunted about money.

At a governors' meeting later in day, I told them Stonehouse story. They were very sturdy. They decided that no money meant no local radio. Experiment would soon cease – staff would go anyway. We would be back to Square 1 with our savings to avoid deficit, including orchestras. Hugh Greene very helpful.

Then on 4 August Curran and I called on the Prime Minister and Stonehouse at No. 10, at their request. We were told that the government wanted an expansion of broadcasting within the available resources and that they were against extension of broadcasting hours. There were no firm conclusions on finance, though the Prime Minister 'had it in mind' that there would be an increase in the combined licence fee to £6 10s, accompanied by abolition of the sound licence fee, coming into effect in the first half of 1971.

I told him that it would be impossible for the BBC to plan on the mere expectation, however genuine, of an increased licence fee in 1971. Unless there was a firm and satisfactory statement now, we would have to close down the eight experimental local radio stations. Secondly, in the absence of additional money the economies would have to proceed. What the

Prime Minister had suggested was an indication of an intention which this, or any other government, might not honour.

Eventually, the Prime Minister yielded the point that it could be stated now that the named increased licence fee would operate from a named date. I pointed out that this would mean the BBC running into a deficit which could now be calculated. Curran pointed out that it would certainly be necessary to secure agreement by the Musicians' Union on a number of points, including an increase in needle time and the freedom of the BBC to negotiate joint working and sharing of costs of some orchestras with other bodies. The Prime Minister accepted this.

In seeking the views of the governors by post, I included a personal interpretation of the Prime Minister's thinking :

> I suspect that the Prime Minister was operating within the framework of a known dislike on the part of a number of his colleagues to raising the licence fee before the election. He wanted local radio to develop and he was seeking somehow or other to meet our requirements without proceeding forthwith to an increased licence fee from 1 January next. It would be recognized between the Post Office and ourselves that we were running into a deficit of a certain size, in our view of the order of £4 million by 1974. If this plan is accepted there will, I suspect, be public criticism of this as a political device; some of this criticism would come to us but much would go to the Prime Minister. On the other hand, he is aware of this and probably feels he cannot be helpful to us in any other way. Forgetting this criticism, we should have succeeded in gaining the acceptance of our plans at the cost of a known deficit which if it were not liquidated by subsequent surplus would fall to be dealt with at the next consideration of the licence fee.

With varying degrees of reluctance, the governors decided to accept the package, even though it meant a departure, as Bellinger pointed out, from the principle of no-deficit budgeting which the governors had so recently approved.

On 14 August the PMG announced that the BBC would be authorized to introduce a general service of local radio, increasing the number of stations to forty; that the BBC had decided not to restrict Radio 3 to VHF; that the BBC would revise its proposals with regard to their orchestras : that there would be no increase in hours; that the combined TV and radio licence would be raised to £6 10s on 1 April 1971, the sound-only licence being abolished. The press reaction to Stonehouse's announcement of these decisions was in no way hostile. While one paper saw it as a victory for me, another as a win for Stonehouse, most regarded it as reasonable compromise.

The new plans for radio published and the licence fee decided, it was reasonable to expect a period of relative calm in which the radio planners could begin the complicated task of translating 'Broadcasting in the Seventies' into programmes. But it was not to be. Three months after the publication of the policy, a protest body called the Campaign for Better Broadcasting was formed.

We received about a thousand letters on the subject of 'Broadcasting in the Seventies' from the public in three or four months, a small post bearing in mind that the average daily post of the BBC, on all subjects, is a thousand letters a day. *The Times* apart, the newspapers seemed bored with the whole affair. Then, in February 1970, some seven months after publication of the proposals, the controversy took on a new and much more serious face. *The Times* published a letter from over a hundred members of the BBC staff protesting against the new proposals embodied in 'Broadcasting in the Seventies'. Other critical letters followed. Later, Hugh Greene weighed in with an effective attack on the rebels. The governors, resenting the stories that I was the wicked author of the offending proposals, wrote to *The Times* to say that the proposals had the unanimous support of the Board of Governors and the Board of Management.

A wider protest movement, we were told, had begun in the previous October at both the Conservative and the Labour Conferences. According to one observer, some of the most distinguished programme makers from both the BBC and ITV had held large private meetings to which they invited MPs and ministers. They had argued that the whole structure of broadcasting in this country was in need of fundamental revision. An advertisement appeared in the *Guardian* signed by a number of well-known broadcasters calling for a Royal Commission 'to review the structure, finance and organization of broadcasting'.

What had begun as a revolt against changes in radio generally, and the Third Programme in particular, was developing into a fundamental attack on the whole system, BBC and ITV alike. The bureaucracy had taken over from the producers and was positively hostile to participation by anyone else : some of the people in control of broadcasting constituted the most immediate threat to broadcasting standards – these were some of the charges made.

By the weekend following the staff letter to *The Times,* the temperature had lowered somewhat :

Diary 13 February
On Saturday there was a supporting leader in the *Express* and a fair and helpful article in the *Financial Times.* Sunday press not too bad. A. J. Taylor attacks the intellectuals in the *Sunday Express.* God preserve us from our friends. The *Sunday Times* published two pieces, one of which says we have not gone far enough. The *Observer* piece is regarded by the BBC as satisfactory. Side swipes at me don't worry them – and why should they?

The following week came a debate in the House of Lords, opened by Lord Gladwyn :

Diary 22 February
Things are easing up somewhat. The House of Lords debate had an element of anti-climax. Gladwyn opened with a feeble speech. The government spokesman, Lady Llewelyn-Davies, was cautious and non-committal. Lady Stocks, in her innocent way, tried by innuendo to blame my appointment for staff unease; Francis Williams followed same line. Goodman was terrific and challenged my critics to produce evidence. Strabolgi was excellent. Eddie Shackleton, winding up with his usual charm and ability, included one little bombshell. Reith, before whom so many had bowed (and who was present for much of the debate) loathed the Third Programme. Not a bad day. When Goodman had finished, the debate was over. What an extraordinary man he is ! He

has every reason to dislike me. The company he advised, TWW, had lost its ITA contract and the company he gathered for the Yorkshire contract failed. Yet he sailed in to my defence. Incidentally as a patient and unwearying chairman he is leading Musicians' Union and us to agreement.

At the same time a new group had been set up to press for a Royal Commission on broadcasting :

Diary 17 March
The main features of the past fortnight have been
1   The death of the Third Programme controversy largely killed by the House of Lords debate.
2   The start of a new campaign by a group called the 76 Group, headed by Stuart Hood, Phillip Whitehead and, in the background, Hugh Jenkins, MP. An all party meeting of MPs is to be held today to listen to leaders of this group. On the face of it, the group asks for a Royal Commission to consider the whole structure of broadcasting, adding a side swipe at the management of BBC and ITV. This is fair enough. After all, the chances are that we shall see an enquiry of the Pilkington kind set up in the next twelve months or so. What peculiar virtues a Royal Commission has, I don't know : I associate a Royal Commission with prolonged delay. Anyway, Stonehouse has already said that he has it in mind that the enquiry should be set up about the middle of this year after his technical committee has reported.
. . . I doubt the wisdom of setting it up so soon because of the anxiety it creates inside the BBC. 1971 seems early enough. No government in the run-up to a general election ought to select and appoint so important a body. It ought to wait until after the election.

Looking back over the prolonged controversy surrounding 'Broadcasting in the Seventies', it is natural to ask what went wrong. I was wholly convinced that the policy expressed in this document was soundly based. It was logically argued and persuasively presented; the product of prolonged study by able and experienced men. It would bring, I was convinced, new hope and vigour to radio. Yet it had aroused serious and genuine misgivings in the minds of a number of creative people of high reputation in radio as well as criticisms by some distinguished outside figures.

In part the internal misgivings stemmed from fear rather than fact, for one had to conclude that the critics inside Broadcasting House could not believe that, in practice, the policy would live up to its published prospectus. There had, they also averred, been a great deal of discussion but very little consultation with programme makers.

Although I realized that often a charge of failure adequately to consult really means a failure to accept the views of those consulted, in this case there seemed to be substance in the criticisms. If not wholly to satisfy the critics, it was imperative to speed up the preparation of the detailed programme schedules : this would answer the first misgivings and improve the procedures for internal consultation so as to minimize the second. Ian Trethowan and his colleagues, quick to appreciate the nature of the difficulties and the need for these parallel steps, set to work on them. As this course was followed and the new programme schedules were evolved, the internal critics were mollified and some of the external critics shamed. Neither would dare to repeat their criticisms today now that the policy has found expression in actual radio programmes. Indeed, that radio is now arousing an even wider interest and appreciation is due in no small part to 'Broadcasting in the Seventies', and to the sturdiness of such men as Frank Gillard, Ian Trethowan, Howard Newby and Tony Whitby who stuck to their jobs in the kitchen, despite the rising temperature and the babel of voices.

16

Greene: My Assessment

Sir Hugh Greene left the director-general post on 1 April 1969 and returned to the BBC in the role of governor on 11 July.

The competitive attitude to ITV had been a spur to the BBC, dating from the time when the BBC awoke from its trance of smug self-satisfaction and belief in its own divine righteousness to find that it had only 30 per cent of the television audience and ITV had 70 per cent. The BBC had had to fight hard to get on roughly equal terms with its opposition and Greene had led the fight. In the mid-sixties most of the higher command of the BBC really hated the commercial competitor that had robbed them of their exclusive power. It was the television service, the dominant influence in the BBC, which set the pattern of bitter antagonism to the competitor, and Robert Fraser took the brunt of this animosity at first. Later I received my portion.

Greene had seen that during my spell at Brompton Road I had strengthened the role of the Authority at the expense of the director-general and no doubt he feared that I would seek to do the same at Portland Place and as a result lose something of his public standing. Bearing in mind also that the Authority had actually lunched with and listened to Mrs Whitehouse, he was wary of my approach to controversial programmes. This was part of the background of suspicion and animosity against which I began at the BBC. Not unnaturally I resented the mood of courteous hostility that greeted me and it was some time before my resentment died.

Yet, for all the initial hubbub, Greene and I worked together amicably and sensibly. Indeed I enjoyed our spell together. Although Lord Normanbrook once told me, in a mood of exasperation, that he 'could do nothing with Greene', I had no such experience. But I did not get to know him well, nor, I suspect, does anyone, even those who have worked closely with him for years. An approachable man, there is a central area in him which no one sees.

As to how he reacted to our association, I cannot in the nature of things have direct evidence, apart from the statements he made to the press and the letter he sent to me at the time of the announcement of his retirement from executive office. Some of those close to him have told me that, in the light of experience, his fears were progressively allayed. He even told a former ITA colleague whom he met at an international conference that he was 'beginning to like the old boy'. But, if our working together did allay his fears, the change was temporary and did not last throughout his governorship and certainly ceased when he retired from the board.

My assessment of Hugh Greene is that he is a man of obstinately rigid judgements, seldom failing a friend or forgiving an enemy. Despite his intermittent hostility to me, I have never faltered in my admiration for much that he did. His contribution to the BBC and to broadcasting was outstandingly brilliant. I said, at the farewell dinner the governors gave to him on his retirement as director-general, that there were three dominant elements in his achievements. In fair weather and foul he had adhered unswervingly to the principle of the BBC's independence. He had met the competition which was created some fourteen years before head on, matching it million for million, without blurring the public service concept. Consistently and relentlessly, he had supported the creative mind and the atmosphere in which creative ability can thrive. A born leader, he can exhibit both a considerable maturity and a juvenile capacity for mischief. He loves to be thought outrageous. Unpompous and unstuffy, an apostle of joy and pleasure, he passionately believes in total freedom within the law, whatever it involves and wherever it leads. An ace, if low-brow, professional, with reactions as apparently slow as his bulk is great, he has the discernment of a top-grade politician.

In the weeks before the day of Greene's retirement, a series of four articles on the BBC appeared in the *Sunday Times* over the name of Kenneth Adam, the former director of BBC television. I cannot improve on Greene's description of them. 'I have seldom in my life read so much poisonous nonsense,' he told Quentin Crewe of the *Daily Mail*. 'There were 27 errors of fact alone in Mr Adam's first article,' he told the *Daily Telegraph*.

A curious incident involving Greene occurred at a governors' meeting in the autumn of 1969. It was the practice of the BBC to send every week to the chairman and vice-chairman copies of the minutes of some internal weekly meetings, the Board of Management, the Television Programme Review Committee and the corresponding committees reviewing the output of news and current affairs and radio. I found these minutes both interesting and instructive, revealing both the vast range of problems confronting management and the remarkable vigour and thoroughness with which post mortem examinations were conducted on programme output. Indeed, if I had a doubt about something I had seen or heard, some similar misgiving was almost certain to have found expression through a member of one or other of these committees. The more I knew about how the machine worked, the more confidence I had in its efficiency.

The background of the incident was that one governor had commented on what he called the inadequacy of the reports of the work of the Board of Management given by the director-general. Did they never discuss programmes? This led me to ask the governors whether they would like to receive the Board of Management minutes, as did the vice-chairman and myself : not for discussion but for information.

The fat was in the fire. Immediately Greene opposed, to be followed by May Baird and Glanmor Williams who argued that if this were done the director-general might be undermined. Presumably the circulation to the chairman and the vice-chairman did not undermine him but to circulate them to other governors would. My view was that a sight of these minutes would increase and not reduce the confidence of the governors in the management machine. It was not an interference in management to know what management was doing.

Seeking a compromise I suggested deferring the item until

the next meeting, when samples of the actual minutes could be seen and governors would know what they were discussing. Even this modest and non-committal suggestion was opposed by some governors so I put it to the vote. Five voted for seeing sample minutes at a postponed discussion and five against. I voted, making it six in favour. My diary comments: 'How the senior staff resent the Governors showing the slightest sign of governing. Unimportant in itself, it has become a symbol of Board of Management resentment.'

Before the next meeting, I learned that Greene had been lobbying some governors against the circulation of Board of Management minutes and that one governor who had voted for the motion had been persuaded to his view. So I withdrew the item until another day. In fact, another day came, as I shall describe later, and the essence of my proposal was accepted. It worked very well without undermining anybody.

A later episode which embarrassed the Board of Governors occurred in August 1970. I read in the press that Hugh Greene had agreed to become creative consultant for a series on Thames Television. The publishing firm, Bodley Head, of which he is chairman, had sold Thames the rights of a book edited by Greene on which the programme would be based, and he would be creative consultant to the series.

The first I knew of this appointment was when it appeared in the press following a press conference at which Greene revealed the news. This was not a breach of the standing order on governors' broadcasting, which read as follows:

> While in office Governors shall not normally broadcast on any service, BBC or other, except officially on matters affecting the Corporation when the Standing Order No 11 shall apply. But this Standing Order shall not prevent a Governor broadcasting in circumstances and on matters wholly arising out of his or her non-BBC activities and in no way related to his or her Governorship or to the BBC. No fees shall be payable for any broadcasts which Governors may give. The same principle of non-payment shall be extended to contributions to BBC publications.

As the standing order did not expressly cover the point as

to whether a governor broadcasting on Independent Television is entitled to take fees, I thought it would be as well to extend the standing order in this respect for the sake of clarity.

Greene's action raised other points. He had always condemned commercial television vigorously and his appointment had aroused our producers. Can a man be a governor of the BBC and, at the same time, advise its commercial competitor on programme-making? At the next meeting of governors I decided to raise this question and I prepared a note which included a draft new standing order covering the point. I gave Green advance notice of my intention.

When my note was discussed at the next meeting of governors, Greene strongly defended his action. He argued that a writer selling his work is entitled to ensure that it is properly presented by advising at the production stage. He was not a writer but the compiler of an anthology of detective stories. None of the governors supported Greene. One suggested that he had been invited to accept this post in order that Independent Television might have the newsworthy cachet of gathering to its fold an ex-director-general. Greene did not refute this. There was general agreement that a standing order should be prepared. At this stage Greene asked what was the legal standing of a standing order? What if he broke it? What steps could follow? He was promised that the advice of our laywers would be obtained; their answer did not give him a leg to stand on.

Greene then raised the question of his appearing at a press conference on Tyne-Tees. My own immediate reaction was that this was permissible but we sent for the full standing orders to discover that it was not, unless Greene refrained from speaking about the BBC. He agreed, now more gracefully, that he would accept only on the understanding that he did not discuss the BBC (the real reason, of course, for inviting him).

In April came the unveiling of Greene's portrait.

Diary 24 April
I unveiled Hugh Greene's portrait by Ruskin Spear in the Council Chamber. I don't think he wanted me to do it, but I insisted. The first suggested date for the ceremony was Easter Tuesday when it was known I should be away! As I

drew the curtain there was a gasp from the audience of BBC colleagues – a gasp which meant astonished delight that the artist had captured the real Greene . . . Greene referred to it as a caricature.

Early in August 1971 Hugh Greene told me of his intention to resign his governorship. I was not surprised. Because of other commitments, he had not been attending the board regularly. When he had attended, he had not taken much part in its discussions. No doubt a desire not to embarrass his successor as director-general had been a factor in his relative silence.

Diary 5 August
Hugh Greene came to see me as arranged. In one respect I guessed aright that he had come to tell me of his intention to retire as a governor. In another respect I did not. I had formed the impression that he was looking for an excuse to resign. I thought this time that the Ombudsman proposal would provide him with just such a peg; in fact he did not mention it. [The Ombudsman proposal is explained in chapter 23. Greene opposed the suggestion that there should be an Ombudsman to whom those aggrieved by a broadcast could appeal.]

He told me that he was soon to be appointed as chairman of Greene King Brewery – he is already a director – and that although the post would be non-executive there was a good deal of promotional work to be done in the area and that he would have to spend more time in and around Bury St Edmunds. As this would mean more absences from the board he thought it best to resign.

He added that he thought that the end of August was a good time, because in October the programmes on which he had been acting as a consultant would begin to appear on Independent Television and he expected that they would cause quite a sensation. This being the prospect he thought that there should be a distance of time between his retirement and the appearance of the programmes. He added as an afterthought that he would, of course, as a freelance be free to do more broadcasting, and be paid for it.

The discussion was entirely amicable.

17

Another Clash with Mr Wilson

Charles Curran had a Sunday night tête-a-tête with the Prime
Minister at Chequers on 7 December 1969. He told me the next
day that they had roamed far and wide in their discussion and
Curran was pleased with it.

But on Tuesday the position had changed and the Prime
Minister was angry. The BBC had declined the Prime Minister's
suggestion to put him on *Panorama* the previous evening. The
BBC had argued that it ought not to give a political leader who
had spoken in the House that day an opportunity to say it all
again to the public without a balancing appearance by the
spokesman for the other side. We had done this very thing on
the day of the Queen's Speech : we had been criticized by
Harold Wilson for putting on Mr Heath and had agreed that
we were wrong to do it (see next chapter, diary entry for 30
October). Having resolved not to do it again, that was the explanation for refusing Wilson's suggestion that he should go on
Panorama and offering him an alternative on another night.

But on the night for which we had refused Wilson we did
put on – on the subject on which he (Wilson) wished to speak,
Biafra – Patrick Gordon Walker, Edward Du Cann and
Auberon Waugh. As soon as the programme was finished,
according to Charles Curran's report to me the next morning,
the Prime Minister spoke to him on the telephone at his home.
He was, Curran said, hopping mad. The good work of Saturday night had been destroyed. It was clear to him that Curran
was not in charge of affairs at the BBC. Charles Curran rang
me straightaway to tell me this on the same night, and ten

minutes after he had finished Wilson's private secretary rang me asking me to come down to No 10 the next day.

I dutifully attended at No. 10 at noon the next day. Unusually, in my experience, the Prime Minister was not in a good humour. Twice in five weeks, he said, the Prime Minister had been refused an opportunity to come to the screen, one on the fifth anniversary of his government taking up office and now in *Panorama*. Any pretence that we could not put him on during the debate was destroyed by the fact that we had put on others. This had led him to re-think his whole relationship to the BBC. Mrs Wilson had been denied the screen except as Cliff Michelmore's selected interviewee because Ted Heath was a bachelor. The more he thought about it, the more he felt that the BBC was prejudiced against him and was failing to perform its duty as a public service. He then recited from his extraordinary memory all the items of difference of recent years that I had heard so often before, plus a few I had not heard of.

When he had finished I said we had better get clear the *Panorama* position. The last time I had been in his room he had criticized bitterly our putting Heath on the screen on the night of the Queen's Speech. Two chances for one : it was unfair, and so on. We had accepted that we were at fault and decided not to do it again. Two wrongs do not make a right. As for the rest, I said it both astonished and depressed me that he should see in the BBC a conspiracy against him and his government. He had said that he did not include Charles Curran and me in the conspiracy : but we were ultimately responsible. He had described a BBC which I did not recognize.

It became clear that there would be no useful outcome of the meeting. When I told Harold Wilson that Michael Stewart had been invited for Thursday night and suggested that if he wished he could replace Michael Stewart, he declined.

Later, I told the director-general that we must be scrupulously careful to maintain impartiality. We may make mistakes; indeed, on the night of the Address we had made one, but this did not justify the slightest suggestion that we were deliberately anti-government or pro-government. I told him that we should make no gesture at all at fence-mending, the Prime Minister must be left to make the next move.

18

A Chairman's Diary

I was often asked 'What does the BBC chairman do?' Previous
chapters have, I hope, given some clue to the variety of problems which occupied me. After all, the chairman and governors
are responsible for everything the BBC does.

One thing I did which I had never in my life done before.
I kept a diary. It was not for posterity but to help my memory,
which fades like everybody else's as I grow older. Also, it gave
therapeutic relief to my feelings! Some extracts from my 1969
diary illustrate my earlier remark that life at the BBC is never
dull.

8 January
With Curran and Gillard I received a deputation from the
Newspaper Society. They suspected that we might be favour-
ing advertising as a source of finance for local radio. I told
them plainly that, in my view, we should resist advertising
in any part of our service. It was time they woke up to the
danger of a commercial service to the provincial press.

10 January
Spoke to magazine editors off the record. Only two telling
questions. What was my role as chairman? Secondly, if competition had done so much good to the BBC, why not commercial radio? I admitted the logic of this but argued hope-
fully that I did not think the public wanted it.

27 January
Visited Lime Grove. Ted Heath on *Panorama* : at his best –

revelling in detail and relaxed. Later an argument developed. To Grist, Amoore, Webster, Dimbleby, Mossman, Rowlands, Hylands and others, I floated the idea that party political broadcasts should go. To a man, they were against abandoning them. They argued, firstly, that more party political stuff would be expected in their current affairs programmes and, secondly, that politicians had the right to address the public directly. One of them said, to my surprise, that party politicals were popular! Behind all this I detected unease, and more than a suspicion that the BBC would not defend belligerent interviews – belligerent, that is, to the interviewed: I gave them the governors' view. But clearly references to the governors left them cold.

20 March

Programme on old schools last week in which Ted Short had appeared. In the broadcast version we cut out his reply to critical comments on three schools. Short's PRO had insisted on knowing in advance names of three schools to be mentioned in the film. Our people say he was told their names only on the understanding that he should not tell Short. He told Short, and Short answered the criticism (two schools to be replaced next year and one to have £10,000 spent on it). How bloody silly can the BBC get? Of course an Education Minister invited to a programme in which are to be named three schools as outworn, is entitled to know their names in advance and to reply without having his reply cut out. We were criticizing a man and we cut out his reply. I insist on simple statement before this week's programme remedying deficiency.

25 March

Anthony Wedgwood Benn spoke at Radio Industries Club (of which I am president). He spoke with astonishing fluency. The trouble is that ten minutes after he had sat down, I hadn't the slightest recollection of what he had said.

6 May

Lunch with PMG at GPO. A lush lunch with a strong PR flavour. Other guests include Lord Stokes. Stonehouse hosted with considerable panache, using the occasion to sell PO wares. One day he will be a business tycoon.

16 May

Phoned at home by Tony Whitby [Secretary of the BBC]. Mrs Whitehouse, through solicitors, had threatened prosecution (of BBC) for obscenity if we repeat *All My Loving* on BBC 2 on Sunday. Talked with Robin Scott [Controller, BBC 2]. There was a scene (raping a banjo!), probably obscene but Scott could defend it.

I decided not to intervene. It would be fatal to yield to Mrs Whitehouse on her threats. The process would never end.

2 July

Attended *Any Questions* session at Commonwealth Press Union Conference with Roy Thomson, Geoffrey Cox and Bill Barnetson. Ludo Kennedy presided. One or two questions loaded against TV. We were indulging in instant and superficial news while press was deeper and more contemplative. Roy Thomson said companies like TWW losing their contract should have compensation. I asked about the millions he and others had taken out of TV and pooh-poohed the idea of compensation. Gavin Astor asked whether showing of news films of horrors of war would enhance national morale or reduce it. I said I did not know. But our prime duty was to show what was going on in the world whether it embarrassed or not. He said my answer was terrifying. Perhaps I overdid it.

27 October

D-G told me that PM had asked him (and Harman Grisewood, Kenneth Lamb and, if he wished it, others) to go to dinner at Chequers next Sunday. I got suspicious but discussion was hurried and I said I would think on it.

28 October

Saw D-G. I told him I was suspicious of PM's invitation. An invitation to him for a tête-a-tête made sense : he could look after himself. What made me suspicious, at the beginning of a run-up to a general election, was that he (the PM) was suggesting who should accompany him – in fact, the BBC people dealing with the political arena. I rang the PM's private secretary and expressed my doubts and suspicions. When he told me that the PM would be accompanied by his press secretary and political secretary, I nearly exploded. This was wrong ... He said he would tell the PM.

29 October
PM's secretary rang to say PM accepted advice, adding that PM assumed that it would apply to other party leaders. He would dine with D-G alone.

30 October
Saw PM at his request about Heath's broadcast on day of opening of Parliament. To give Leader of Opposition a second chance on TV on day when he and PM had spoken in the House is unfair, particularly with five by-elections on the following Wednesday. He is right in his criticism and I said so.

25 November
Spoke to Army Staff College on broadcasting. To a man, they are anti-permissive and believe that BBC is undermining morals, decency and the rest. One (with news and current affairs in mind) urged external censorship but did not say by whom.

In the evening, spoke at Swedish Broadcasting Dinner. I really did leave my speech notes in the office. Gave a better speech in consequence.

19

Sensitive Politicians

It was virtually certain that 1970 would be an election year. The BBC began to brace itself for its trials, having learned from painful experience that the run-up to an election is a very sensitive time. To many politicians a programme is impartial if it leans to their direction and hostile if it is truly impartial.

The mildest of breezes began to blow in February. The director-general was invited to call on the Prime Minister to discuss the presentation of the forthcoming White Paper on the Common Market and from this the talk went on, pleasantly enough as Curran told me, to refer to Ted Heath's recent appearance on television. The latter had recently appeared on *Panorama* for fifteen minutes (compared with Wilson's fifty minutes the previous week) – there had been an item on Heath's sailing success and there had been ample publicity for the Tory Party's weekend conference on policy at Selsdon Park. Then the discussion had passed to the theme of law and order and a suggestion was made that Jim Callaghan might be invited to broadcast. My diary carries on the story:

8 February 1970
Separately, the Government Chief Whip, Bob Mellish, asked about the appearance of the Prime Minister and Heath last weekend. Pressure had been applied both to us and ITN to send cameras to the PM's meeting on Saturday. Both had declined. On the other hand for Heath's meeting at Llandudno on Saturday we did send a camera. The result

was a still of Wilson on the one hand plus a report and a live appearance of Heath on the other. Mellish asked for details of the time devoted to each and a transcript of what they said. This may lead to nothing but it may blow up into another exercise in friction and pressure.

There was an unfortunate sequel to the director-general's exchanges with the Prime Minister. Curran had told Wilson that the Common Market issue would be dealt with in an explanatory or expository way on the day of publication of the White Paper on the subject, on the ground that information should precede argument. He had given an instruction to this effect, through the editor of news and current affairs. In fact, nothing of the sort happened and the BBC let the director-general down. The PM did not complain about this though no doubt he had stored it in his capacious memory. The matter was raised at the next meeting of governors :

Diary 12 February
The governors were appalled but uncertain as to what to do. Eventually it was agreed to suport D-G's suggestion that a full and serious programme on the Common Market should appear either on *Panorama* or *24 Hours* next week. It raised the whole question of the authority of the D-G over the programme makers. For my part, I suspect that whenever an instruction or request or guidance goes down from Broadcasting House, the instinctive reaction of Lime Grove is to do as little as possible to carry it out.

For a month or so, all was quiet on the political front. Then came a blast from the opposition. Iain Macleod accused the BBC of showing bias in a statement on the result of the Bridgwater by-election, a charge which I knew to be wholly unfounded as I had heard the statement three times. Peter Hardiman Scott, who made it, had spoken with impeccable impartiality as he invariably did. I wired to Macleod asking him for the evidence for his charge but received no reply. At least this unfounded charge reminded the government side that there were some who thought the BBC was pro-Labour !

In March 1970 there began some discussion with the Home

Secretary on an exceedingly important subject, violence on the screen. Curran and I, and Aylestone and Fraser, met Jim Callaghan at his own request. Callaghan spoke of the relationship between television and violent crime. He accepted that too little was known about the general effect of violence on the individual viewer, apart from the maladjusted child, and that obviously more research was needed. His concern was with the interim period before fuller knowledge became available. He had read our two Codes on Violence, adding that he thought that both services fell short of the standards laid down in them. Could we offer any suggestions? It was agreed that we should meet again in about a month's time when we would reply to Callaghan.

Before the next meeting with the Home Secretary we got together with Aylestone and Fraser to exchange ideas. The position of the ITA as a supervisory and not a programme-making body was easier to explain and defend than that of the BBC. They did not propose to modify their arrangements. It was more difficult for us, for though the Code was distributed to the staff, the rest was left to the producers under the system of 'upward reference'. We trusted in God and the programme maker. We agreed to exchange documents before we met the Home Secretary again.

Callaghan, I thought, had raised a very real issue, easier to describe than to solve. Though little of scientific value was known about the effect of violence, assumptions could and perhaps should be made until scientific study came up with solid and accepted findings. Furthermore, we ourselves could contribute by our own study and research. I knew that for some time David Attenborough had been mulling over the idea of an advisory body on social research, including the impact of violence. Was this likely to be of intrinsic value to our programme makers and, if so, should it be part of our reply to Callaghan? The governors decided that it should.

A fortnight later the director-general, David Attenborough and I, together with Aylestone and Fraser, again met the Home Secretary, having sent to him the day before a note explaining our procedures relating to the Code of Violence and reporting our decision to appoint a small advisory committee of experts which would meet regularly with our television people and generally oversee and encourage research. It would advise the BBC on the current state of knowledge of the social effects of television, with specific regard to the effects of violence. It would consider ways in which, through existing or newly commissioned research, the BBC might be advised to modify its Code. It would be attended by senior representatives of the programme side of the television service and by the head of audience research.

Callaghan seemed to recognize that we made a constructive proposal, though he wanted a joint advisory committee to both television services. In reply I explained how a monolithic service like ours needed a quite different system from a supervisory body which did not make programmes but which controlled companies at arm's length. My diary completes the report of this meeting :

5 May

I invited David Attenborough to speak.

Callaghan looked surprised to see so young a man and began by asking what his job was. Anyway when David got going he was very effective – clear and cogent. All in all, our proposal would, I think, have been accepted as concluding the matter for us – but not for the ITA. Aylestone described the Authority's system of control and offered nothing but a continuance of the present position. Callaghan turned on him, threatening to set up some sort of viewers' council – or at least to give it serious consideration if the ITA did not come up with something better. In the end he asked him to look at the matter again, and us to consider with the ITA some joint apparatus. My impression, though I may be wrong, is that we have averted an external body. What worries me is the very real public belief, that television plays some part in encouraging violence.

In May Stonehouse announced the new Pilkington, the Annan Committee, a few days before the dissolution of Parliament, only a week after he had been talking to me rather vaguely about a Royal Commission, with Rab Butler as chairman. The Tories responded by indicating that they would not be committed by this announcement if they won the election.

Sir Hugh Greene (left), director-general of the BBC until his retirement from that post in March 1969 with Sir Robert Fraser, director-general of the ITA until October 1970.

Frank Gillard and Lord Hill at the news conference held on 10 July 1969 to announce the BBC's plan for network radio and non-metropolitan broadcasting.

Frank Gillard   Lord Hill

Sir Charles Curran, director-general of the BBC since Sir Hugh Greene's retirement.

H.M. the Queen with Lord Hill at the opening of the BBC's fiftieth anniversary exhibition.

Professor Sir Michael Swann with Lord Hill whom he succeeded as chairman of the BBC in January 1973.

As I reflected at the time in my diary, there would be one good result from this announcement. The critics of the BBC would have to get down to the daunting task of putting forward constructive proposals for the reform of broadcasting, a more difficult exercise than the sniping we had recently experienced.

Then there came the news of a general election to be held on 18 June. As usual a meeting of the parties and the broadcasting bodies was promptly called to consider the party political broadcasts. Shorter broadcasts were agreed upon but a number of our other suggestions were not. The parties would not agree to broadcasts with participating audiences. They rejected our proposal of serious political discussions 'in depth' on the BBC on Sunday nights. Indeed they made clear that they would kill this proposal if we proceeded with it by declining to provide contestants. My diary of 3 June records my reaction to this refusal : 'What hypocrisy! Politicians criticize us for trivializing politics, for not treating at length and in depth, and when they get the opportunity, they back out.'

The parties did not, however, object to three election forums, one for each party leader, with questions sent in by viewers, though Wilson insisted on thirty-five minutes for himself and Heath, not the forty-five minutes we had proposed.

On the whole there was little trouble for us in the course of the election battle, though there were two significant incidents. The first related to a *Panorama* programme on Monday 15 June. The director-general mentioned this to the Prime Minister and said he thought we ought to do foreign affairs, asking, of course, for the Foreign Secretary, Michael Stewart. The PM in reply made it pretty plain that he wanted Healey, saying that he thought defence should be the subject chosen.

Curran conveyed this view to the *Panorama* people via John Crawley, then editor of news and current affairs. But they, off their own bat, had already approached Michael Stewart on the subject of foreign affairs and he had accepted, but later he withdrew. When it was thought that Stewart would do it, however, Alec Douglas-Home had been invited for the Tories and had accepted. So a new situation arose. Not being able to get Stewart, the BBC reluctantly went for Healey, only to find that

F

Alec Douglas-Home was opposed to a discussion with him. In the end, Healey and Home did separate pieces from different parts of the country. It was not a great success.

As it had announced that Stewart and Home would do the programme, the BBC had to make public that Stewart had withdrawn. Wilson's press people, seeing the dilemma, briefed the press that Wilson had said that he had no objection to Stewart appearing as well as Healey. Then the next morning Wilson referred at his press conference to what had happened, saying in effect that it was for the parties to nominate speakers and subjects and that he had made it known to us at the highest level that he thought the subject should be defence and that Healey should be the spokesman. The BBC issued a statement in the following terms :

> In view of some statements which have been reported in the press the BBC wishes to make it clear that, party political and party election broadcasts apart, the parties do not nominate speakers or choose issues in BBC political programmes. The BBC takes the initiative, and in the case of the election editions of *Panorama* offers the parties the opportunity to comment on the major issues selected and consults the parties on speakers before inviting them to take part.

But not a single newspaper published this statement though David Wood of *The Times,* on being told of the matter, wrote a good piece.

Then, on the eve of poll, came another spot of trouble. In the 5.50 pm news, we broadcast a piece of film depicting Heath warning that devaluation would be the inevitable result of a Labour government and a slightly longer piece of Callaghan replying to this. All we gave of Wilson in this bulletin was a film of him leading a drum and fife procession. Within a few minutes, Wilson was on the telephone from Huyton, first to Lamb and then to Curran, complaining bitterly that man for man Heath could not be balanced by Callaghan.

Curran decided that in the 8.50 pm bulletin, bearing in mind that it was the eve of poll, all three leaders should appear and that a piece of film should be found on the cutting room floor of Wilson making a speech. In the result, the 8.50 pm news was, of itself, balanced, although added to the 5.50 pm news perhaps over-balanced in Labour's favour.

Wilson rang Curran after the 8.50 news to say that he was still unhappy and that he would have to consider whether he would give the BBC facilities at Huyton on election night. The director-general replied that if he did not give the BBC facilities he would not appear on anybody's screen, for Granada were on strike. Ah, Wilson replied, that means that you are exercising your monopoly. No, said Curran, in fact we have already offered to Independent Television the pictures we take of you at Huyton. Wilson then murmured about our future relations, adding that he would deal with us after the election.

On the evening of election day, I went to Television Centre about nine o'clock. It was a fantastic sight. Few people realize the immensely complicated organization behind the gathering and announcement of general election results, punctuated by running comment and psephologists' calculations. I asked Robert McKenzie what he thought the result would be and he forecast a Labour Party majority of eighty. Everybody I met thought the Labour Party would win.

Two senior BBC people I met expressed the view that, until a day or two before, the BBC's own interests as distinct from any other considerations were likely to be better served by a Labour victory. At least we should get our local radio. But, in the light of the events of the previous forty-eight hours and Wilson's threats to deal with us after the election, they said that the BBC's interests would probably be better served by a Labour defeat.

I went on to Broadcasting House to meet the radio staff and then settled down there to await the results. Amongst those there were Tony Greenwood, Kenneth Younger and, later on, Eddie Shackleton and Alun Chalfont. As the results came in their faces were a study in surprise. Tony Greenwood managed to disguise his delight at being out of it all, particularly as his old seat was lost to the Tories. Eddie Shackleton bore up well, saying simply that he would have to look for a job the next day. Chalfont just looked depressed.

20

Threats to Radio

When the general election was over and Edward Heath was installed in No. 10 Downing Street, we awaited with interest the new government's attitude to the BBC plans for extending local radio over the whole country. In my diary of 24 June 1970, I noted:

> The Tories are committed to commercial radio but have not made clear whether they will allow the BBC plan to continue to fruition. They may say that we can have our local radio, but that there should be a competitor. What I fear is that they may hold up our plans or even bring them to a halt altogether while they prepare the commercial alternative.
>
> A lot depends on who is to be Minister of Posts and Telecommunications. Today, Wednesday, it emerged that Paul Bryan was going to another job. Thank God for that. I pray that the new minister is not Eldon Griffiths.
>
> What does a Tory victory mean for the BBC, apart from local radio? There is a piece in the *Sun* this morning which suggests that Heath is going to cut the BBC down to size, allocating to us the minority, the serious, the cultured – and leaving to commercial the mass, the trivial, the escapist. We must wait and see.

On 1 July I called on the new Minister of Posts and Telecommunications, Christopher Chataway. The one theme of the meeting was commercial radio and it soon became obvious that

Chataway was wholly committed to this clear-cut item of Tory policy. I recorded some impressions in my diary :

2 July
Chataway would like to put an immediate stop to the BBC's local radio plans. He seemed surprised that, in respect of the dozen already approved (in addition to the original eight), the buildings are going up, the staff had been appointed and we were well forward with it all. He seemed to think that it would be enough that local radio should be wholly commercial, the BBC confining itself to the rest. He referred to our licence fee embarrassment as if to suggest that he could kill two birds with one stone by pushing us out of local radio, so saving us money. Our line must be that local radio is an essential part of the public service. If we are to have a competitor, so be it, but to divide the country into parts so that one has BBC only and another commercial radio, is a nonsense.

A few days later the Minister of Posts and Telecommunications visited our London Training School of Local Radio. Ian Trethowan told me that Chataway was greatly impressed and used words to suggest that he would try and persuade his colleagues to agree to the twenty stations without officially closing the door to further stations.

About this time BBC radio staff were worried by the government delay in increasing the licence fee and by reports that radio programmes would have to be reduced. On 21 July 1970 I wrote in my diary :

Dined last night with senior radio staff. Most of them would prefer advertising on radio to cutting of services. Obviously they were thinking of their jobs as much as the principle involved. Some seemed to think that it would be possible to have advertising on Radio 1 and avoid it spreading to the rest.

I told them plainly that I was strongly against it and urged upon them not to express views in favour. If, ultimately, the crunch came and we had to choose between some other source of income and cutting services, the problem could be looked at afresh. For my part, I hoped that the question of advertising would never arise.

My opposition to advertising on the BBC had been forcibly expressed some months earlier, as my diary for 24 April 1970 records:

> Governors' meeting. Main item a discussion on advertising (about which I had learned some members of the staff were wavering after so much delay in increasing the licence fee). I led, urging that at no time and in no way should we accept advertising revenue.
> Unanimously agreed.
> Fulton said it was one of the best days for the BBC.
> Odd that I – a suspect in this matter of advertising – should be the strongest advocate of undiluted public service.

On 10 August Chataway announced that we were to get our twelve new stations on VHF only, making twenty in all. Attached conditions at first sight looked forbidding. Frequencies might be reassigned. The government were not permanently committed either to the BBC operating local stations or to an increase in the licence fee beyond that already promised for 1 April 1971. I was much relieved:

Diary 10 August
My guess is that he (Chataway) has been convinced that the general pattern of the future should be competition between public service and commercial local radio. I just don't believe that once it is established he will be able to destroy BBC local radio.

The limitation to VHF is annoying but provided the two services compete on equal terms in relation to wavelength we cannot decently complain. This decision of Chataway's is very gratifying when one bears in mind what he said to the D-G and me some weeks ago. It was pretty obvious that he then had in mind giving us one part of the country and commercial radio the other part, at least at the outset. The argument against this, that he would be creating two monopolies in place of one, seems to have convinced him. His visits to the training school and to Brighton seemed to have clinched his attitude. In terms of population, the bulk of the country will be covered by the 20 stations.

The future of Radio 1 and BBC local radio were in question again in the autumn of 1970 when Curran and I saw Chataway about finance. I told him we were heading for a deficit of £48 million by March 1974 and would need a pound increase in the licence fee, over and above the £6 10s due to begin on 1 April in the following year.

Diary 28 October

Chataway immediately began to ask whether we should not cut some of our services, such as Radio 1 and local radio. I reminded him that, while he was responsible for the allocation of wavelengths, we were responsible for programme content. If the wavelengths of Radio 1 were taken away we should have to introduce pop material into the other services in order to remain comprehensive. We had to make an appeal to the young, however little the stuff appealed to us personally. Anyway, the savings would be only three-quarters of a million pounds a year. About local radio I argued that this was not merely an addition to radio. It was an element in a new structure in which we destroyed the old regions and replaced them by local services appealing to the local community.

Chataway said that a further increase of the licence fee was a political impossibility. We agreed to resume discussion when the scrutiny of our estimates had taken place.

The following week Christopher Chataway lunched with the governors. Rather to my surprise, Chataway asked whether there ought not to be changes in what the BBC offered to the public. Should it not confine itself to the kinds of programme which only a public service would provide, leaving other programme areas for other people – presumably Independent Television and commercial radio? He said that it was virtually impossible for the government to agree to an additional pound on the licence fee.

All who spoke after Chataway, governors and senior executives alike, disagreed with him. On his doctrine, the BBC would hand over types of programme at which it excelled – light enter-

tainment and sport included – to Independent Television ! Staff
and governors, once they recovered from their astonishment,
did very well in demonstrating to Chataway their horror. In
winding up, I said that we were appalled to hear what he had
said though we were grateful for his candour. I thought that
Chataway was taken aback by our reaction.

When the minister had departed, I asked the governors to
remain, saying that we had been given warning signs of a fundamental battle. What Chataway had said was so similar to what
Ted Heath had said the previous year that we must assume that
a new government philosophy on broadcasting was developing.
My own reaction was that we must prepare to defend ourselves
on this basic issue and to use publicity for the purpose. Once
informed, the public would reject this pernicious doctrine. To
allow it to succeed would destroy the BBC as a comprehensive
broadcasting organization. A week later, my diary reported the
beginning of our counter-offensive :

12 November
Publicity wise, this has been a good week. Huw Wheldon
replied effectively to Michael Peacock in the *Sunday Times.*
This morning there appeared in *The Times* a piece by
Charles Curran dealing with BBC finance and with the Chataway argument that the BBC should confine its broadcasting
to those things commercial companies would not do. These
articles represent a good start to what I believe should be a
more positive phase in expounding the qualities of the BBC
instead of merely defending itself against attacks.

A fortnight later, a governor told me, on what seemed to be
good authority, that Chataway was thinking of abolishing our
local radio, throwing it all into the lap of commercial radio, no
doubt as a way of reducing our expenditure and reducing our
case for a higher licence fee. Maybe it had also been urged upon
him that commercial radio, as it was emerging, looked as if it
would not be so profitable as its advocates had hitherto assumed.
This would have meant a reversal of the decision of the previous August when Chataway had approved twelve additional
local stations, making twenty in all.

Our apprehensions were not relieved when the following

Sunday we read in the *Sunday Times* that the Minister was thinking of reversing his decision to allow BBC local radio to continue, a line which was further developed in the next day's *Guardian*. The time had come, I put to the governors, for a deputation of governors to go to the Minister to find out what really was afoot.

Diary 17 December
Our main preoccupation this week has been with the possible intentions of the Minister, Christopher Chataway. A story appeared in the *Guardian* suggesting that Chataway is still thinking of abolishing local radio. We doubt whether this is true, preferring to think that his covetous eyes are on Radio 1. He could embarrass us by withdrawing the frequency used by Radio 1, 247. Presumably the idea behind this is that commercial radio, by concentrating, as it is almost certain to do, on pop music, would make more money without the competition of a BBC pop music channel. In other words, make commercial radio more viable, which means more profitable, by destroying the competition of the BBC.

We discussed tactics at the governors' meeting this morning. We resolved to oppose the destruction or diminution of local radio and the assault, by way of the withdrawal of a wavelength, on Radio 1. We decided to ask the Minister to receive a deputation forthwith (he has agreed to do so on Monday next).

It seems to me that the governors must be seen to be actively opposed to these changes and to express their opposition to them before the Minister has made up his mind. I have a niggling fear that unless we do this our next contact with the Minister will be the occasion for him to explain what he has decided to do.

So just before Christmas a deputation from the governors, consisting of Sir Robert Bellinger, Dame Mary Green, Lord Constantine and myself, accompanied by Charles Curran, Ian Trethowan, Jimmy Redmond, the director of engineering, and Colin Shaw, the secretary, called on the Minister.

I said in opening that speculation in the press about the future of radio and some of the Minister's answers in Parliament were arousing apprehension in the minds of the BBC staff, as in our own. I stated that given a licence fee of £7 from 1 July next (this is the date the Minister had mentioned) we could maintain existing services probably until 1975, including twenty or so local stations, so that financial considerations were no reason either for destroying BBC local radio or for doing anything else. The BBC had taken no part in the arguments for or against the introduction of commercial local radio, regarding this as a matter for government and Parliament. Local radio was a logical extension of the BBC's services, not something additional to be removed without consequences. The move into local radio was an integral part of the development of non-metropolitan broadcasting.

I then outlined three separate schemes under which it would be possible to provide matching numbers of BBC and commercial local radio stations. I went on to say that we had heard that he had his eyes on the frequency of Radio 1, 247, a medium high-powered frequency, on which to provide a national commercial network. Radio 1 provided 45 per cent of the BBC's total listening audience and was a card of entry for many young people to the BBC's other services. I elaborated on the consequences of taking this frequency away, saying that I hoped that he had not got it in mind to destroy local radio and/or Radio 1 in order to make commercial radio more profitable.

As my guess was that the commercial people were finding the prospect not as lush as they had thought and that their real purpose was to get a monopoly in local radio and a monopoly of pop by the destruction of Radio 1, I put the straight question to him as to whether he wanted a medium high-powered frequency in order to create a national network for commercial radio or in order to put us out of pop. He replied that he was not seeking to deprive us of Radio 1 – he just wanted to know whether there was a frequency. He then went on to give a comprehensive survey of the many problems confronting him, his current thinking on them and the licence fee possibilities.

Chataway was in first-class form. He had studied the whole matter, including the complicated subject of frequencies, very thoroughly. In the end I promised, as much in our interests as his, to supply an aide-mémoire setting out our arguments pretty thoroughly. Although he described this as a private meeting it was clear from the *Financial Times* the next morning that he or someone on his behalf had given his views on a number of problems we had discussed to the press, either after or before he met us. My diary gives my reactions to this meeting.

23 December

Inevitably our local radio staffs are getting agitated. They are sending telegrams to me and talking to the *Guardian* about militant action. We have to keep in mind that our main objective is to preserve existing services not only for their own sake but because Chataway is clearly reflecting Ted Heath's notion that the BBC should concentrate on those things that a commercial service cannot do as well – in other words concentrate on the dull and serious and leave the lively and the entertaining to commercial radio. This doctrinne we must resist. Our job as a public service is to cover the whole field. The assumption that a commercial service will, for example, do light entertainment better than a public service is refuted by our experience in television. So far so good. I suspect that January will be a lively month while the government makes up its mind what to include in the White Paper. And now to hell with it for the next ten days.

In the aide-mémoire we subsequently submitted to the Minister, it was argued that the case for an increase in the licence fee in 1971 had been made out. We had been promised by the previous government that the combined licence fee would go to £6 10s on the following 1 April. The minimum we needed was £7 early in 1971. On such a fee the BBC could afford to continue the twenty local radio stations, though there would have to be some slowing down of the capital investment programme.

Whether there should be a competitive system of radio was a matter for the government, not the BBC. What the BBC was opposed to was the destruction of BBC local radio : in any case, such destruction was not necessary in order to provide air space for commercial radio. There was no need to eliminate the BBC local stations in order to make frequencies available for a sufficient number of commercial stations. There could be made room in the ether for both services, in both medium wave and VHF.

On the suggestion that the frequency (247) used by Radio 1 should be withdrawn so as to facilitate a national commercial network, it was plainly stated that the BBC could not contemplate shedding its pop music output. If 247 were lost, other ways of broadcasting pop music would be found even if that meant reducing the number of channels from four to three, with pop music occupying by day the frequencies used by Radio 3, confining the broadcasting of serious music to the evening. However it was done, it would mean the squeezing out of some minority interests and a reduction in the employment of musicians. In any case, the use of 247 was not essential to the creation of a national commercial network and an intensive study would be begun for another high-power medium wave.

Once the aide-mémoire had been despatched to the Minister, the search for another high-power medium wave began. The one we first had in mind was a wavelength that had been on offer to the Foreign Office for the external services for some time, without their showing any particular haste to claim it. But now that we wanted it, we discovered that there was a new sense of urgency in the department about accepting the long-standing offer! So that alternative was virtually lost to us.

When Jimmy Redmond told me of this on a Thursday, I asked him to find another wavelength by the following Monday, for I feared that if we did not produce an alternative high-power medium wave, we should lose 247 and Radio 1. He said this was impossible. I replied by saying that in that case I should like it by Tuesday. The computers began to hum and by Tuesday an appropriate wavelength was found which could be offered, though not without some loss of coverage to our domestic services, especially Radio 3. We put in the offer and awaited the outcome.

Then I invited Chataway to lunch to go over the whole position. We dealt first with finance and I thought I convinced him that with a further ten shillings increase in the following April, over and above the ten shillings already promised, the BBC could, at least for a while, maintain its existing services, including twenty local stations. On the other points a note to my colleagues records what I then judged to be the state of play.

At the moment, the Minister's main purpose is to make commercial radio financially viable even at our expense. With this purpose in mind, the Minister still favours taking over the Radio 1 frequency, despite the arguments we have adduced against it. This is not because of the saving but in order to provide a national basis for commercial radio. There is a reasonable chance of staying in local radio but the prospect of preserving Radio 1 is more doubtful.

*   *   *

So, at the end of 1970 the BBC seemed seriously threatened.

At the beginning of the year, strangely, references had been made in a book by Harman Grisewood to an earlier threat to the BBC – but this time references that appeared totally unfounded :

Diary 19 February
A very interesting lunch with Freddy Bishop (formerly Eden's principal private secretary, deputy secretary of the Cabinet and a permanent secretary of a department) and Harman Grisewood. Freddy asked for the source or sources of the references in Grisewood's book to Anthony Eden's threatened take-over of the BBC and his request to David Kilmuir to prepare a plan for it, at the time of Suez. It soon became clear that Harman's one source for this allegation was something said to him by William Clark, now in Washington. He did not check because he could not, Clark being unwilling to search his papers, lodged in a bank, for confirmation. Grisewood was rather shaken to realize that there seemed to be no evidence for his assertion other than what Clark had said to him. There was nothing in Eden's papers, or Kilmuir's papers, in his recollection, in my recollection (I was Postmaster General at the time) or in the recollection of others to support the statement. Nor is there anything in the BBC's records, as I was assured on enquiring. In fact there was no plan or document relating to a take-over of the BBC. True there was irritation in the minds of Eden and some of his colleagues at the broadcasts of the external services during

Suez, but the only outcome of this was the allocation of a Foreign Office observer to the external services headquarters at Bush House.

*   *   *

When 1971 began, my continuing preoccupation was with the licence fee and the preservation of local radio and Radio 1.

We had demonstrated that, even with the twenty local radio stations, we could live on £7 from July next without unbearable deficit and that there was room in the ether for competing pairs of local radio stations on medium wave and VHF (and more commercial stations if international agreements were invoked). We were about to demonstrate, too, that a high-power medium wave could be made available for national commercial radio, so rendering unnecessary the withdrawal from the BBC of 247.

But now, to complicate matters, the Post Office decided to charge us more for collecting the licence fee and other jobs. This would add £8 million to our deficit by 1975. An unhappy coincidence or a crafty ploy to demonstrate that we really could not afford the twenty local stations?

Diary 5 January
Robens' resignation is reported this morning following, it is stated in the press, a row with the government on hiving off. Maybe, before very long the press will be talking about the sacking or resignation of Hill because of his opposition to the hiving off to local radio and Radio 1. We shall see. In any case, I am not going to be put off by threats of that kind.

During January we awaited ministerial decisions. As I was going to Australia to bid goodbye to Laporte staff (I had retired from the Laporte chairmanship the previous October), I called on Chataway to enquire when the decisions would be announced. If the White Paper were published in February, I would cut my Australian visit short. I had formed the impression that he would recommend that the 247 wavelength be withdrawn from us. So, at the governors' request, I wrote to Chataway asking that 'the BBC should be given the opportunity to make its observations on any particular proposal which affects it before firm decisions are reached as to what should be said in the White Paper'.

Chataway said that his secretary would warn my secretary if it should be decided to publish the White Paper during my absence. In fact all went well. I had no need to return from Australia before the arranged date of 3 March.

While I was away the government announced that, in place of the ten shillings increase promised by the previous government from 1 April, there would be an increase in the licence fee of £1 from 1 July. And in mid-March there came the White Paper on commercial radio. The two proposals we most feared had been dropped. There were to be sixty commercial radio stations and twenty BBC stations. Medium wave would be available to both, priority being given to commercial radio. The controlling body for the commercial stations was to be the ITA renamed IBA. Chataway, with his usual courtesy, told the director-general and myself about the contents of the White Paper some hours before publication.

Diary 27 March
D-G was inclined to be grateful. I am afraid that I plunged in to criticize the suggestion that, in the allocation of medium waves, there should be a priority for commercial radio. Could it happen, I asked, that in an area where we and commercial radio operated, the enemy would have medium wave and we would not? Yes, it could, replied the Minister.

It was months before the Minister was persuaded that commercial radio should not have priority in the allocation of medium wave. Indeed, he eventually agreed that the BBC could use medium wave for local radio before commercial radio began.

21

Clashes with Management

March 1971 was a month of gentle breezes. For example, there had appeared in *The Times* a leader in which the BBC was criticized for its reluctance to make available copies of broadcast scripts. It quoted an example. The secretary of an examination board had been refused a transcript of a television programme in which it was very interested, called *Test for Life*. *The Times* thought an important principle was involved.

For some time I had been uneasy about the BBC's resistance to applications for scripts and I had mentioned the point to Curran and others. I told the governors that I had been troubled by the rigidity of the current policy, even though discretion was regularly exercised, for example, in the supply of scripts to Members of Parliament. I thought that, although there were practical difficulties, the principle should be that where requested by a participant in a programme or someone responsibly involved in the issues raised by a programme we should make a copy of the script available, if there was such a copy, with or without charge. The director-general drew a distinction between the individual who had actually taken part in a programme and an individual who might want a transcript for the purpose of attacking the BBC. The director of public affairs, Kenneth Lamb, opposed the idea that the BBC should supply transcripts to a person or persons not directly involved in the programme.

A lively discussion followed in which Curran nearly lost his temper, telling the vice-chairman, Lady Plowden, that something she said was 'prejudiced', whatever that might mean. By a majority of five to three (the minority including Greene and Glanmor Williams), the board approved my proposal that, in principle, where an appropriate script existed, it should be made available to participants and those responsibly involved in a programme or its contents, and asked for a paper setting out the practical problems.

After the meeting I told Curran that I regretted his near loss of temper and his remark to Lady Plowden and that he must learn to accept the decisions of governors on matters within their scope. This was something which every chief officer had to accept. Provided that he had been given the fullest opportunity to express his own views and to give his advice, he must accept the ultimate decision of his masters, whether he liked it or not. This was something I had had to do when I was a chief officer and something with which every good chief officer has to live.

Curran told me later that within management there was a feeling of frustration and resentment at the governors' decision and this would find expression at the Board of Management. I told the director-general that when a policy decision had been reached by the governing body, management had to accept it, and that any attempt by the Board of Management, meeting that day, to frustrate the governors' wishes would raise serious issues. The minute of the Board of Management which discussed the transcript issue was cryptic :

> MD Tel briefly reviewed discussions of transcript policy by the Board and by Board of Management. At the moment little could be said (and that only privately). Management was now considering the practical, legal and economic implications of a desire to be somewhat more liberal in providing transcripts on request.

At the next meeting of the board, a fortnight later, practical details of the revised policy were approved, including a provision that at its discretion the BBC should make a charge where the script was supplied for the personal interest of the enquirer rather than that of the BBC. Despite the fears of management the revised policy worked well.

At this same meeting, two other mild but warming breezes

blew. Governors had complained of the placing at 11 pm on Sunday night of a programme to which they attached great importance, *Talk Back*, the nearest the Corporation had so far got to a correspondence column on the air. It was too late, they had said. Curran told us at this meeting that it was impossible to change the time, giving us technical reasons. I said, somewhat testily I fear, that the professionals ought to be able to rearrange things so as to place the programme at a better time than 11 pm on Sunday. As I wrote in my diary, 'No use amateurs like us getting drawn into all the technical problems of planning. Clearly this was a wrong time and it was for management to put it right.'

The second breeze was yet another illustration of managerial unease when the governors came within sight of making a decision, however minor. The governors had on their agenda a guide-line document on the criteria to be observed in the handling of news and current affairs, prepared by management for the General Advisory Council. It was an excellent document, clear, cogent and beautifully written, and the board liked it and said so.

One governor asked whether the presence of cameras was not liable to incite demonstrators to demonstrate and, if so, should not this point be mentioned? To what extent does the prospect of the cameras appearing provoke the organization of demonstrations which would not otherwise take place? What was the BBC's position on the artificially created scene and ought this kind of problem to be dealt with in the document? It was generally thought that it ought.

I asked who was the BBC for the purpose of the document? It was properly emphasized in it that the BBC must not editorialize and that it must be impartial. So who was the BBC in this context? Who were the people who, reading this admirable document, should realize that they were the BBC in the context of their programmes? Was Jack de Manio the BBC when he talked after the morning news? Was Bernard Braden the BBC when he uttered in *Braden's Week*?

To my surprise these questions raised a good deal of bureaucratic dust. The director-general did not think the questions could be answered. Eventually I got impatient, perhaps unnecessarily so, and said if no one else would draft some paragraphs, I would. What for example was the point of defining criteria unless one defined the people to whom they applied? The board agreed that drafts should be prepared on all the points raised. In due course the amended document went to the General Advisory Council where it was much appreciated. The theme of most of the comments there was that the principles of the documents were fine, but were they being applied?

Diary 24 April
It will be interesting to see if a document prepared within the BBC and with internal circulation proposed by management will have a better fate than 'Broadcasting and the Public Mood' which was stifled by management because it was essentially a governors' document. I suspect it will.

Looking back, I suppose the background to these modest breezes was that the governors as a whole were becoming clearer as to their role and firmer in their decisions than they were in my first two or three years. In the previous year the governors had had their way over another matter. This time it was a minor personal point involving a general issue. In a Saturday night quiz programme there had been rude references to Marion, my wife, to Paul Fox and to me. Paul Fox and I have to put up with this sort of thing. But why a reference to my wife? It was in the following terms : 'Now this is the last of these quizzes, and I've been asked to deny rumours that the other three weeks have been cancelled because Lady Hill stayed up too late one Saturday and William Rushton over-excited her.'

I said to the governors that the remark was unimportant and I was confining my remarks to a point of principle. It was a recorded programme and so could have been edited. I asked them to assume for a moment that a rude reference to the chairman's wife should have no place in this programme. But it had happened. Had we any power to prevent things that were undesirable?

The director-general was clearly embarrassed. He said if instructions were given by him that this or that sort of thing must not take place it would almost certainly find its way to the press. I remarked that our fear of internal communication going to the press should not prevent us from doing the right thing.

> What did it matter [I wrote in my diary] if the press learned of an instruction that there were to be no rude references to the chairman's wife?
>
> I did not force a conclusion, for this is but a small illustration of a greater problem. Small wonder that the politicians have begun to say that the top of the BBC has no control whatever over the programme-making level.

Some governors had been clear and firm from the beginning, like Tom Jackson. Others had gained strength as their experience of the BBC grew. Lady Plowden had arrived as vice-chairman some four months before. As charming as she was able, once her view was formed she expressed it with candour and courage, often in the process causing flutterings in the Corporation dovecotes. Her appointment and those of Roy Fuller, Bobby Allen and George Howard in the months to come, different though their outlooks were, gave the board a new strength which will become increasingly evident in this record.

Robert Bellinger told the board of his impending retirement at the end of May and I thanked him warmly for all he had done. To money matters he brought a wealth of knowledge and experience which no one else could contribute. Unpopular at the start because of his direct methods, he came to gain the respect of everybody, staff and governors alike. 'I am very sorry he is going,' I wrote in my diary.

A crucial change for the better had also occurred in the General Advisory Council. Lord Aldington, Toby Low of old, had recently become its chairman. The governors invited him to lunch soon after his appointment:

Diary 30 March
Toby Low raised an important question. Why was the BBC so unloved, particularly in important circles? It had its victories, such as 'Broadcasting in the Seventies'; the increase in the licence fee; and it looked as if it would win another in the impending White Paper. Yet to many people it was unloved and unlovable.

Naturally and properly, in the discussion that followed, it was argued that at least in political circles the BBC would be in danger if it were not to some extent unloved. To be loved by the government of the day would probably mean that it was leaning in its direction. Nevertheless I felt, as did some others, that there was something in this point. We do from time to time unnecessarily annoy or affront people who would otherwise be our friends. There are many serious and fair-minded people who believe that we deliberately and persistently knock at authority and institutions. Party bias is probably unusual and accidental. But the destructive tendency, even if it is only a curl of a lip or an occasional phrase, permeates some of what we do in current affairs. I suspect, too, that sometimes sex and bad language are indulged in for the sheer professional joy of pressing the boundaries of permissiveness.

Interestingly, I discovered that others in the BBC agreed with me in this.

Diary 27 May
Last night I paid my regular six-monthly visit to Uplands [where BBC staff courses are held]. I followed the usual technique of a short preliminary statement followed by questions. The general impression I got was of a lively group whose morale was high. One man asked me whether I recalled my visit to Manchester soon after appointment. On that occasion, he said, I had told them that the BBC was arrogant to the public. Had I changed my mind? I said it was a little less arrogant. Nowadays it even apologized sometimes.

I found on this and on other visits that when I said that we sometimes offended the older section of the community unnecessarily and at times appeared even to set out deliberately to do it, the conference agreed. Perhaps this is due to the small number of producers and directors who attend these conferences. They consist mostly of administrators, engineers, doctors, accountants; indeed they are drawn from all parts of the BBC.

22

Yesterday's Men *Episode*

The saga of *Yesterday's Men* began on 10 June 1971 when the *Evening Standard* printed a story about a recently recorded interview of Harold Wilson by David Dimbleby. On being asked how much he had earned from his recently published memoirs, Mr Wilson asked, said Londoners' Diary, that the interview be stopped and then angrily demanded 'to be put through immediately to Charles Curran, to whom he had made it quite clear that he did not wish this part of the interview to be broadcast under any circumstances'. The story, with or without embellishment, was taken up by the whole press next morning.

Basically, the story was true. The previous November, David Dimbleby had written to Harold Wilson inviting him to take part in a programme 'about the political and personal nature of the job of Opposition' and Mr Wilson had agreed to see him. In April, after the shooting of the film had begun, Dimbleby had written again to say that the film 'will be about the defeat and its impact in political and personal terms and about the problems Opposition poses'. Later Miss Angela Pope, the producer, and David Dimbleby, the interviewer, saw Mr Wilson and told him that they had in mind a responsible and serious programme in which they would wish to interpolate some personal details insofar as these were relevant.

Early in May Harold Wilson was interviewed. According to a taped record, the following exchange took place :

DIMBLEBY : Many of your colleagues have told us that they

are suffering financially from being in opposition, but you are said to have earned something between £100,000 and £250,000 from writing this book. Has that been a consolation to you over this time?

WILSON : I would not believe any of the stories you read in the press about that. My press handling for a long period of time has been one of rumour. If they got the facts, they twisted them. Anything personal – if they did not get the facts, they invented them. So you can dismiss that from the case right away. I think I got a fair compensation for what I wrote, but I would not accept any of those views. I get a salary as Leader of the Opposition.

D : You could not set our minds at rest on the vexed question of what the *Sunday Times* actually did pay you for it?

W : No. I do not think it is a matter of interest to the BBC or anybody else. If you are interested in these things, you had better find out how people buy yachts. Did you ask that question? Did you ask him how he was able to pay for a yacht? Have you asked him that question?

D : I have not interviewed him.

W : Well, has the BBC ever asked that question?

D : I do not know.

W : What has it got to do with you then?

D : I imagine—

W : Why do you ask this question – if people can afford to buy £25,000 yachts? Did the BBC not regard that as a matter for public interest? Why do you come snooping with these questions?

D : It is only that it has been a matter of speculation—

W : All I am saying—

D : . . . and I am giving you an opportunity, if you want it, to say something about it.

W : It was not a matter of speculation. You are just repeating press gossip. You have not put this question to Mr Heath. When you have got an answer from him, come and put that question to me. This last question and answer are not to be recorded.

D : By any standards—

W : Is this question being recorded?

D : Well, it is, because we are running the film.

W : Well, will you cut it out or not?

(WOMAN'S VOICE – Angela Pope)

W : All right, we will stop now.

(WOMAN'S VOICE – Angela Pope)

W : No, I am sorry. I am really not having this.

ANGELA POPE (speaking over): . . . Yes, of course we will.

W : I am really not having this. The press may take this view. They would not put this question to Heath. If they put it to me . . . If the BBC put this question to me without putting it to Heath the interview is off and the whole programme is off. It is a ridiculous question to put.

ANGELA POPE : Obviously, we will have . . . [two words unheard] . . . cut out the question and answer.

W : Yes, and I mean it cut off. I do not want to read in Miscellany or the Times Diary that I asked for it to be cut out.

ANGELA POPE : Can we go on, then?

D : Are we still running? May I ask you this then – Let me put this question and if you find this question offensive then—

W : To ask, if your curiosity can be satisfied. I think it is disgraceful. I have never heard such a question.

JOE HAINES (Mr Wilson's press officer): Let us stop it now and talk about it.

D : No, I think let's keep going, don't you?

ANGELA POPE : Let us go on to the other section.

W : I think we will have a new piece of film in and start all over again. If this film is used or if this is leaked, then there is going to be a hell of a row.

D : Well, I certainly would not leak it. I am not in the practice of—

W : You may not leak it but these things do leak out. I have never been to Lime Grove without it leaking.

JOE HAINES : I think you should stop.

These exchanges fall roughly into two parts, the first two questions asked by Dimbleby and the answers given to them, and the explosive exchanges which followed (subsequently regarded as the third question and answer).

The next day there was a conversation on the telephone between Joe Haines and the BBC's then editor of news and current affairs, John Crawley, on the extent of the deletion promised to Mr Wilson by David Dimbleby and Angela Pope. Joe Haines understood the agreement to be that all three questions and answers would be omitted. John Crawley, on the other hand, had no doubt that the assurance related only to the third question. The story is taken up by my diary entry for 17 June, the day of the governors' meeting and of the showing in the evening of *Yesterday's Men*.

17 June

It has been a busy twenty-four hours. When the incident in the programme *Yesterday's Men* concerning Harold Wilson's income from his memoirs was reported to me by D-G two or three weeks ago, he told me that the questions on this subject were to come out, Wilson having been so assured. Today he said that the assurance given to Wilson – in fact it was given by John Crawley to Wilson's press adviser, Joe Haines – was that it was only the third question that should come out, and that the television people proposed to include the first two questions and the answers.

I reminded him of his talk with me and the different impression he had then given. He said he would ring up John Crawley, who is in Helsinki, to get from him his version. In fact, he got Kenneth Lamb to ring up Crawley who was on a boat between Helsinki and Leningrad. John Crawley replied that the assurance he had given did not exclude putting in the first two questions. Yesterday I said to D-G that in view of the confusion about the extent of the assurance given, and bearing in mind the impression he gave me in the talk referred to above of what the assurance was, we should interpret this generously so as to avoid at all costs an allegation of a broken word. He agreed and said he would have the first two questions cut out.

Yesterday evening, following talk with Huw Wheldon and Desmond Taylor, D-G changed his mind. He told me his instinct was still to leave out the two questions but, nevertheless, he proposed that they should be kept in. Last evening there were further talks between D-G, Huw Wheldon and Wilson's advisers, including Lord Goodman.

Now the objections were threefold. Firstly, that the photograph of Wilson's houses should be excluded on the grounds of security of Wilson and his family. Secondly, that the title *Yesterday's Men* was misleading and should come out. Thirdly that the questions on pay for the memoirs should come out.

Goodman talked of the possibility of an injunction to prevent the programme going on. Roy Jenkins came through on the telephone to say he withdrew his consent for the inclusion of his piece, although if the Wilson questions came out he would withdraw his objection. This morning Jim Callaghan came through in similar vein. That is where matters stood in the early hours.

I was staying at the flat at the BBC following a dinner and Mrs Marcia Williams tried to get me so that Wilson, accompanied by his solicitors, could speak with me. The telephone girl had already informed Mrs Williams that I was on the telephone to Charles Curran and would ring her when I had finished. I had to indulge in the subterfuge of getting her to tell Mrs Williams that I had gone home, whereupon Mrs Williams said he would ring me at home in about an hour's time, which would have been about 1 am. I rang my wife straightaway and told her not to answer the telephone during the night. My purpose in all this was to avoid being put in the position of having pressure applied to me.

As I saw it, the main issue was, what was the character of the undertaking we had given? At all costs we must keep our undertaking.

To come to this morning. Arrangements had been made to show the programme – in advance of this evening's programme – to the lobby and the television critics. Charles Curran and I agreed that the matter should come to the governors who, before discussing it, would see the film. This we did this morning.

At the governors' meeting we concentrated on the central issue, that of the pledge. D-G gave the history of events and I added an account of his conversation with me weeks before, not to embarrass him but to indicate that he had then been of the view that all three questions were, on the undertaking which had been given, to be omitted. D-G said that, although John Crawley was utterly reliable, he also thought that Joe Haines was honestly giving his version of the undertaking.

After a short discussion the governors, Greene dissenting, decided that in the circumstances of the confusion about the character of the undertaking, we were bound to honour it as Haines had interpreted it, as covering the three questions. As for the other demands for a change of name, omission of the still photographs of the three houses – these were rejected. I asked whether there was any governor who felt that, having seen the programme, the whole thing should be cancelled. The answer was 'no'.

There the matter rested. We now await the press reaction. The press people who saw the film this morning did not raise any question of moment. But I learn that the *Evening Standard* is on the trail and I suspect we may be attacked for having yielded to political pressure. In fact we have done nothing of the sort. A pledge was given (wisely or unwisely) and we have honoured it. Any pressure to do more we have resisted.

Then, on the evening of 17 June, the programme was at last shown to the public. I thought it fascinating television. The title *Yesterday's Man* was tough, but then these were the words used by the Labour Party to describe their political opponents at the general election. The opening song by the Scaffold, 'Humpty Dumpty', was biting stuff but bearable. The overall impression of the programme as a whole was, I thought, favourable to those who took part, especially Jim Callaghan. The names of Angela Pope and David Dimbleby were not given in the titles at their own request: I thought this childish but unimportant. The only point which worried me was Dimbleby's reference to Mr Wilson's 'privileged access' to government papers (which culminated, quite rightly, in an apology from the BBC to Mr Wilson as the following pages will show). Overall I felt relieved, but not for long.

Someone at the BBC, it seemed, had leaked the three offending questions and answers to the press – apparently an anonymous voice had read them out over the telephone to selected newspapers. This gave the controversy a new life. But the comments on the programme itself were mostly descriptive and, on the whole, favourable, particularly in the eyes of the political writers who gave substantial extracts from it. Harry Boyne of the *Daily Telegraph,* for example, said that to students of politics, the programme must have been one of the most interesting ever shown on British television. The *Sun* said that the BBC, by agreeing to omit the three questions, had caved in to Wilson.

The next day the mood changed as the protests of the opposition grew. Mr Wilson, it was reported, was consulting his lawyers. *The Times* attacked the BBC, saying that the programme was 'too shallow to be tolerated' and the *Daily Telegraph* wrote that the Scaffold's ditty 'was well beyond the fringe'. Bob Mellish, the Opposition Chief Whip, said there was 'a limit to how much a democracy can abuse, insult, sneer and jeer', adding darkly that if the BBC went on with this type of campaign 'we must counter it by whatever activities we have at our disposal within the party machine'. The *Guardian* said that the producer had produced 'a giggly, gossipy, documentary full of snide visuals and engagingly crass questions of the would-you-stab-Harold-in-the-back-or-front variety'.

To aggravate matters, on the evening following the transmission of *Yesterday's Men* there was an interview of Mr Heath which, by comparison, was gentle and bland. The two programmes were seen as a package, one purporting to balance the other. That they were not so intended did not help. More fat was in the fire.

A day or two later came much more serious criticisms. It was alleged that there had been misrepresentation of Tony Crosland's house, that the title of *Yesterday's Men* had been deliberately concealed from the participants and that there had been deliberate over-recording to achieve results wholly at variance with professed intentions. The BBC governors had been kept in the dark about the tape recording of assurances to Mr Wilson. The members of the Shadow Cabinet had been 'conned'.

Ian Waller in the *Sunday Telegraph* summarized the criticisms by saying that the row fell into four distinct parts. Did the BBC deceive Mr Wilson and his colleagues? Was a distorted picture presented of the way Labour ex-Cabinet ministers were living, by the way the filmed interviews were cut and presented on the screen? Was there a breach of faith by the BBC. Who was responsible for leaking the questions and comments by Mr Wilson which were not shown in the programme? One Shadow minister was reported as saying that 'we should never have agreed to take part had we known how it was to be presented'.

These allegations of deception were a much more important matter than the programme itself. There were charges for which the evidence could not be seen in a viewing of the programme : something much more was needed to discover their truth or falsity.

It seemed to me, after consultation with the vice-chairman, that such charges warranted a detailed enquiry and Charles Curran unhesitatingly agreed. I asked him to set one up and he instructed Maurice Tinniswood, the director of personnel, assisted by Desmond Taylor, the recently appointed editor of news and current affairs, to make 'an immediate enquiry into the facts'.

Later in the week the *New Statesman* published a leader, in which it was alleged that the BBC had released a programme which was grotesquely and indecently different from that in which former ministers had agreed to participate, which achieved its effect, first, through deliberate fraud and, secondly, by the even greater fraud by which fragments were snipped out of the interviews they gave and juxtaposed in order to give a false impression of what they meant and even of what they actually said. The writer condemned 'this licence to distort and misrepresent which the BBC concedes to its producers'. The governors were criticized for letting the programme go out. The *New Statesman* was glad that I had started a full enquiry, adding that they were under no illusions what the likely effects would be.

While these charges were being flung around in the press, Harold Wilson's lawyers had not been inactive. First came a request by Lord Goodman for me to meet him. I jibbed at this and anyway I had arranged to go to Medway Local Radio on that day. Curran lunched with him the next day and learned that Wilson was considering a libel action concentrating on David Dimbleby's reference to Mr Wilson's 'privileged access' to government papers. If we made the appropriate apology or retraction that would end the libel action, leaving only the general issues.

When the director-general told me this, I took the view that we could not sensibly deal with this in isolation. If Goodman would set down his suggested words of apology then they could come, together with the investigators' report, to the governors. Goodman accepted this suggestion. Then came a long memorandum from Goodman's firm addressed to the governors, in which the whole history of the programme was recited, and deception and misrepresentation were alleged in a wealth of detail.

On 7 July a special meeting of the board was held at which the report of the special investigator, Maurice Tinniswood, was considered, together with a first rough draft of a possible report by the governors which I had prepared. That the investigation had been both thorough and meticulous was evident from the Tinniswood report, as it was from the public statement based on it which the governors issued. Some governors thought the draft before them was too mild and wanted a severe condemnation of those who had made the programme. Eventually, however, the draft was approved with little change.

To my regret, one salty little paragraph was removed. One of the criticisms by a participant was that the fee offered by the BBC had been too high. I wanted to include a sentence to the effect that in fact only two participants had complained of the fee and both had said it was too low! The matter of the suggested apology on the 'privileged document' reference was referred to our legal advisers.

In its report the board concluded that the questions to Mr Wilson about the earnings from his memoirs were both permissible and proper for a BBC reporter to ask, adding that no one was bound to answer questions put to him in a television interview or, for that matter, to appear in a television programme. The board's decision to eliminate them had been solely on the grounds of some misunderstanding of the scope of the promise given by the BBC to Mr Wilson's representatives. The scope and range of the questioning of the participants had conformed to the description of the programme given to them and no major area of the questioning covered in the seven interviews had been omitted. On the subject of editing and cutting, the material selected for use in the transmitted programme had been fair and there had been no improper intercutting.

On the other hand, the title *Yesterday's Men* ought to have been conveyed to the participants who should not have been left to learn of it for the first time in the *Radio Times*. The theme music and the illustrations, the report went on, did so colour the presentation that the participants should have known of them in advance, and the tone given by part of the programme was too frivolous in comparison with the main content of the programme, though the general charge of trivialization in current affairs programmes was rejected. As for the leaks, though all the evidence pointed to the BBC as the source – and the governors condemned them – there was no proof. Considered as a whole, the errors that occurred were cumulative rather than individual and the board regretted them.

With this in mind, the director-general would consider the general implications of the report and in particular 'will review the levels of responsibility and the means of internal consultation within the field of current affairs'. The report ended with a re-statement of the principles which the BBC sought to apply in its news and current affairs programmes.

The principles are simple : they are based on the fact that the BBC has no editorial opinion, and on the requirement that what is broadcast should be fair, just and true. The application of them amid conflicting claims is difficult, and it is subject to continuous review by a process of internal criticism. Errors are usually the result of failure to apply correctly principles the BBC has itself laid down.

The basic principle in current affairs programmes is impartiality – a self-imposed requirement from the BBC's earliest days. Much depends on interviewers, who are not required to be without personal views, but who should be able to put those views behind them. By thorough homework they must equip themselves to ask the questions that an intelligent and sceptical viewer or listener would wish to have asked, if necessary with persistence. Deference is not required, but courtesy is.

Participants in current affairs and documentary programmes should be told what sort of programmes they are invited to join and the general intentions behind it. When material has been recorded it should not be edited unfairly so as to give a different impression from that intended by the contributor. Nor should it be used in a programme of a different kind without obtaining prior consent.

Politics is a minefield. There is inevitably a divergence between the aims of politicians and the aims of journalists, whether of the press or of broadcasting.

The politician may want to expose his views of the truth, whereas the journalist wants to expose all the truth as he knows it. Nevertheless, each needs the other, and ground rules have been developed on which trust and understanding rest. This incident has impaired that relationship, and the BBC greatly regrets that this should be so. It will play its part in restoring understanding.

We shall, however, do nothing that could put at risk the independence of the BBC. Broadcast journalism has special obligations, but it cannot surrender to any individual or party or government – any more than can the press – its right of independent editorial judgment.

The report had a mixed reception in the press. Headlines included 'BBC defends Dimbleby', 'BBC rejects charges', 'New Labour fury', 'BBC refuses to apologise over controversial Yesterday's Men'. In the leader columns the *Guardian* rebuked both sides concluding that 'the BBC will have to be more careful next time'. The *Daily Telegraph* thought that the BBC had often forgotten of late their duty to put fairness and objectivity before sheer entertainment value. The *Daily Express* said the governors were right to take the public interest as their guiding principle. The *Daily Mirror* argued for 'an effective and accessible watchdog' like the Press Council. *The Times* thought the incident raised the problem of the procedure for enquiry into complaints, concluding that if the governors could not build up confidence in their ability to act as a court of complaints, then an exterior body on the lines of the Press Council would have to be created. The *Sunday Times,* on the other hand, thought that the mere existence of a broadcasting council would intensify the leaning towards a self-censorship and 'in determined hands could become an instrument of censorship proper'. The *Economist* thought the programme was best buried and forgotten.

The BBC can never win. To ignore criticism is arrogant and high-handed : an enquiry into charges made is an exercise in covering up. Superficial abuse does not worry me, but there are other kinds of criticism which the BBC ignores at its peril.

Some critics say that governors should never preview a programme. I disagree. Previewing can only be rare; discussion of programmes by the board is bound to be almost invariably after the event. This is as it should be. But to lay down an iron rule that governors should never preview, whatever criticisms are being currently made, is, I think, unwise. In law the governors are the BBC and they should not be hamstrung by a rigid rule of this kind. They should be the judges of when they wish to see a recorded programme in advance of transmitting. Incidentally during my five and a half years of chairmanship, two programmes were previewed by the governors – *Yesterday's Men* and a *Man Alive* on housing and the Rent Act. One programme, *The Question of Ulster,* was discussed by governors in advance of transmission. All three were transmitted. The result of such previewing, although rare, was both to inform and strengthen the position of the BBC in the controversy which might follow. Defence in retrospect is not as convincing as approval in advance.

Reflecting on the sequence of events, a nagging question kept recurring in my mind. Whose role was it to protect those who believe they have been unfairly treated by the BBC? Strictly speaking, the answer is the governors, for they represent the public. But, as in this case, it is often necessary and right for the governors to defend the staff of the BBC when they have

G

been unfairly attacked. The more we were seen in this defensive role, the more difficult it was to be seen to be, if not actually to be, the trustees for the public. It was this which led some people to advocate an external supervisory body.

At the governors' meeting on 14 July, Curran proposed a change in the headship of current affairs in television. He had had this in mind for some time in order to give John Grist a new area of activity after a long spell in current affairs. He also proposed to strengthen the control exercised by the editor of news and current affairs and to add to the team someone with recent knowledge and experience in the parliamentary field.

In September, Curran told the board of the new dispositions in news and current affairs, the fruits of the overhaul he had begun some months before. The editor of news and current affairs, Desmond Taylor, would have a closer and fuller responsibility for all current affairs programmes, spending more of his time at Lime Grove. John Grist, who had led the current affairs group in television, would succeed Pat Beech as controller English Regions. Brian Wenham, editor of *Panorama* (and a great success in the role), would become head of the current group. Curran thought the new appointments and the re-drawing of lines of responsibility would have a visible and significant effect on *24 Hours*.

Wilson's threat of legal action still rumbled on. In mid-July, I received a letter from Mr Wilson's solicitors demanding an abject apology, 'trailed' on the air and in the *Radio Times,* plus the payment of his costs and a contribution to a charity named by him.

Diary 23 July
In short we were asked to grovel. The nub of the matter is the phrase 'access to privileged documents'. According to Wilson this means the improper use of documents in his memoirs. For myself, I was a bit uneasy when I heard this phrase. Nevertheless, Counsel's advice is that we should have a good defence to any action. So we're not going to grovel. Incidentally, Wilson's solicitors demanded a reply within 72 days, obviously meaning hours.

Our lawyers replied to Wilson's lawyers offering a cautious statement by the BBC. It accepted that Mr Wilson had conformed with the usual practice, in relation to access, of former Prime Ministers and former Cabinet ministers. It had been represented to the BBC that certain words in the broadcast might suggest that he had made advantageous use of privileged or secret documents in an unjustifiable fashion. The BBC had no intention of conveying any such impression and 'would be sorry if the words had been so understood'. In early August the matter was settled.

Diary 5 August
At long last we have reached an agreement with Wilson's solicitors. He has accepted our phraseology, which can be described as a grudging apology. But we resisted his demand for a contribution to a charity of his naming and that for a trailing of the statement we propose to make. Today comes the news that he accepts the position. We propose to make the statement tomorrow, Friday, night, and to send it to the press so that it appears on Saturday morning. We are doing this to avoid a legal action.

I confess my own view of the words 'privileged access' is that they might imply abuse of privileged access, so I am rather glad to see us emerge from this with no more than a grudging apology.

Whether this means that Wilson will now come to our screens or not, I don't know. For the last few weeks he has appeared only on Independent Television, making it clear that he is not appearing on our screen until this matter is settled. His refusal to appear on our screen is something we have borne with fortitude.

Throughout this series of events, Harold Wilson was not at his best. He could, with his customary skill, have told Dimbleby to mind his own business. For once, he was caught napping, something which rarely happened. During my association with him, I came to admire his immense intellectual agility and political skill, and to be grateful for his courtesy and kindness.

Edward Heath as Prime Minister was a very different sort of man. He joined the governors for lunch in September.

Diary 26 September
Prime Minister was pleasant but uncommunicative. If Wilson, on his last visit, had 'buried the hatchet but marked the spot', with Mr Heath we just did not see the hatchet but had a feeling it was there. His letter of thanks dwelt mainly on the theme that the food and drink were excellent (which they weren't).

23

Complaints Commission

Early in 1971 I had raised in the board the possible value to broadcasting of an external scrutinizing board, a so-called council for broadcasting.

In a discussion on the subject in the series *Ad Lib,* participants had argued that some form of protection for individuals wronged by broadcasts was desirable. This prompted me to raise the matter. In a paper to the board I instanced six situations in which individuals might allege injustice. They were the juxtaposition of extracts from interviews; the editing-down of lengthy recordings; the reconstruction of incidents; inadequate reporting; an unfair line of questioning and misconduct by staff.

The director-general thought that such situations were rare and existing machinery was sufficient to deal with them. Others were not so sure. The secretary was asked to produce a paper for the next meeting. As always, Colin Shaw, the secretary, produced an excellent analysis of the problems covered by the six illustrations. Misconduct apart, all the other instances are examples of alleged abuse by the BBC of its editorial position. The first step was to discover the facts and test them against existing policy rulings. For example, early in the previous year the director-general had reaffirmed the rule that persons interviewed should always be told of the use to be made of their contribution to a programme : they should not be required to give lengthy interviews of which only a fragment is, unknown to them, intended for inclusion. A misuse of material obtained at interviews was a breach of known policy. On unfair questioning in news interviews, the policy line was necessarily less specific and could be summarized in a quotation from the policy guide-lines: 'The reporter is not a personality: he is seeking usually, simple, direct, and brief answers which will illuminate the subject which is the news.'

Some other questions remained. While, when damage had been done, the complainant was entitled to an apology with or without a right to reply, even a financial payment, what of the complainant's position when no breach of the Corporation's policy is revealed? Would he not feel that justice had been denied him? Would such a complainant benefit from the existence of an outside court of appeal? If such an outside body supported his complaint, it would have no power to punish the broadcaster. Would it be tempted in such circumstances to harden the terms of its verbal condemnation, with the danger that it was unjust to the broadcasters?

The paper raised some practical difficulties. A broadcasting council would have to be staffed to deal with complaints. It would require recording and play-back facilities. It would duplicate many of the Corporation's own functons. Yet there was an element of public criticism the BBC could not ignore, criticism which could be met by various forms of visible justice. A clearer public statement of the BBC's policy would go some way to remove popular feeling that the BBC permitted its staff to operate without adequate rules of conduct. More opportunities might be given for providing redress for grievances within the programmes which gave rise to them. Television, following radio's example, could develop programmes carrying listeners' correspondence, though such programmes were more difficult in a visual medium. When the board discussed this paper there was a refreshing tendency to recognize that we were confronted by a real problem.

The director-general, with his Board of Management, were asked to look into the whole question of redress and to come back to the board with their ideas. Eventually, in July, management proposed a new complaints procedure. There would be an Ombudsman to whom those aggrieved by something in a broadcast could appeal: the verdict would be published by the BBC.

The case for a new complaints procedure for broadcasting was closely argued in the director-general's paper. No organization should be judged in its own cause. Some sort of remedy should be available for grievances which, although real, generally fell outside the scope of the law. Justice needed to be seen to be done. Hitherto, whenever an external body had been proposed, the BBC had argued that the governors were 'the trustees of the public interest and that it would be unsatisfactory and confusing to have two sets of trustees'. But the public could not easily understand how the governors could be wholly impartial in matters affecting programmes for which they required to take ultimate responsibility. Further, the governors' response to grievances was usually made in private. *Yesterday's Men* had stimulated fresh demands for an appellate body. This might lead a government to establish a body which would erode the BBC's independence. The parallel with the Press Council was far from perfect. Broadcasting accepted an obligation towards balance and impartiality which most of the press did not.

The paper made some suggestions for discussion. Complaints, from individuals or organizations, should be heard by the appeal body only after the broadcasters had failed to provide an answer satisfactory to the complainant. In return for publication, complainants should waive their rights to legal action. Complaints should be laid only after transmission. Adjudications should have no mandatory force, leaving the authority of the BBC unimpaired. The ITA should be asked to consider whether it would participate. The paper asked the Board of Governors to consider whether the extent of public concern justified a new complaints procedure. Was a single individual or a panel of three the desirable composition of the body? Did the suggested plan safeguard the BBC's independence?

Greene who was absent wrote opposing it and Glanmor Williams expressed substantial doubts, but most governors liked the plan. We spent a good deal of time going over details. It was accepted as fundamental that the plan should not weaken the BBC's independence.

I liked the general principles. I was convinced that a broadcasting council, in the terms in which some were advocating it, was unworkable and undesirable. To some, it was a device for the control of broadcasting by politicians; to others it was a means of imposing their own attitudes and ideas. Some wanted workers' control – broadcasters' control – over the medium. Yet, the case against a broadcasting council should not blind us to weakness in our existing structure. If a complaints machinery would make a broadcasting council less likely, all the better.

The next stage was to perfect the details and devise a formal scheme. I arranged a talk with Curran, Trethowan, Attenborough, Crawley and Shaw.

Diary 3 August
I called together this morning the director-general; managing director, radio; director of programmes, television; the chief assistant to the director-general; and the secretary to discuss the scope of the proposed Ombudsman. After a good deal of argument we agreed that a general category of complaints, whether called unethical or not, was too vague and concluded that the scope of the Ombudsman should be limited to complaints about injustice or unfairness or misrepresentation. We discussed the appointment of the Ombudsman and who it should be. On balance we thought that if the ex-Ombudsman, Sir Edmund Compton, could be persuaded to do it that would help us with the public. The general view was that the appointment should be made from outside, say by the Lord Chief Justice. The director-general and I discussed it afterwards and thought another possibility was an Ombudsman committee of three, consisting of the ex-Ombudsman as chairman; Horace King, until lately the Speaker of the House of Commons; and a retired judge, appointed by the Lord Chief Justice. I think this has merit.

I put to the group the basic question as to whether we should do this thing. Would it be interpreted as another clever BBC device for resisting change? Would people believe that we really had departed from our old attitude? Would it really influence the present mood in the Labour Party? All agreed that it was a good thing to do.

Meanwhile the press continued to air their views about a Broadcasting Council.

Diary 5 August
There is a piece in *The Times* this morning by Julian Critchley which gives the game away. It emerges that his main concern is with the BBC's 'excessive moralizing and its addiction to the rhetoric of crisis'. He criticizes 'those producers who, at the time of the election, regarded the whole electoral process as no more than an insignificant farce'. In short, he reveals that it is the resentment of politicians at what he regards as a more powerful and less responsible medium that lies at the heart of his pressure for a broadcasting council.

And I started to make the necessary approaches to the people concerned.

Diary 16 August
At the office I saw, by invitation, Edmund Compton and Horace King, and put to them the proposed complaints procedure. They liked the procedure and both indicated, Compton after a two-day interval, that they would become members of the proposed troika, or three-man commission. The Lord Chief Justice's office was closed so I made no progress there. Indeed, I have had another thought. We could approach the ex-Lord Chief Justice, Lord Parker, directly. If he agreed we should then have a commission of the ex-Lord Chief Justice, the ex-Ombudsman and the ex-Speaker of the House of Commons – and no one could throw stones at such a trio on the grounds of lack of impartiality. I will try and contact Lord Parker.

Lord Parker agreed and the three commissioners-designate met with Curran, Shaw and me on a Sunday morning in mid-September to discuss their reactions to the draft terms of reference. Then the governors approved the final draft and we were ready for publication on Wednesday 29 September, the director-general to address a meeting of staff (his liaison committee so-called) the previous day. We informed the Ministry of Posts and Telecommunications of our intentions, sending them an advance copy of the announcement.

Then, to our surprise, ministerial rumbles began on the day before publication day. A senior civil servant spoke to Curran on the telephone in what the director-general called 'uncivilized tones'. There had been no time to minute the Prime Minister he said. It would be discourteous to proceed with plans for publication on the following day. Curran told me of this conversation on the telephone to Llandudno where I was addressing the Royal Institute of Public Health.

I replied that the decisions were ours and did not need government approval. The only question which mattered was the allegation of discourtesy and I had no objection, on this score, to a delay in publication until the following Tuesday, 5 October. Curran agreed and said he would inform the Ministry. By the end of the week there was no word of any kind from the Ministry – and there were signs of a leak in the press. The *Guardian* had published a story, though it was not entirely accurate. On the Saturday, the *Observer* rang me at home and it was evident that it had the full story, including the names of the commissioners, for publication the next morning. Curran and Campey (head of publicity) advised issuing the announcement on Sunday for Monday's papers and I agreed, asking that the Ministry should be told what we were doing and why. This was done. It became evident from the press next morning that the Ministry had issued some guidance to the press, which *The Times* summarized in the following paragraph:

Mr Chataway is thought to see the announcement as initiative by the BBC and not necessarily as something he would have supported or encouraged, preferring that more consideration had been given to the whole concept of a Broadcasting Council.

I reacted, perhaps over-reacted, in my diary.

4 October
This gave the government's game away. Despite the statement in Parliament there really was something on the move

in the direction of a broadcasting council. Possibly even for announcement at the Tory Conference. They regarded us as having killed or at least injured their fox.

Another inkling of this was given to me in a casual conversation with a civil servant. When I asked him how the government was concerned with this, he replied almost indignantly, 'of course it pre-empts the idea of a broadcasting council'. This, too, could only mean that the government was considering creating such a body, despite Chataway's parliamentary statement. Perhaps the idea of pressing us to delay was to give them the chance to get out their announcement first. I can think of no other explanation of the government's annoyance and the government's statement. Anyway the governors' decisions, for that is what they are, are now published and this morning's reaction has not been too bad.

The Times described the scheme as a modest concession to a growing demand for a broadcasting council, adding that it did not go far enough. The *Daily Telegraph* saw it as a reasonable plan, though it would not in any way satisfy those who had been pressing for a broadcasting council. The provincial press on the whole welcomed the move.

Greene, who by this time had resigned his governorship, said in a letter to *The Times,* that he was 'horrified' at the establishment of a commission. He saw it as a 'short-sighted attempt at appeasement' of the movement which wanted a broadcasting commission. It would make the staff more timid and less adventurous. It was 'the deplorable surrender by the present Board of Governors of responsibility and authority'.

On the day this letter was published I was to speak at a luncheon of medical journalists and I took the opportunity to reply. I quote from my speech.

Was there, we asked ourselves, something in the argument that the BBC is both the judge and defendant? Is justice always seen to be done?

The commission is not a broadcasting council : it is a move in the direction of being fair. But the setting-up of our commission is being used by the advocates of a broadcasting council to reactivate the arguments for controlling the broadcasters. Control. Censorship. Suppression. However the words are packaged in the clamour for a broadcasting council, those are the ones built into the argument.

The subject of taste is not covered by the commission; nor should it be. Taste is always a matter of one's own opinion. The responsibility for it in the BBC rests with the governors, aided by a General Advisory Council drawn from many sides of life. Would they be helped by the views on taste of an outside body, particularly if a proportion of that body were committed to one level of taste, one morality?

The BBC must, in the interest of the public and other media, be free to portray in a responsible way the world as it is. It makes mistakes; of course it does. That is the price of the intellectual and creative freedom it gives to its staff, on which the life and the excellence of broadcasting depends. It is fallacious and dangerous to pretend that the errors inherent in freedom can be prevented by an external regulatory or controlling body with no responsibility for the creative process.

I just do not believe, knowing the BBC staff, that they are such timid characters that they will be less adventurous and less liberal – I use Sir Hugh Greene's words in *The Times* this morning – simply because in certain circumstances someone else may comment in public on the BBC's defence of what it has done. After all, this is no new experience for them.

A few days later I called on Chataway.

Diary 8 October
First I asked what he had got to complain about. The decision to appoint the commission was our business though we would have welcomed comment. He made a number of minor criticisms. D-G had told the permanent secretary that we wanted to make a statement before the political conferences. But we had not communicated to him the exact date, though his officers knew it. Then he criticized us for not telling him of the early release.

I was able to reply that if he had a press office which kept open after 5.30 pm he would have known. In fact, George Campey had great difficulty in finding his press officer; his

number was not in the book and in the end he had to ring
No. 10 to find it. He phoned his home and his wife said he
was expected back soon and that he would ring back. It was,
in fact, two hours before he rang back. Chris smilingly
accepted this.

Then I came to my main purpose of the visit. When we
had last spoken in his room in July I had asked him whether
his recent answer in the House of Commons meant that he
was moving his ground on a broadcasting council. Suspicion
was widespread in the BBC that something was afoot. I
thought it possible that Ted Heath might be thinking of
including this item in his speech at the conference. I did not
feel able to tell him that we had some information that Ted
Heath had asked Bryan Forbes [the film-maker] to draft some
possible terms of reference for a broadcasting council.

Chris came quite clean. There would be no change in his
position; he was opposed to a broadcasting council. The conclusion I formed was that something had been going on at
the Prime Minister's level, at least to consider a broadcasting
council as a possibility. I know from experience that Prime
Ministers often dart here and there and ask for ideas and suggestions. It may have been no more than that.

All in all, reaction to our move seemed fairly favourable,
despite the opposition of Greene and of those who were advocating the setting up of councils for purposes other than our
own.

Diary 14 October
This has been a week largely concerned with the repercussions of the 'three wise men' story. There have been some
comments on Greene's letter, most of them unhelpful to him.
What has struck me has been the absence of any rebellion
on the staff.

It is difficult to do the right thing in this world. We have
seen over the past week advocates of a viewers' council
criticizing this scheme because they believe it pre-empts the
case for the viewers' council. There have been those who say
it does not go far enough, conveniently forgetting this project
was not launched in order to set up a viewers' council.

Today Mrs Whitehouse's book came out and the press has given a certain amount of publicity to her allegation that in a talk with James Dance, my predecessor Lord Normanbrook had said that there was a deep rift between him and Greene and that if the viewers' council reconstituted itself on a democratic basis he would reconsider his attitude to it. Mrs Whitehouse had inferred from this that a viewers' council was in the bag once her body became really representative. Normanbrook's letter may have invited some such an interpretation. She adds, quite accurately, that at the subsequent meeting with me – she was accompanied by two others – I disabused her mind of this idea. The matter now seems to be dead. The next phase will be an effort by Julian Critchley to get the Conservative Party 22 Committee to present, to quote Critchley, 'a pistol at Christopher Chataway'. We shall see.

However, the General Advisory Council did have cause to complain, with regard to the Complaints Commission. Their complaint was made at the October meeting, the best I had yet attended. The quality and interest of its discussions had steeply risen since Lord Aldington had succeeded to the chair. He had the knack of stimulating free and frank discussion while remaining in full charge of a meeting.

Diary 18 October
The main discussion was on the Complaints Commission. Underlying it was some resentment that the General Advisory Council had not been consulted, although the chairman and the Business Committee had been. I had some sympathy with this criticism. The plain fact is that the D-G and I forgot the Advisory Council. We ought to have suggested to the chairman of the GAC that he should call a special meeting of the council. Technically we had a good answer – that the board reached the decision to appoint a commission the day after the last meeting of the GAC and, therefore, that it would not have been appropriate to have mentioned it last time. What we had done in between meetings was to consult the chairman who consulted the Business Committee.

There was not widespread satisfaction with this reply. Just at the time when we were anxious to extol the virtues of the uses of the GAC, we ought to have advised the chairman to call a special meeting. Frankly, we did not think of it and there it is. As far as the Complaints Commission itself was concerned, one or two expressed their doubts. But, on the whole, our judgement was accepted.

24

Responsibility or Censorship?

At the governors' meeting on 21 October a new venture was launched. For some time, we had felt the need for fuller and franker discussions with the senior staff about some of the larger problems of broadcasting, without the formality which necessarily characterized meetings of the board, and in circumstances in which we could freely discuss them, not as governors and executives, but as men and women who, whether amateurs or professionals, were all involved in the business of broadcasting. The opportunity to make a start in what became known as colloquies arose at this meeting.

Diary 21 October
The most interesting discussion at the governors' meeting took place as planned on the question of taste and we decided to have a discussion with the senior people in television and radio about the whole subject. We are going to have it in an afternoon session following the next governors' meeting.

I accept the general argument that the role of the BBC is to mirror the world as it is and to risk offending people when this is necessary. But I do think that from time to time there are scenes, or words, or, indeed, actions which are not necessary to the programme and which cause unnecessary offence. We have to cater for all groups and all tastes. What we should not do is *unnecessarily* to give offence where this cannot be defended on the grounds of realism or fact.

We have dealt with violence through the new Advisory Group on the Social Effects of Television. We are dealing with complaints of unfairness and injustice through the commission. What remains is the area of taste and sex which is a main ground of those who advocate a viewers' council.

We will have this discussion in a fortnight's time – a colloquy as we are calling it – and see where it leads. I hope it will lead to a voluntary decision by the senior executives themselves to take discreet steps and so avoid a breach between the governors and our creative staff.

This may sound like timidity but I have learned from experience that ideas which our senior staff people have formed or believe that they themselves have formed are more likely to be effective than *obiter dicta* from above. Any thought that the governors are out to clean up television will produce an obduracy or a resistance which will negate its efforts. Anyway, we will try it.

About this time the board received its first report of the work of the Advisory Group on the Social Effects of Television which had been set up in April 1970, initially for a period of a year. The main work of the group, admirably chaired by Charles Longbottom and with a distinguished membership, had been in advising on revisions to the BBC's Code on the Use of Violence in Television Programmes, the outcome of which would be a new Code early in 1972. It had scrutinized the research being undertaken in this country and overseas and was about to consult researchers engaged in long-term work covering the development of children. It had met a number of senior staff working in drama, news and current affairs and children's programmes and was now considering problems associated with the portrayal of sex in programmes. Although its work was not spectacular, the group was clearly fulfilling a useful role by making a wide range of outside experience and knowledge available on a regular basis to those making editorial decisions in television. The board readily agreed to extend its life for at least another year.

It is not every day that one quarrels with a bishop. But everything has to happen a first time. In the autumn of 1971 I publicly disagreed with the Bishop of Southwark – indeed, so angry was I that I used some pretty strong language.

There had been criticism by him of a *Panorama* programme on the Church of England which led to some correspondence between him, Curran and Lamb. The details of it were complicated and I was not involved in them.

Then one Thursday evening I received at home a letter from him saying that he proposed to make his recent disagreement with the BBC the subject of his address to the Synod. As the director-general figured largely in the correspondence and time was short I rang Curran on the Friday morning and asked him to ring the bishop to thank him for his courtesy in writing to me of his intention and expressing the hope that he would give both sides of the dispute.

In his speech to the Synod the bishop's version of his exchanges with Broadcasting House and his attacks on one of our staff ('pompous, pathetic and insulting') and on those who made the programme to which he objected really aroused me. I publicly described his criticism as uncharitable, unfair and, in important respects, untrue. The words were strong but those which first came to my mind were even stronger.

The bishop wrote asking me to justify my words, which I did in reply. He wrote describing my letter of justification as misleading, frivolous and inadequate. I replied that as he saw fit to make such unwarranted and distasteful allegations I did not propose to continue the correspondence. Anger, I confess, is a poor guide in controversy.

In November the governors returned, in a two-hour debate, to the perennial problems of taste, language and sex in our programmes. A successful colloquy had taken place and we now discussed what had been said.

Diary 4 November
I began by inviting every governor to express his view. The majority of governors felt that from time to time there were scenes and words, not essential to the context, which were calculated to offend. Huw Wheldon, Ian Trethowan, David

Attenborough and Howard Newby replied. They were skil-
fully and sincerely defensive, though not altogether convincing to everyone.

I took the line that the BBC was risking its independence by
not taking sufficient care to exclude unnecessary and unjustifiable material calculated to offend. At the end of the discussion, not quite clear as to the next step, I suggested that we
resume the discussion in two months' time, subsequently asking that the executives should produce a considered reply to
what governors had said. It may be that at long last we have
begun, through this preliminary discussion, to secure greater
care *not unnecessarily to offend*. We shall see.

Yet another controversy about the BBC's handling of Northern
Ireland arose in November, too. The Board of Governors
had discussed some aspect of programmes about this unhappy
province at almost every meeting. It was perhaps inevitable, in
circumstances approaching civil war, that those who sought to
report what they found, however faithfully, should be under
fire. There had been frequent allegations of bias, or misrepresentation, even of encouraging the terrorists by interviewing
members of the IRA. Too little had been reported of the large
part of the province which was at peace. Criticisms had been
made by Northern Ireland ministers, Members of Parliament at
Westminster and the press both here and in Ulster. A member
of our reporting staff had gone to prison rather than identify
IRA men he had interviewed.

To reduce the danger of error, the director-general had instructed that no IRA member should be interviewed without
his express permission, subsequently delegating to the editor of
news and current affairs the power of approval. He had introduced a system of greater editorial supervision.

Although the amount of criticism had declined, the situation
was still delicate and the mood uncertain. Then, at a meeting of
Conservative backbenchers, the attack on the BBC was resumed. Some backbenchers pressed the Home Secretary,
Reginald Maudling, to impose some form of 'patriotic censorship' on BBC television and newspaper reporting of the
Northern Ireland troubles. According to newspaper reports, Mr

Maudling had responded by saying that he would speak to the chairmen of the BBC and the ITA.

The following week the governors met at Bristol, the day before I was to meet the Home Secretary at his request. It emerged in discussion that the detailed arrangements for the supervision of programmes which had been reported to the governors a few weeks before had been suspended by the director-general. The governors were not pleased.

Diary 23 November
On the way back in the train, I told D-G that nothing less than a restoration of the high-level responsibility for *Panorama* and *24 Hours* would suffice. He agreed. He said he would speak to the people concerned before he left for Japan the next morning. The day after I took this up in his absence with John Crawley and Desmond Taylor. In the television area, editor, news and current affairs, or, if we so decided, Brian Wenham, head of current affairs group, should be responsible for all Ulster items and similar arrangements should be made for radio.

Then I called on the Home Secretary. He was his usual cheery self. He told me what had been said at the Tory backbenchers' committee, in fact the Home Affairs Committee. We did not discuss censorship after Reggie had made it clear in a single sentence that he had no use for it. I suggested, as a sensible procedure, that I should reply to the points of criticism made at the meeting of backbenchers in a letter to him which would be published. In this way I could make the reply to the criticisms which I was anxious to make. He agreed and I subsequently wrote the letter, some sentences of which, to my surprise, were to lead to further criticism. Here are some of the salient paragraphs :

If the people of Northern Ireland were denied full news by their own country, they would be thrown back on Dublin and other sources – newspapers, radio and television. The BBC already undertakes a scrupulous editorial watch at all levels. We believe that if we went beyond that it would do nothing but harm and we would reject any such suggestion, from whatever quarter it might come. Its immediate effect would be to destroy the credibility of all our reporting.

It is evident that those who have gone on record as demanding censorship of the BBC would want to censor the whole press as well, since suppression would have to be total. In essence, those who are demanding censorship are, whether they realize it or not, demanding propaganda and the death of all truthful reporting. Censorship breeds rumour, because then nobody knows how to recognize the truth.

We see it as our over-riding responsibility to report the scene as it is, in all its tragedy, to all the people of the United Kingdom, including the communities of Northern Ireland. We do not side with the Catholics or the Protestants. The BBC and its staff abhor the terrorism of the IRA and report their campaign of murder with revulsion.

About a third of the citizens of Northern Ireland are Catholics. Many of these, while not approving the terrorist tactics of the IRA, are openly hostile to the presence of the British Army, and critical of the policies of Stormont. These are citizens of Northern Ireland and of the United Kingdom, and their opinions must be represented. Often what they say will be most unwelcome to the majority in Northern Ireland, to the troops, and to many in the rest of the United Kingdom. But it belongs to the reality of the situation.

In short, as between the government and the opposition, as between the two communities in Northern Ireland, the BBC has a duty to be impartial no less than in the rest of the United Kingdom. But, as between the British Army and the gunmen the BBC is not and cannot be impartial.

Soon after this letter was sent, a meeting of television and radio journalists passed a resolution : 'We deplore the intensifying censorship in the television, radio and press coverage of events in Ireland and we pledge ourselves to oppose it.'

A week or two later, at a cocktail party which the BBC gave to trade union leaders, Tom Rhys, of the Association of Broadcasting Staffs, and Percy Jarrett, of the National Union of Journalists, drew me on one side and criticized the BBC for lack of impartiality. We were, in fact, taking sides, they argued, by the editorial control which was being exercised over reporting from Ulster. They could not accept the last sentence of my letter that 'as between the British Army and the gunmen the BBC is not and cannot be impartial'. There was some element of logic in their contentions, I suppose, but it was the kind of logic I could not accept, as I told them with emphasis. But I had no doubt they were sincere when they told me that some of our reporting staff were criticizing not only the editorial control but what they saw as a lack of impartiality between the forces of law and order and their opponents.

A little later the same two men came in a deputation to put the same point to me and John Crawley. The question which nonplussed them was one put by John Crawley : 'Should we have a reporter attached and accredited to the IRA?' I heard little more of this criticism.

Diary 2 December
There has been a curious reaction within the Corporation to the letter to the Home Secretary. In it we said that we were agin the gunmen, impartiality does not apply to them – or words to that effect. We are not impartial as between gunmen and those they gun. I would have thought that this was a fairly self-evident proposition for anybody with a sense of responsibility. Not so for everyone, it seems. Some of our journalists are moaning, it seems, about this kind of impartiality. Rhys, of the ABS, last night told me that he thought we should have said that we regard the gunmen – not with revulsion, the word we used – but with compassion. The doctrine of impartiality should apply as between the murderers and the potentially murdered. I suspect this is a piece of journalistic punctilio. In part it seems to be the characteristic attitude of some towards instructions that come from their superiors. They should be allowed to decide what we broadcast. They should not be called upon to refer a particular category of material to their superiors for discussion, even if their superiors are journalists.

What they don't seem to see is that we are fighting a battle against censorship, control, regulation, intervention from outside. The claim of programme makers in news, current affairs or in any other field that they should decide what goes on the screen or emerges from the microphone without guidance or instruction from above, is just the sort of claim that brings external control nearer.

I had yet another reminder of the BBC's unpopularity with some Conservative Members of Parliament and of their firm belief that the BBC was biased in its reporting :

Diary 2 December
Last night I attended, at their invitation, the Tory Party Broadcasting Committee at the House. About 30 attended, some of them new faces. Criticism of the BBC came from all sides. More than a third of the time was devoted to treading the old ground of Ulster, despite the answer to the allegations contained in the letter to the Home Secretary. The BBC was slanted in favour of the rebellious; it knocked established standards, and so on and so on. None of the charges was new and most of them were without foundation yet the fact of the matter is that there is a general unease in the Tory Party, if this meeting was in any way representative.

Some of them had no idea of how the Corporation works, or the principles on which it is based. Although I replied with vigour I cannot pretend it was to much avail. One man even complained of bias in music. Sir William Glock favoured some kinds of music at the expense of others.

I told the governors this morning that, justified or unjustified, our reputation, at least with this group of parliamentarians, was lower than I have known it in my steady contact with this Committee over the last eight years or so. I asked D-G to take some steps to give these critics, or a number of them, an opportunity of seeing how the Corporation works. But this is but part of the solution.

It may be that the BBC is always crucified whenever there are big public controversial issues but that our name is mud, at least with these Members, was left in no doubt. I don't pretend to have influenced them and the only good that was done is that they let off steam.

In the end I told them that I could only think that these widespread criticisms stemmed from a feeling that Westminster was growing weak and the broadcasting medium was growing strong. I added that the broadcasting of Parliament would do something to rectify what they believed to be the situation. Some nodded approval of this, but it was the only kind of approval I got last night.

25

What Governors Do

Have the BBC governors any real power? I was often asked this by new governors.

Critics of the BBC were, as always, divided. Some said we were too weak, others considered us too strong. Some accused us of being impotent; others of dictatorially interfering with creative freedom.

It has been said that I was appointed by the government to curb the director-general and to control programmes. Well, was I? One man wrote to me, 'God's bloody teeth, man, do you not realize that you, and your fellows, are permitting complete licence by anarchists, traitors, and any dissident faction and kidding yourselves that these are intellectuals.'

There had been so many attacks on the BBC during 1971 that, at the last meeting of the year, I invited the board to discuss the whole question of its role, circulating in advance a paper on the subject designed to provoke discussion. In some respects, I wrote, the responsibilities were clear-cut and efficiently carried out, as in finance and appointment-making. Most problems arose in the exercise of its responsibility for programme policy : the establishment of an external supervisory body would not, in my view, solve them. The governors were amateurs, not professionals, and naturally enough on many matters of mood, standards of taste, they were divided. The handling of creative people was especially difficult and delicate. Yet the creative spirit was the engine of broadcasting. As, in effect, non-executive directors, who in law *were* the BBC, they were inescapably

responsible for what was broadcast. Yet, properly and inevitably, their scrutiny of programmes was almost always retro-
spective. How could the trustee role of representing the public
be reconciled with the responsibility of the governors for what
was broadcast?

I reflected on the discussion which followed in my diary:

20 December

My predecessor, Lord Normanbrook, dealt with the subject
of governors' responsibilities and duties in speech and in published form, in a way that it is difficult to better. The snag is,
if snag it is, that when he wrote it the governors were not
being criticized for failing in their role as trustees for the
public. Increasingly in recent months critics of the BBC and,
in particular, the advocates of a broadcasting council, have
been saying that the governors are so wrapped up in the
running of the organization and the defence of their staff
that they fail in their role as representatives of the public.

'How can the two things be reconciled?' is sometimes
asked. 'As they cannot be, there should be an external body
which really is the voice of the public,' so the argument
runs.

At first sight it is not easy to refute, yet it is important to
refute it in order to demolish the case for a viewers' council. Already a good deal has been done to demolish that case.
There are those who want in some way or other to control,
to regulate and so to censor. This has been pointed out. There
are those who say that we are unfair to individuals without
giving them a chance to reply. This has been dealt with by
the Complaints Commission. There are those who argue
that an external body is needed in order to impose standards
of taste. So far the weakest part of our position has been the
difficulty of reconciling the public trustee role with that of
running the Corporation. Anyway I have made an effort
to bring this out and to invite discussion in the paper. In
fact, because of the weight of other business discussion on
the paper was postponed until January.

Both board meetings in January 1972 had useful discussions
on the governors' role. The governors broadly accepted Lord

Normanbrook's propositions and then discussed whether these
were being fulfilled.

Among the points made were that governors should be more
frequently consulted in advance about controversial matters;
that the board were being seen as apologists for the BBC, rather
than as public trustees; that the appointment of senior staff was
the most important of the Board's responsibilities; that the
executive should recognize that the governors, though further
from the coal face, were nearer to the customers; that there
should be closer contact with junior staff.

In winding up, I said that we were amateurs and not professionals and our role was policy not management. Governors
should not underrate what they have achieved: there was now
much tighter financial control, there were flourishing radio
services and there were closer relations with the staff.

I put another paper to the next meeting, listing some practical suggestions. The director-general said he would provide
as much advance information as practical on programme policies, major programme projects and possible controversies. The
old subject of the circulation of minutes of some management
committees was raised. This time the general view was that it
should be done: the director-general's view remained unchanged. I suggested a compromise: a fuller report by the
director-general to the Board of Governors on matters of
importance coming to the Board of Management and a précis
of discussions at senior staffs' programme review committees.
The compromise satisfied both the director-general and the
board.

Diary 18 January
The governors' meeting last Thursday was one of the most
interesting I have attended. There were two new governors
present: Roy Fuller, Oxford Professor of Poetry, and Tony
Morgan, managing director of a refuse disposal company.

What was interesting was the way in which most
governors sought to strengthen the governors' role in one
way or another. More information, more opportunity to discuss controversial or likely to be controversial decisions in
advance, and so on. I found myself steadying the tide and

reminding governors that we were amateurs presiding over professionals.

There are two sorts of attack on the governors. One line is that the governors are the tools of the management and the programme makers; that they are impotent; that they do not represent the public. The other line is that the governors are interfering with the experts, that the chairman is taking over the role of the director-general, and so on.

How long it has taken to strengthen the role of governors! Wilson and Short may have expected that my appointment would briskly lead to a more effective board. If they did, they have had to wait an awful long time for it. Maybe it is that I have got a little wiser in handling matters.

Among the letters I received at this time was the following:

Dear Sir,

I am writing in utter disgust at the way you are doing your duty. You have no control over the BBC staff and programmes. Be man enough to resign.

(Signed)
Only one of hundreds of thousands

26

'The Question of Ulster'

A storm of a severity unprecedented in my experience broke
upon me and the BBC in January 1972 because of a television
programme on *The Question of Ulster*. The Home Secretary
publicly urged the BBC and privately urged me not to screen
it. Our rejection of this plea is of such importance that I now
tell the full story.

Plans for a major discussion programme on Ulster were discussed inside the BBC during October 1971. It was felt that the
time was ripe for a long and thorough programme that would
look below the surface of violence and coolly examined solutions being offered. Waldo Maguire, the BBC's controller,
Northern Ireland, helped to draw up an outline. The intention
was a programme that would look to the future and not let participants apportion blame for the past.

The programme would be live, under a neutral and judicial
president, leading a three-man 'tribunal'. It would begin with
a short historical setting of the scene, after which representatives
of the government, the Labour opposition, and the Northern
Ireland government would each make a statement of their
policy. There would then be eight Irish speakers – two from the
Republic and the rest from Ulster, giving four each to these
antitheses : Protestant/Catholic; Loyalist/Republican; Right/
Left; Moderate/Extreme. Each would make a statement, a
verbal précis of a written declaration of policy circulated to all
the other participants in advance of the programme. After such
statement, the politician would be questioned by members of
the tribunal, to clarify his policy. Expert witnesses would also
be available for the president to question on matters of fact.

'You've got three minutes to get out!'

At the end the president and his colleagues would sum up their views on the propositions they had heard, not judging between them but setting them in perspective.

The word 'tribunal' caused controversy. It was alleged that the programme infringed the government's sphere by trying to set itself up in judgement on solutions to Ulster's problems. A document for internal use said the programme was based on the procedures of United States Senate Committee hearings, in which testimony is examined and sifted. In fact, it was not envisaged that the tribunal would make any sort of adjudication. Lord Devlin agreed to be the president.

The director-general and I were fully involved in the plan. It was discussed with the Stormont government of Mr Brian Faulkner, who was invited to make an opening statement. Not till then were approaches made to the other proposed participants.

The alarm bells began to ring on 9 December when it was learned that Mr Faulkner had doubts about the wisdom of the programme while people were being killed. He was critical of the proposed casting on the ground that the eight Irish speakers proposed included only one Ulster Unionist, Mr Baillie, Minister of Commerce. Nevertheless, the assumption remained at this stage that if the programme went on, Mr Baillie would represent the views of Stormont in the main part of the programme, with Mr Faulkner making an opening statement in the introduction.

At this stage the Home Secretary, Mr Maudling, who had specific responsibility for Northern Ireland, asked me to go and see him and accompanied by the director-general I went to the Home Office on 13 December. The meeting was private, but since a fairly full account of it was published in the *Daily Telegraph* later that month no confidentiality remains.

The Home Secretary, who looked unusually stern and was accompanied by a grim-looking permanent secretary, said he was seriously disquieted by the project, which he regarded as potentially dangerous, quite apart from his view that it had a built-in bias. Of the eight Irish participants in the main part of the programme, only one would represent the Ulster Unionists, with seven expressing various dissenting views. Only one favoured internment.

I replied that the programme was a genuine attempt to present a fair picture from a variety of angles. I thought the programme would be valuable, and could not agree to abandon it, though the governors would consider Mr Maudling's views about balance. It was decided that by a change of placing and by the allocation of additional time, the special position of the majority party in Ulster could be better reflected in the programme, and in the event it was.

Then on 11 December newspaper stories about the programme began appearing first in Belfast and later in Dublin and London. The first London story, in the *Daily Mirror* on 16 December, said the BBC had called the programme off after representations from Stormont that it might be inflammatory. This was untrue.

The proposed programme was discussed on that day at the Board of Governors. One governor expressed the fear that there might be discussions, even negotiations, going on between governments of which we and the parties in the discussion were unaware and in this respect we ran a risk. The board decided to proceed, while leaving open the question of how the Unionist viewpoint might best be put, to meet the charge that the programme was weighted against it. Right up to 23 December there seemed good reason to expect that either Mr Baillie or some other minister from Stormont would take part in the programme, but on Christmas Eve it was learned that no representative of the Stormont government would be allowed to take part.

From now on the programme was a centre of controversy in the press – the *Daily Telegraph* campaigning against the BBC's alleged irresponsibility and willingness to serve as a propaganda vehicle for those who advocated violence.

During Christmas there were discussions involving the director-general, myself and those working on the programme. On 28 December the BBC issued a statement :

> The BBC believes such a programme to be in the public interest and that the suppression of views, however unpopular, would be both unwise and dangerous. Clearly such a programme depends on the willingness of governments to co-operate in providing authoritative spokesmen. Mr Faulkner had not asked the BBC to ban the programme. If, however, it be true that the Stormont Government is now unwilling to co-operate, then the programme cannot proceed in the form planned for January 5th, and fresh thought will have to be given to its preparation for a later showing. The BBC recognises the formidable difficulties of producing such a programme but is confident of its ability to do so. What the BBC cannot accept is that it should be diverted from its public purpose of presenting all points of view by a campaign of pressure by a newspaper or anyone else.

This was, of course, widely reported and commented on. Opinions were divided, *The Times* saying 'The programme should be shown', the *Guardian* : 'Lord Hill should not give up', the *Sun* : 'Stop this mock trial', the *Daily Telegraph* : 'The project in its present form is demonstrably ridiculous. The BBC should scrap its original ideas and start again.'

A few days before the programme was due to be screened, I

called two meetings – one in the morning of the senior staff involved, and one in the afternoon of available governors and staff. Despite the earlier statement that without Stormont co-operation the programme could not proceed as planned, it was thought that the programme could yet be saved, and the executive producer of the programme, Richard Francis, was asked to continue to try to get an Ulster Unionist MP as a spokesman. On Sunday, 2 January, a comparatively little known Unionist MP at Westminster, Mr Jack Maginnis, agreed to appear, and indeed needed no persuasion, since he thought the programme would be valuable and was anxious that the Unionist case should be heard.

On Monday 3 January I presided over another meeting with five governors and others at Broadcasting House, and, subject to consultation on the telephone with absent governors, the go-ahead was given. After telephone consultation, the position was that of the twelve governors nine were in favour, two were unavailable, and one abstained.

Next day the Home Secretary took an unprecedented step. He sent me a letter, by hand, saying that he would later send it to the press, declaring that he believed the programme 'in the form in which it had been devised could do no good and could do serious harm'. The contents of the letter, which arrived in the late afternoon after I had left, were telephoned to me when I arrived home and I dictated a reply to be sent immediately saying, 'If we shared your fears that such a programme would worsen the situation in Ulster we would not dream of proceeding with it. On the contrary we hope and believe that it will be of value in widening understanding of the issues involved. No good purpose can be served by our declining to air conflicting views as to the future.' It also said : 'The three distinguished men who will question the politicians will not be reaching a conclusion or forming a judgement. They are not a tribunal in that sense.' Both letters were prominently published next morning, the day of the programme, Wednesday 5 January.

As a result of the newspaper campaign and the Home Secretary's letter, the programme got a much bigger audience than would normally be expected. At 9.20 pm seven and a half million viewers tuned in, including nearly two-thirds of the population of Northern Ireland. Telefis Eireann relayed the programme live throughout Eire. It proved to be what it was planned to be : a sober and low-temperature examination of eight different proposals for the future of Ulster, with no attempt by Lord Devlin or his two colleagues to give judgement. Lord Caradon said on the programme : 'We may have been dull, but not dangerous.'

More than half the viewers who started stayed to the end at a quarter past midnight – a higher rate of 'staying power' than on previous marathon programmes. Whereas telephone calls to the BBC were 10 :1 against the programme beforehand, they were 5 :1 in favour afterwards. Several critics wrote or telephoned to say that they had been wrong in their opposition to the programme. One fringe benefit of the programme was that with so many people watching, Northern Ireland had one of its quietest nights for weeks.

The press continued to be divided after the programme, though a number of hostile critics or waverers were won over. The *Daily Mirror* ran its own strange course. It had opened the ball in London papers by saying, quite wrongly, that the BBC had called off the programme. On the morning of transmission it supported the BBC under the headline 'Carry on BBC'. On the following day it attacked the BBC and its chairman under the headline 'Lord Blunder of the BBC' – not on what the programme had turned out to be (for the leader must have been written before the programme started) but on the principle of the matter, on which it had supported the BBC the previous day.

The *Daily Telegraph* seemed disappointed at the restraint of the programme, but thought the question whether the programme might have done harm remained to be considered. The *Daily Express* remained hostile. But in general the kicks were directed at the government for trying to suppress the programme, and not at the BBC for broadcasting it.

The Times gave a measured judgement, saying the programme lived up to neither the extravagant hopes nor the worst fears. 'The most that can be claimed is that it made more apparent the intransigent and incompatible attitudes of different parties, and the substantial obstacles that remain in the way of a solution. But that in itself was a valuable exercise. Those who watched the programme from start to finish must have emerged with a deeper understanding of the complexities of the Northern Irish situation.'

It won approval from the *Belfast Telegraph,* a newspaper which had often criticized the BBC for giving too much weight to the Republican cause. This time it said, in a leading article : 'What was all the fuss about? That is the common reaction to the much-maligned BBC programme on Ulster, which failed signally – to some people's evident disappointment – to raise more heat than light . . . The formula for the programme, which was the subject of so much criticism from Stormont, turned out to be perfectly suited to a rational debate . . . It was not dull, as Lord Caradon modestly suggested it might have been, and neither was it harmful.'

After the programme, the Home Secretary said the programme might yet have done harm, because it could serve only to harden attitudes. He was referring no doubt to the statement by Mr Gerry Fitt, MP, of the Social and Democratic Labour Party of Northern Ireland, that he would not take part in any talks before internment was ended. Yet he had said the same thing in the House of Commons five weeks earlier.

The whole affair undoubtedly heightened a feeling of resentment in the government and among many Conservative MPs against the BBC. With hindsight, it is possible to pick out some pitfalls that could have been avoided. The use of the word 'tribunal' was unwise. It enabled those who were hostile to the idea of the programme to represent it as an arrogant attempt by the BBC to set itself up in judgement and decide the 'right course' for Northern Ireland. There was never any such intention. In fact, at one time it was suggested that Lord Devlin and his colleagues should be termed a panel, but this was rejected on the ground that it had connotations of panel games and entertainment programmes.

Another pitfall became apparent in the programme itself. The participants were all told that they could illustrate their spoken statements with film or stills or diagrams. Some did, and some did not, and the result was that some emotive film of violent

scenes made a disproportionate effect. To many people it looked like unfairness. This could have been minimized by a plain
statement that all eight speakers had been told that they might
illustrate their statements and that some had decided not to do
so. It might even have been better not to make the offer in the
first place.

There were some positive lessons too. Internally, the procedure was impeccable. The proposal was carefully worked out
and discussed with plenty of time to work out the details. Since
the programme was bound to be controversial, the director-
general and I were informed of the plan at an early stage, before
irrevocable decisions had been taken. To the participants the
ground rules were explained in detail, so that everybody knew
who else was taking part, and what form the programme would
take. Contact between the most senior levels in the BBC and
those producing the programme was close, and in the final
crucial stages there was daily discussion.

All these are matters of detail. More fundamental was the
demonstration of the technique of veto by abstention. It very
nearly succeeded. Without a representative Ulster Unionist
voice the programme could not have been put on in the form in
which it had been devised. At least one other promised participant would have withdrawn, and the structures would have
disintegrated like the spills in a game of spillikins. But in any
case, the BBC would not have wanted to proceed with a programme in a form that would manifestly have failed to give
the Ulster Unionist view at first hand, as was the case with the
other participants.

Anybody has the right to decline to appear in a television
programme. A government can decline to make an authoritative spokesman available. Whether it is reasonable for a
government and a party to try to extend that authority to the
point of forbidding individual elected members to appear is
another matter. Had the attempt succeeded the programme in
its planned form and on the announced date would not have
been possible, but planning would immediately have started on
another programme that sought to examine rival solutions in
another way.

The programme was of the greatest importance as a demonstration of the BBC's will to back its judgement against any pressure – and the pressure was great. It demonstrated something else : the independence of the BBC. This was perhaps as valuable to foreigners as to the United Kingdom, where that independence is taken for granted. Even though the Home Secretary so firmly and passionately believed that the programme should not be broadcast, he said both publicly and privately that the final decision must be that of the BBC. My letter to the Home Secretary said that if the BBC shared the Home Secretary's fears the programme would be dropped. But since the BBC believed that the programme would be valuable, it would exercise its right to make decisions for itself. I find it hard to believe that when the history of this section of the tragedy of Ulster comes to be written, the BBC's decision will be judged wrong.

The day after the programme, Waldo Maguire, the controller in Northern Ireland who had carried for so long a heavy burden with so much verve and courage, wrote me a letter which delighted me :

As the man who proposed the Ulster programme in the first instance, may I say how grateful the overwhelming majority of the BBC staff are for the courage and wisdom with which you steered the project through the formidable hazard and on to the screen.

I sincerely believe that the future of free and independent broadcasting in this country was at stake and any weakening of your resolve would have been a disaster.

I hope you will treat with contempt such vicious and myopic attacks as in today's *Mirror*.

The entire BBC is behind you in your determination to maintain free and responsible broadcasting.

Some months later, Hugh Cudlipp, whom I met at some lunch, said the *Mirror* attack on the day after the broadcast had been wrong and he regretted it.

Not unnaturally my diary entries on *The Question of Ulster* and its repercussions are fuller than usual.

6 January

Last night the programme came, with Ludo Kennedy in the chair, Robin Day having withdrawn a few days before. Ludo did exceedingly well. The trio were in no sense a tribunal : Devlin and his colleagues did not express conclusions. The extracts from Maudling and Faulkner were well done, despite Faulkner's protest in the evening press that it would be wrong to take extracts from what he had already said. It was a good programme that was fair and sensible. There has been an obvious Home Office briefing to assert that the programme worsened the situation and had polarized views, and so on.

Harold Wilson was first-class, refraining from using the occasion for party politics. Paisley, after his initial typical blast, was reasonable under questioning. In television terms, the star was Bernadette Devlin, with her captivating flow of oratory. Sir John Foster, almost like a would-be lover, coyly demonstrated her irrelevance to the issues under discussion, save under the heading of social reform. Blaney, the man I feared most, was almost throughout apparently reasonable. A valid criticism could be that he was not more rigorously questioned but, then, that might have turned it all into an argy-bargy. One of the expert witnesses, General Hackett, began to be awkward but the chairman, Ludo Kennedy, dealt with him. The constitutional and economic experts were good.

For me, the crucial questions have been – could such a programme inform? Could it do it without polarizing views or worsening the situation? If the answers to both questions were 'yes', it was our duty as a public broadcasting body to put it on, despite heavy pressure by a minister. That Reggie Maudling felt strongly I did not doubt, for I have never seen him in such a mood as I found him when D-G and I went to see him. I have no doubt that we were right in resisting government pressure to drop it. It may not be what Kenneth Adam, of all people, said was the BBC's finest hour but at least it was a stand which had to be taken. Government, after all, has power to ban a proposed programme. It did not do this.

The D-G, despite being in ill health over the past week,

had been sturdy throughout. What effects the event will have on that small minority of our staff which has been grumbling that the BBC has been exercising patriotic censorship in Northern Ireland, I don't know, though I am pretty sure that the governors' stand will help to strengthen the morale in current affairs generally. Why R.M. intervened with a public letter the day before, I don't know, unless it was the act of a desperate man. Could it be that we were getting together people who had hitherto declined to meet him and each other in a round table talk?

Already the Tory Broadcasting Committee is crying out for the director-general or myself to go to the earliest possible meeting of their committee after the return of Parliament while their memories are still lively. We will go, of course, but in our time. Alas, there are no medals in this world and the rampage will go on for some days yet, maybe longer.

There may be cries for my resignation, which they will not get : if they want to get rid of me they will have to sack me. If they do sack me because we have rejected the pressure of government they may not find it so easy to find a successor, or, on the other hand, they may put in a government stooge for the purpose. One cannot help reflecting that when I was appointed here the accusation was that I was a government stooge put in to quell the BBC and keep it under control. In the event we had a bloody row last year with the Labour Party over *Yesterday's Men* and now a bloodier row with a Conservative government over this programme. The sweets of responsibility are delightful – but not all.

My diary a week later recorded that letters pouring in revealed a majority in favour of the BBC's action. It is anger and criticism which usually spur correspondents on programme matters. Normally there are far more letters of criticism than support. What was reassuring was that so many of the supporting letters put their finger on the principle of the BBC's independence. A number said that they learned something from the programme, even going so far as to describe it as very interesting, or fascinating.

Of course, there were the usual letters of abuse. 'Monstrous,' one of them wrote. 'Whose side are you on, the people of this country would like to know? You, the ex-Radio Doctor – one of the gutter peerage – who draws his thousands a year in comfort and safety, while our poor boys out there die in their youthful innocence. When is someone going to do something about the treacherous scum which makes up the BBC today?'

Another: 'It took between five and six centuries to rid Britain of priestly domination. You seem bent on putting Britain back under its yoke. May God preserve us!'

Still another: 'You have given comfort to the men who are killing our lads in the Army in Ireland. In fact, you give comfort to all the enemies of this country. You stir up, you misrepresent. The sooner they clamp down on you the better. And clamp down they will, make no mistake. You abuse the freedom (like the miners) this dear old Country has given you. Your time is running short.'

One evening angry callers rang the BBC to complain about another TV programme on Ulster. In fact, it was not on BBC but ITV. One irate caller, when told he was complaining to the wrong people, said: 'I'm bloody sure the BBC must have been behind it somewhere.'

A fortnight after the programme, there was a tally of correspondence about it, with the following result.

	FOR	AGAINST
Before programme	33	230
After programme	487	169

27

Unpopularity

'Harold Wilson came to lunch,' my diary recorded on 18 January 1972.

He was bland and pleasant. I opened by asking him whether he thought that the new abrasiveness between Westminster and BBC was due to the growing feeling in Parliament that its stature and strength are falling, and those of the media are rising at the expense of Westminster.

He thought not but that the relations between the BBC and Westminster were bedevilled by the fact that a proportion of Members were never asked to broadcast. Then he listed some of our less peaceful exchanges over the last few years. It was a deft display.

A few days later I had lunch with a senior minister. He did not disguise the government's displeasure with the BBC in general and with me in particular over the Ulster programme. I recorded my reactions :

Diary 23 January
This government, no less than any other, wants to bring pressure on us and the most inconvenient person to bring pressure on is a former colleague. Aubrey Jones was a Tory Member, but soon after he went to the Prices and Incomes Board he became unpopular with the Tory Party. Alf Robens become unpopular with the Labour Party, even to the extent

of a motion put down urging his dismissal. I have been pretty successful in becoming unpopular with the Labour government when they were in and with the Tory government today.

I am pretty sure that Heath would like to get rid of me but that it is not easy when the issue is the BBC's independence. In any case I am on the last lap and they will probably think they have got to be patient.

Less patient was one writer of a letter to me. He said, 'I hope you get slung out on your neck soon, you sanctimonious hypocrite.'

In mid-January, the Minister of Posts and Telecommunications told me of the announcement he intended to make, postponing a decision on ITV 2 but agreeing to end all limitation on broadcasting hours. I wondered what he would say if asked whether an enquiry into broadcasting would be set up. He replied that he would parry the issue. I had a pretty firm impression that he was in favour of an enquiry but that the Prime Minister was still holding to the view that the government could and should decide broadcasting issues without the help of some external body. The argument for this view is quite strong. Again and again a problem is put to a Royal Commission or a departmental committee in the hope it will go away for the time being. Then the commission or the committee reports and the government is still faced with the task of deciding what to do.

I told him that, while I recognized the strength of this argument, there were two good reasons why there should be an enquiry. First, it was a form of public accountability, important both to the public and to the BBC. Secondly, though the various suggestions being bruited around for weakening the BBC, varying from a viewers' council to the break-up of the organization into parts, would probably come to nothing, the staff of the BBC was inevitably affected by public agitation for them. Their morale was very important to us. The sooner such notions were disposed of, the better. A further advantage of an enquiry of the Pilkington kind was that the BBC would have the opportunity to argue its case to an independent body, even though the final decisions still remained with the government.

What, he asked, about a Green Paper? I pointed out that when a government produced a Paper, Green or White, there was a certain commitment from which it was not easy to escape. For example, Margaret Thatcher had issued a Green Paper on student finances. Now that she had decided to postpone a decision she was being accused of climbing down. I formed the impression that Chataway favoured an enquiry, though a short sharp enquiry by relatively few people, but that he had not yet got his master's approval.

Finally, we chatted for a while about the Ulster programme. He was rather vague about it, merely saying that he thought the form of the programme was not suitable; the questioning by Devlin and colleagues was not right. He preferred questioning by professionals.

A few days later we were criticized for the news bulletin reporting the Derry shootings. I had thought the bulletin balanced and fair, though the picture material was inevitably horrifying. Some people, alas, cannot stomach the broadcasting of any anti-British material without its being clearly condemned, although they have come to expect it in the press. In their belief, a British Broadcasting Corporation should report events from the British angle in a pro-British way. In some moods, I am tempted to share this view, but I know it to be wrong. It is the responsibility of broadcasters to report what happens, not what we think should happen.

About this time I had a conversation with a parliamentary colleague who had the previous day talked with the Prime Minister. He said that the PM was against a broadcasting enquiry of any kind. That was not the view of all his colleagues. One group, led by Hailsham, wanted a root-and-branch enquiry. Another, represented by Whitelaw as well as Chataway, wanted a short, intense enquiry by two or three people. I asked if the PM had mentioned the BBC. He said, it seemed, in one terse sentence : 'The BBC's in a mess.'

It is becoming pretty clear [I wrote in my diary] that the PM has got a deep-seated dislike of the BBC. I gather from reports of other conversations he has had that he is not very specific, he just makes scornful references rather than detailed criticisms. This is part of the general Tory picture.

Behind the specific examples of lack of balance they quote, there is a belief that in its factual journalistic programmes generally the BBC seeks to be destructive not only of the Establishment but of everything established. This is one criticism which I have felt for years has something in it. We are living in an 'anti' world as far as the young are concerned and we have our share of anti's. Another line is that we should exercise a patriotic censorship. These critics just do not accept that our job is to report the world as it is, warts and all, and that those who make news by attacking the established order have to be reported no less than those who defend it.

In mid-March Peter Walker rang me up to say that from what he had heard a *Man Alive* programme to be broadcast called *Landlord and Tenant: Up the Rent* was going to be an unfair attack on the Bill. I told him what I would have told any other serious complainant, that I would have the matter looked into. In Curran's absence I asked John Crawley to offer to call on the Minister to explain what was afoot and to repeat the invitation to him to participate, which he had declined. Later, John Crawley rang me up at home to report that he had seen Peter Walker who was far from mollified and that the programme was, in Crawley's view, just defensible.

I asked him to arrange for one or two governors to see it on Monday morning at ten o'clock and I asked Bridget Plowden and Tom Jackson to join me. We met together with the D-G, John Crawley, David Attenborough and the man in charge of the programme, Desmond Wilcox. When we had seen the programme, Bridget Plowden thought it was biased, Tom Jackson thought it fair and I thought it unbalanced. It depicted two Labour Members of Parliament addressing meetings but no interview with a Tory Member of Parliament. There were two Labour municipal leaders in the programme and no Conservative municipal leaders. Inadvertently the property owners had been allowed to be interviewed while drinking some sparkling fluid, either champagne or gin and tonic.

The D-G was uncertain, saying that with rents as the subject there was bound to be an emotional or other bias against the Bill. We were confronted with the same old position. The programme was virtually made and we could only be effective by the extreme step of withdrawing it altogether. The alternative was to recognize that it was not completely balanced and to ensure that in the following programme – fortunately it was a two-programme series – a minister was given an opportunity, say ten minutes at the beginning and five minutes at the end, to say what he wished and so restore the balance. This was agreed.

The attitude of Desmond Wilcox in the discussion appeared to be that the contents of the programmes were his business and he could not see why we were having this special showing. Fortunately, Huw Wheldon, who came in late and had not seen the showing, sensed the position and dealt with it effectively.

In March 1972 we were back – rather unexpectedly – to wavelength arguments with the Minister. Curran, Redmond (director of engineering) and I called on Chataway to put the BBC's view. Curran and Redmond were at their most effective. In the White Paper, Chataway had said that our twenty local stations would cover 60 per cent of the population on medium wave in the day-time and that commercial radio's sixty stations would cover 70 per cent. It was implicit in this plan that if these figures were to be achieved, our few stations, rather than the more numerous commercial stations, would have to have the wavelength with the greater penetrating power of two available wavelengths. Chataway proposed, despite the White Paper, to give the one with greater coverage to the commercial bodies. This meant that to achieve the White Paper figures for population reached we should have to increase our transmitting power sixfold at very considerable additional cost. Chataway argued that the opposition to commercial radio was not only our local radio but our national networks, particularly Radio 1.

I replied that he knew this before the White Paper was issued, that he was now departing from that White Paper and in the process involving us in very substantially more expenditure. What was more, though this was not our business, his proposals meant that the four first stations of commercial radio would cover 50 per cent of the population. Was he still going to call it local radio? Even worse than this, the London area, extending far outside London – from Luton to the south coast – had in its area of coverage a number of places that were to be offered their own local radios, like Luton. How were they to be viable?

Diary 9 March
My own impression is that this is pure politics. Chataway dare not let commercial radio fail and so, for a start, he was creating four big companies of a regional rather than a local character which were bound to be successful financially, and giving little thought to the viability of the smaller companies that would fill in the rest of the country.

If local radio has a justification it is in relatively small areas, with local stations serving really local communities. Some of our own areas are too big. How can Birmingham, for example, be really local to Wolverhampton, though we have no alternative because we are limited to 20 stations. Commercial radio, on the other hand, having 60 stations, had the opportunity to be more local. On the contrary, it is to be less local.

At today's meeting of the governors it was decided to incur the expense of strengthening the signals, not only of our local radio stations, but of Radio 1. The strengthening of Radio 1 is necessary because local radio, with its competing pop, will, unless we strengthen our Radio 1 signal, be heard in many areas much more clearly than our own. The governors did not much like the additional expense, one of them saying, in effect, that if we had money to spare it should be spent not on local radio, but on increasing our coverage of our network radio and television programmes.

We must make sure that the Newspaper Publishers Association, headed by Arnold Goodman, knows about this because these four stations, covering half the country, will be near national in character and will, no doubt, carry a lot of national advertising at the expense of the national newspapers. I do not think that the medium-size provincial newspapers will care because they will get less competition with their local 'smalls'. The really local newspaper will hardly get a look-in.

The problem of programme taste was discussed by the governors and senior executives twice in early 1972. I referred to it in my diary.

16 February
It really was a successful discussion justifying the colloquy method. The purpose is not to reach decisions or pass resolutions, but an exchange of ideas to enable the executive and the governors to put their ideas into a common pool. On the executive side, Wheldon, as usual, was brilliant though wordy; Attenborough was clear and cogent; and, to the surprise of some who had thought him shy, Howard Newby was exceedingly good. Both his basic approach and his choice of words were very impressive.

I found particular pleasure in the success of the colloquy for, after feeling around for some long time, it seems that we have found a way of exercising our function of public representation without irksome exchanges or friction between the governors and the staff. After all, the other method which was followed in the case of 'Broadcasting in the Public Mood' was a failure. The governors were seen by the staff to have pronounced and, in consequence, hackles rose and the document was suffocated. The method that would obtain in most other organizations proved unsuccessful here. The colloquy, on the other hand, at its first attempt has proved successful.

This is due in part to the new arrivals on the board. Lady Plowden is gaining strength. What has happened to her has happened to most of us. We begin with clear-cut ideas, usually critical ones, only to find that things are not as simple as they seem. Of course the danger is that governors will go too far and be nobbled.

But many members of the public were by no means satisfied with us. Early in 1972 the Festival of Light found its way to the board agenda. This body claimed to speak on behalf of 'several millions of people'. The Festival was intended, its spokesmen said, to promote the views of many people that 'in Christ there was a joy not represented adequately in the mass media'. A deputation we received said the BBC was not always fair to the case for purity and Christian values. They spoke of the effects of the mass media on the young and questioned whether teenage programmes for schools ought to be quite so neutral in their moral attitudes. One of the visitors said that there seemed to be certain background assumptions in our programmes that people would be promiscuous, that programmes should not moralize and that monogamy should not be commended. Another asserted that a recent sex education series had been produced without sufficient thought for deprived children.

We put questions to the deputation, aimed at a clarification of their views. The most telling came from David Attenborough who asked whether the BBC should base its programmes on, for example, the philosophical assumptions underlying Christian marriage to the exclusion of other philosophical assumptions about marriage. The reply from the leader of the deputation, Colonel Dobbie, was that programmes should be based on the assumptions held by the deputation, another member adding that the freedom of the artist needed to be reconciled with a sense of responsibility to the rest of society.

After further exchanges I suggested that the Festival of Light should set down its views on paper in rather more detail, the BBC replying to them in writing. This was agreed and some three months later, their statement arrived and was put before the governors. A considerable discussion followed. There was a lively moment when Curran said that the Festival's statement could not be circulated to the staff without being destroyed by derision, to which a governor retorted that that was a trouble with the BBC, it ignored the feelings of a large number of people.

Some points in the Festival's document were regarded as fair, indeed they had often been expressed in board meetings. For example, it was said that nowadays some creative artists wanted to use artistic freedom to go to lengths which were indefensible for broadcasting. Eventually it was agreed that the secretary should prepare a draft reply in the light of the discussion.

My mail bag at this time contained the following letter :

Lord Hill,

Why don't you get your *filthy* TV shows cleaned up. It's *dirty scum* like you that corrupt youth. Have you no sense of *decency* or *shame*? Having seen 'Man at the Top' I consider the sooner your kind and the playwrights have your mouths cleaned the better. No wonder this is now a third rate country. How *stinking rotten* can you get?

Man at the Top was, of course, an ITV programme.

28

Unease About News

I had been brooding for some time about the BBC's handling
of news and comment. Inevitably, the BBC is liable to be disliked because it has to report unpleasant facts. Sometimes the
BBC, being only human, makes errors. Could these be reduced
by changes in the control structure?

In March 1972 I presented to the Board of Governors a
paper on the organization of news and current affairs. It was
to be one of the ventures in which I failed to carry others with
me. As it relates to a crucial area of programming, perhaps I
may be forgiven for giving it in full :

1   Two or three years ago the area of BBC broadcasting to
come under the strongest fire was drama, with sex,
language and violence as the favourite targets and a
Viewers' Council as the recommended remedy.

2   Today the main target is News and Current Affairs.
Yesterday's Men, although related to one particular
party, seems to have aroused some politicians of all
parties to resent the ridicule and the artfulness which
they believed they detected. Inevitably Ulster has
dominated the criticisms of recent months. A recent and
new development has been the criticism attracted of
bias by the News itself.

3   This note refers only to News and Current Affairs in
both television and radio. There are various brands
of criticism. Some critics adopt a right-wing posture,
remind us that we are the British Broadcasting Corporation and advocate a patriotic censorship in news and

current affairs, particularly in Irish matters. Others accuse the BBC of a persistent left-wing bias, even seeing a Communist inside every microphone and camera. A smaller but growing number of critics detect in our journalistic efforts generally a steady intention to attack the established and the traditional, less on a party political basis than on that of a general knocking policy. And there are those, more sophisticated critics, who regard our programme makers as an uncontrolled and uncontrollable body. Neither the Governors, nor the top management, are in effective charge, they say.

4   Much of this criticism must be rejected as based on an entirely erroneous view of our functions as a broadcasting service and of our essential role as a truthful presenter of what is really happening in the world. Our job is to present the facts as we see them, not as we would like to see them. We are not an organ of government or a defender of the status quo.

5   From time to time errors do happen and bias is unmistakable, an inescapable result of the delegation of authority and the 'upward reference' principle. Such departures from our overall policy we must recognize – and admit – explaining them on the ground that it is human to err and that there are greater gains than losses in the system of delegation of authority. Even so, one is left with some unease. There is something in the 'knocking principle' criticism. Errors do occur more frequently than one would wish. One cannot entirely reject the argument that there is too much uncontrolled 'freewheeling' in some current affairs programmes.

6   The question I have been turning over in my mind for some time is whether by organizational changes there could be brought more coherence, more top level coordination and supervision to a crucial branch of broadcasting which from now on is likely to be a source of attack on the BBC in a world in which conflict abounds and in which Parliament appears resentful of a medium which it believes, rightly or wrongly, to be more powerful than itself.

7   In practice there are difficulties inherent in the nature
of broadcast journalism. News and Current Affairs are
not easily co-ordinated. Much of what is broadcast is
up-to-the-moment, fast-moving stuff. The principle of
delegation is necessary as well as right. But this does
make more difficult an overall policy control at the top.

8   The Editor, News and Current Affairs, although recently strengthened, tends in the nature of things to be effectively responsible for News but occupies more of a consultant position to Current Affairs. The Programme
Controllers naturally regard News and Current Affairs
as a special area responsible to others. The Managing
Directors are necessarily much less in control in this
than in other programme areas. The Director-General,
with his immense responsibilities over the whole field
of broadcasting, is bound to delegate, though the
appointment of John Crawley as his special assistant
has helped him substantially in this field.

9   This is, to some extent, an old problem. Haley was a
working journalist and anyway, in his day, radio
dominated television and the hazards were less. Ian
Jacob, his successor, was a soldier; eventually he realized
the need for a concentration of responsibility for News
and Current Affairs in a journalist immediately responsible to him. So Hugh Greene, a widely experienced
journalist, was appointed Director of News and Current
Affairs with a seat on the Board of Management. When
Greene became Director-General he retained, in practice as well as in theory, his direction of News and Current Affairs. Since those days Current Affairs has grown
even more in scope, importance and hazard.

10 It would seem to me that in seeking a solution of the
problems outlined in this Note, regard must be had
to certain general considerations : —

(i)   The Director-General's authority, in scope and
character, must remain unimpaired. He is and
and must remain the 'front' man of the BBC. He
must have – and does have – an especial interest
in Current Affairs. The delegation by him of de-

fined areas of broadcasting, subject to his ultimate
authority and responsibility, to a man he knows
and trusts, who does not fail to inform and consult him on matters properly concerning the chief
officer, does not reduce his authority. On the contrary, it strengthens it and spares him from
involvement in lesser issues so leaving him more
time and energy for main issues and overall
policy.

(ii) In the BBC, as elsewhere, effective power lies
with those who have troops at their command. To
over-simplify in the crudest of terms, a good deal
of the trouble into which current affairs has land-
ed us has stemmed from having on the one hand
people with ideas and no power, and on the other,
people with power and no ideas. Put effectively,
in current affairs the people at the top find themselves having to rely for the most part on their
powers of persuasion. The real power lies at a
comparatively junior level.

(iii) One solution might be the intimate involvement
of Managing Director, and the Director of Programmes Radio, in the current affairs operation as
in all other operations. Already their burdens are
heavy in their responsibility for programmes and
a specialised kind of background and experience
is necessary for the political awareness which the
control of current affairs demands. Other and
different talents are so much more important in
the management of a broadcasting service.

(iv) In 1968 McKinsey, proceeding from the managerial aspect and confining themselves to news,
recommended that TV news should become
managerially responsible to MD Tel [managing
director, television] and Radio news similarly to
MDR [managing director, radio], leaving a central service of correspondents etc. under Editor,
News and Current Affairs. The editorial responsibility would remain with ENCA. It was rejected

mainly on the argument that editorial and managerial responsibilities could not sensibly be separated.

(v) To be in effective control of a segment of broadcasting – subject to the overall authority of the Director-General – a man (or woman) needs to have his own budget and authority to appoint his own staff.

(vi) The talents and experience needed in a man or woman to whom there could be entrusted overall charge, subject to the Director-General, of such a sensitive area, are so rare that one must ask in advance whether we have such a person available to us. On the news side we have such a man in John Crawley who incidentally is beginning to gain experience on the political side. But he is to retire before long : he has much other useful work to do in generally assisting the Director-General. In Ian Trethowan we have such a youngish man remarkably well equipped in both respects.

11 After weighing these considerations I would like to put forward a series of suggestions for consideration :

(i) That News and Current Affairs in television and radio, should be regarded as a discrete, coherent and self-contained segment under one senior executive directly responsible to the Director-General.

(ii) That included in this area would be News, *Panorama, 24 Hours* or its successor, *Nationwide, Talkback,* politically orientated documentaries, *Late Night Line Up, World at One, P.M., Analysis* and *Today.*

(iii) That this section or segment should be headed by a Managing Director to whom the Editor, News and Current Affairs would be responsible (under this or another title).

(iv) That this Managing Director, subject to the Director-General, would have comprehensive responsibility in his defined area, comparable to that of the other Managing Directors. Like them, he would have a separate budget. In programme planning and timing, he would agree with the other MDs, any failure to agree being resolved by the Director-General.

(v)   It would be for consideration whether these responsibilities should extend to overseas services. I should have thought not.

(vi) That Ian Trethowan should be invited to fill this post.

As soon as this paper had been written I showed it to Charles Curran who took it away to study, returning an hour later to say that it would not work, and giving a number of reasons for his view. It would mean, he said, that this segment of broadcasting would have its own budget and appoint its own staff. There would be an annual argument on the allocation of programme time and money between the managing directors of television and radio, with the director-general as arbiter, a role which he said he disliked. The lines of demarcation between this segment and the remainder of the output would be difficult to draw.

I thought over his arguments and, as they were mostly organizational in character, I decided, with his agreement, to consult McKinseys. I saw Roger Morrison of McKinseys who, though he made the same points, stressed an additional one – if an unwelcome scheme of reorganization was forced from above, it might well be frustrated in its operation. While he did not reject the plan with its radical solution, he suggested a study of an alternative which would leave the upper structure unchanged and strengthen it lower down by inserting a controller between the editor of news and current affairs and his news and current affairs subordinates. Further, the editor could be responsible directly to the director-general instead of to the managing director of television as at present.

I saw force in the arguments of both Curran and Roger Morrison to the extent that I decided to put Morrison's plan as an alternative to the radical plan. I told Curran of this, adding that I would send the revised document, including the alternative, to Morrison and that I would be glad if he would see Morrison on his own to argue the merits and demerits.

The next meeting of the governors was devoted almost wholly to my paper, to the first version of which I had added the alternative scheme, while still retaining the 'radical' plan. Most of the governors accepted that there was unease about news programmes, although the unease was felt less by the ordinary viewer and listener than by the establishment and the opinion makers. One governor thought everything in the garden was lovely, while another maintained that most of its blooms were terrible. Another said that the 'upward reference' system was not working in current affairs and he doubted whether it was appropriate for so sensitive an area. Most of the opinion makers he mixed with were pretty critical of BBC current affairs programmes.

When we came to remedies I invited the director-general to express his views on the first or radical scheme. He opposed it root and branch, giving mainly logistical reasons, such as difficulties in parcelling out the money and allocating the time. It was apparent that he regarded the notion of a managing director of news and current affairs as diminishing his own status and authority.

In the end the alternative scheme was approved, on the understanding that this decision did not preclude the later adoption of the radical scheme and that the whole matter be looked at again at the end of the year in the light of experience.

Diary 4 May
On the whole I am satisfied with the day's work, for the alternative scheme would never have been produced but for the dismay aroused by the radical scheme. The new scheme does, of course, place a very heavy responsibility on Desmond Taylor, editor of news and current affairs. In one part of the field he is excellent, and that is news : on the current affairs side, where the criteria are different, he is learning fast. Certainly he has the clarity of mind and the cold courage needed for decisive action.

29

The Last Lap

I had a little mid-summer fun with that most regular and frequent correspondent of mine, Mrs Whitehouse. The following is a copy of her letter to me dated 16 June 1972.

Dear Lord Hill,
    I understand that the new Rolling Stones' record, 'Exile on Main Street' is being played on Radio 1.
    This record uses four-letter words. Although they are somewhat blurred, there is no question about what they are meant to be.
    I feel sure you will understand the concern felt about this matter, for it is surely no function of the BBC to transmit language which, as shown in a recent court case, is still classed as obscene. The very fact that this programme is transmitted primarily for young people would, one would have thought, have demanded more, not less, care about what is transmitted.
    We would be grateful if you would look into this matter.
                                    Yours sincerely,
                                    (Mrs) Mary Whitehouse

I replied as follows on 20 June :

Dear Mrs Whitehouse,
    Thank you for your letter of June 16th in which you state that the tracks from the Rolling Stones record 'Exile on Main Street' played on Radio 1 use four-letter words.

I have this morning listened with great care to the tracks we have played on Radio 1. I have listened to them at a fast rate, at a medium rate, at a slow rate. Though my hearing is excellent, I did not hear any offending four-letter words whatever.

Could it be that, believing offending words to be there and zealous to discover them, you imagined that you heard what you did not hear?

Yours sincerely,
HILL OF LUTON

I liked the comment she made to the press on my reply. 'He must have got out of the wrong side of the bed.'

The next few months went unusually smoothly, with no major controversies or internal upheaval. For me, retirement was looming in sight. Strictly speaking the five years for which I had been appointed finished at the end of August, but Chataway had asked me to stay on until the end of November to cover the BBC's fiftieth anniversary celebrations. Later, John Eden, the new Minister of Posts and Telecommunications, asked me to complete the year. I accepted, at the same time making it clear that in no circumstances would I stay after the end of the year. By that time I should be within a fortnight of my sixty-ninth birthday.

A few diary entries during this peaceful phase speak for themselves:

1 June
Things are quiet, perhaps because politicians and press are heavily preoccupied with other events, mainly tragedies.

How often the BBC kicks into its own goal! The night before last there was a programme on the late Duke of Windsor, his kingship, his abdication and all that. Of course we must have A. J. P. Taylor with his predictably contemptuous attack on royalty. The others, Colin Coote, Lady Monckton and Bob Boothby were fair enough. I suppose Taylor's voice has to be heard, but to put it on three or four days after the duke's death and before his coffin had been brought back to this country for burial, was a certain and bad-mannered way of provoking distress in a considerable part of our popu-

lation. It is not enough to say that the BBC should put on
what it likes when it likes. It has to show a sense of responsibility as well as good taste.

12 June
Nothing of particular significance at the governors' meeting. More significant was the lunch that followed with John
Eden as guest. John Eden spoke fluently and well, concentrating his criticisms on what may be called the 'Bourne-
mouth' attitude to the BBC – sex, violence, the British
Empire, undermining establishment standards, and so on. A
fairly good discussion followed. I thought John Eden winced
when David Attenborough said that if the BBC did not give
offence it was not doing its job – one of those generalities that
needs to be elaborated to be understood.

Later in the day I called on Robert Carr. He asked me to
describe the type of experience that was needed for the chair
of the BBC. I said I thought that the chairman needed an
understanding of Westminster and Whitehall without necessarily having worked in either. He needed to give the job first
priority although the demands on his time were probably not
more than half the working week. For the rest, I thought it
was unwise to go into greater detail. The man should have
experience of the world and of organization and then develop
his own style. An overlap period was undesirable.

Only in the last six months have the governors, by their
composition and their attitude, begun really to assume their
proper responsibilities particularly as trustees for the public.
Recent appointments have made all the difference, as has the
disappearance of the last trace of adherents of the Greene
view that the governors were there merely to support what
the executive did or wanted to do.

In June there was a minor incident of some interest. After a
Sunday newspaper had published allegations affecting some
people who worked for the BBC, Curran had invited an outside lawyer to examine the evidence and report. When he mentioned the lawyer's report to the board I asked when it was
proposed to circulate it to governors. Curran said that the lawyer

had advised the most restricted of circulations and it was not proposed to show it to governors.

I reacted a little at this and said that the governors *were* the BBC, that the report had come to me but only that morning and I had not yet had an opportunity of reading it. A governor then suggested that when I had read the report I should decide what action should be taken. When I read the report it became perfectly clear that it had been intended by the lawyer for the governors and that the limitation of circulation which he had advised related to levels below the governors. Our own lawyer confirmed my interpretation. When I received the report I found it had been in the office a month and had already been seen by the director-general and three other executives.

The governors surprised me on one point, though they were probably right. When I asked why it had been necessary to interview the convicted spy, Harry Houghton, on his book of memoirs, I got little support from my colleagues. The test, said the director-general, was whether the item was important or interesting. For my part, I could not easily reconcile myself to an interview with a convicted spy on his memoirs and, incidentally, paying him in the process. But I suppose I am old-fashioned in such matters. We had an interesting discussion, too, about the *Listener*, some of us indulging in a little hypocrisy by praising the intellectual standards of some articles which we did not understand.

In the summer of 1972 we received the first two adjudications of the Programme Complaints Commission, both critical of the BBC. I was glad of these adjudications. When the Complaints Commission was established we were told by some that it was no more than a protective façade, by others that it was too restricted in its scope and by yet others that a body appointed by us could not possibly be independent.

Diary 13 July
Some people may greet the announcement of these adjudications as an opportunity for lambasting the BBC, an opportunity they would not have been given if we had not had the Complaints Commission. It is good that in the first adjudications the BBC is not whitewashed or found not guilty. It will

demonstrate what is the reality, that the Complaints Commission is genuinely independent, that there is a job to be done by it and, incidentally, will remind some of our own people that the Complaints Commission is a reality.

A tiny point arose. When the adjudications came to me today they were accompanied by a draft announcement to be published in next week's *Listener*, the day before the next governors' meeting, to the effect that the BBC has no comment to make at present. I have altered this to state that the adjudications will be reported to the governors. That it should be decided by them what action, if any, should be taken was part of the approved scheme and no one had any right to prejudge what the governors' view could be. I have no doubt that the governors will decide to accept the adjudications without comment, but that is a matter for them.

In August there was a complaint at the board meeting that, despite the promise months before that *The Money Programme* would be modified so as to include programmes on industrial relations, nothing had happened. There was rather a long history to this proposed programme. Tom Jackson had urged that the question of industrial relations should be tackled in a regular series. The executive resisted for some time and then said that changes in *The Money Programme* would be made. The theme of the criticism now was that the management, reluctant to make the changes when the suggestion was first made, was avoiding its obligations to make them. One governor said bluntly that the board rarely intervened in programme matters and it was, to say the least, imprudent to ignore the board's directive in this matter. The director-general was asked to convey the board's displeasure to those concerned. At the next board meeting, some new proposals were put forward by Huw Wheldon, based on the restyling of *The Money Programme* and its renaming as *Money at Work*. (The old title has now been restored.)

Then, in October, the board began the long task of formulating the BBC's views and policies to be expressed in evidence to any commission or committee on the future of broadcasting in this country. It was assumed that there would be such an en-

quiry in the next few months. If on the other hand there were
no enquiry, the discussions would still be useful in clearing
people's minds.

When the governors discussed their powers, the strength of
some of the views expressed surprised me. Tom Jackson, in his
fifth and last year on the board and as shrewd and able a governor as any in my time, put his views bluntly. He had always been
unhappy with a governor's role. The board was like the organ-
izer of a bus trip who staffed the bus and filled it with petrol but
had no control over its destination. He wanted a greater knowledge of programme plans in advance, a wish shared by a
number of other governors.

A new governor said that the governors were not seen to exercise the powers they had. To many of the staff, it seemed,
governors were purely decorative. If the staff did not think the
governors counted, how could the public be expected to do so?
As I listened to these views, I could not help comparing them to
those held by most of the board when I had joined it five years
before.

Later there was a discussion initiated by a member of the
board on the BBC's public image based, as he put it, on the
mounting number of attacks on the BBC, the references in the
press to the need for a strong man to discipline the BBC and the
critical feeling amongst the people he met. Ought not the BBC,
another asked, to be more open in meeting its critics and more
forthcoming when it met them as it had been, for instance, in
the case of the Festival of Light, so demonstrating that the top
layers of the BBC wore no horns?

Another view was that the BBC was sometimes too concerned
with its enemies and did not sufficiently nurture its friends, who
could wither for loss of cultivation. If one believed that the
decline of Parliament was one reason for hostility towards the
media, was this not a good reason for not saying so to parliamentarians who resented being reminded of what might or might
not be true?

George Campey, the BBC's remarkably efficient head of pub-
licity, gave it as his view that the real public standing of the
BBC was higher than might be deduced from the press. The
BBC had always been an Aunt Sally : indeed, criticism of it

was often a form of inverted respect. The very preoccupation of the other media with the BBC was a sign of the latter's strength. Blowing the BBC's trumpet too often could produce a back-fire. Were not a few of the BBC's worst enemies within the BBC, those who leaked to the press in criticism of the body to which they belonged? Leaks were a curse of the business but since they sprang from pique rather than greed they were difficult to check. Altogether it was a frank and useful occasion.

Another October topic was the recommendation of the Younger Committee on Privacy that the Complaints Commission should be empowered to consider complaints of invasion of privacy arising from material gathered for broadcasting but not actually broadcast. My first reaction was that this was a fair point which we should accept. Management, however, took a contrary view. There was enough pressure already by those who, having participated in a programme wanted, for one reason or another, to prevent its transmission. Eventually I accepted this view though I am not sure that I was right. Anyway, the board took the management's advice and rejected the proposal.

My diary reminds me that we were not alone in experiencing an occasional breeze of disapproval :

2 August
ITN scooped us last week by getting an interview in their news with the Prime Minister. Some people here thought that this was an implied rebuke for our having put Wilson on *World at One* a day or two ago. I could not help smiling when I congratulated Bert Aylestone on getting this scoop only to be told that it had led to a spot of trouble. In the last minute the interviewer had told the Prime Minister to hurry up as time was short! The ITN man was not popular! Oh, well, there are no medals in this business.

30

Exit with a Poem

I was now in my last few months, after an innings of over five years, and my mind began turning to some problems I hoped to see resolved before departing from Broadcasting House.

One was a matter about which the board and the director-general seemed to be agreed but about which nothing had yet been done : the transfer of the headquarters of the BBC from Broadcasting House to Television Centre. The opening of the central extension of Westway had brought Television Centre within a ten- or twelve-minute journey of Broadcasting House. It was television rather than radio which provided most of the problems which came to the director-general's desk and the board's agenda.

The director-general tended to be regarded as an honoured and infrequent visitor to the Centre, and to Lime Grove nearby, missing the easy, informal personal contacts with staff which walking the corridors and travelling in the lifts would have made possible. Bosses down the corridor are much more often consulted than those who are four miles away. For some time it had been thought by many, including Curran and myself, that it would make sense for the director-general and his immediate advisers to be permanently installed in the Centre, and I invited the governors, with Curran's agreement, to decide on this translation in principle, recognizing that for physical reasons it would be some time before the changeover took place. They did so decide.

The other problem was Curran's indecision, his preference of words to action. For some time the governors had felt that to get the best from his intellectual vitality and range, he needed at his elbow a chief of staff who would help him to speed up the process of decision and action, so encouraging, on the occasions it was necessary, a more authoritative approach. In this way, the director-general would be strengthened, his burden lightened and the fullest benefit of his extraordinary talent achieved.

After a great deal of discussion and the examination of a number of alternatives, including the appointment of a deputy director-general, the governors decided, in agreement with Curran, to create a new post of chief secretary and to appoint to it a man in whose abilities and strength they had the fullest confidence. Colin Shaw, the Corporation's secretary, was appointed, which gave me immense satisfaction, for Colin and I had worked closely together for some two years and I had learned from first-hand experience what a remarkable man he is.

In November came the event of the year, the celebration of the BBC's fiftieth birthday. There was the visit of Her Majesty the Queen and Prince Philip, the Guildhall Banquet with the Prime Minister as principal guest, the dinner given by the Lord Mayor of Birmingham, parties both in London and outside it. All were a great success.

At the Guildhall, the Prime Minister was generous and relaxed in proposing the toast of the Corporation. In my reply I asserted in unmistakable terms the value to our country of maintaining unimpaired the independence of the Corporation and, at the same time, contested a view on the BBC's role in broadcasting which I believed the Prime Minister to share:

I have heard it asserted that our proper role – the role of the BBC – should be to cater only for minorities. Be serious, cultural – and dull. Leave the big battalions, it is said, to those who know how to cater for them. The commercial services – the argument goes on – know how to bring them in and send them rolling in their armchairs. Let them take over entertainment and sport and the rest. It is not an argument which finds favour with me – nor, I suspect, would it find favour with viewers and listeners.

. . . There have from time to time been attempts to con-

I

test the independence of the BBC. These attempts have been resisted – and the press have been as equally vigilant about the BBC's independence as they have been about their own.

I trust that we – and the country – will continue to resist such pressures. Independence implies an act of trust on behalf of the country and a sense of responsibility on the part of the BBC.

As an act of trust, we put great freedom in the hands of the creative men and women who work within the BBC, men and women who bring to us ideas, imagination and professional skills. Inevitably there are risks in this. Experiments may misfire and judgements may err, bricks or even clangers may drop. But the gains in such a system of intellectual freedom far outweigh the losses.

. . . Much of what we do reflects older values, old certainties, and so reassures. But to give only reassurance in times such as these would be to ignore realities which, sooner or later, would find a way of breaking in upon the audience. A broadcasting service which does not match its audience's experience of life all too rapidly loses the trust of that audience. So I cannot accept that in the next fifty years, the BBC will become much easier to live with than it is now.

. . . We have had messages of congratulation and birthday greetings from broadcasting organizations all over the world. That was to be expected. But what is immensely significant is the underlying theme of these messages – the underlying plea to us which I can summarize in a few words. 'We envy your independence and admire your achievements. Hang on to that independence for our sakes as well as your own.'

In December came my farewells. The first came in the form of a letter of thanks and good wishes signed by all the managers of local radio stations, with a covering letter from Ian Trethowan, concluding with the words, 'They are well aware that but for your own efforts in the winter of 1970/71, BBC Local Radio might no longer exist.'

On 13 December the governors gave their customary valedictory dinner at which, in the absence of Lady Plowden abroad, Henry Dunleath, who joined the board on the day that I did, gave a pleasant and generous speech and Charles Curran supported him in a neat little offering. At the end of the dinner, Roy Fuller, Oxford's Professor of Poetry who had proved so admirable a governor, stood up, unannounced, and to everyone's surprise recited a poem which he had specially written for the occasion. I was as moved as I was astonished. He has given me permission to reproduce it in full :

THE CCC

Dedicated to the Lord Hill of Luton on his retirement
as Chairman of the BBC, December 1972

The year is 1976 :
By a strange quirk of politics
Peace reigns in Westminster; the nation
Is ruled by a joint administration.
The crises of the times were such
That Ted and Harold got in touch;
And even Thorpe and Enoch Powell
Sat sunken cheek by lantern jowl.
The Government, thus broadly based,
Finally fair and squarely faced
A problem that seemed everlasting –
The future nature of broadcasting.
To make that future truly blighted
Two Ministers, Eden and Phillip Whitehead,
Decided there was going to be
One broadcasting authority
Embracing in some mysterious way
Both BBC and IBA.
The name of this amalgamation
Was the Cash Culture Corporation.
(Perhaps those dreaming up the plan
Were thinking of the Ku Klux Klan.)

Who was to be executive head ?
A bastard body, someone said,
Needs ruling by a bastard; so
At once Charles Curran had to go.

Nor would it do, 'twas clearly seen,
Even to bring back Carleton Greene.
Short-listed were the tough or haughty :
Clive Jenkins, Aubrey Jones and Forte.

For TV to aim for excellence
Wouldn't have made any sort of sense;
And Huw had to put his natural gas
To selling encyclopædias.
Trethowan's dismissal was delayed :
Politically he was OK'd,
Yet speaking up for Radio 3
Finished him for the CCC.
Thus through the serried ranks did sweep
The axe; and Lambs were changed for sheep.

A question that couldn't be ignored
Was the selection of the Board.
Quickly discarded were the claims
Of Auntie's gubernatorial names :
Mere ciphers once, they'd grown more vital
And actually changed a programme's title.
One Governor with indecent speed
Sank to delivering mail in Leeds.
Found guilty of composing verse,
Another's fate was even worse.
There was a momentary reprieve
For gallant Ulsterman, Dunleath :
Then 'twas disclosed he played the organ.
Some thought of keeping Tony Morgan :
His expertise with stinking waste
Might suit the new corporation's taste.
He lasted till seen coming out
From some subversive Round House rout.

The hardest task was to secure
A Chairman likely to make sure
The dubious machine would work.
All the old names came up – Sir Burke,

Toby and Blessèd Arnold – but
Some had employment, some lacked guts.
(The BBC's Chairman of the day –
Whose startling name I need not say –
Had been kidnapped in '73
By the Welsh Language Society;
Since when there had been little news,
Even from Dr Tegai Hughes.)
Then Downing Street saw that one man
Might well bring off its cunning plan.
He in the past ('twas very odd)
Had served first Mammon and then God
In this same field of broadcasting,
Yet managed to advance the thing.
And prior to that he did not shirk
Making the nation's bowels work.
And so a group of anxious men
Trek to a pub in Harpenden
And with the great man plead and beg
Over some pints of Watney's Keg.
They urged him to become a martyr,
Dangled the ribbon of the Garter,
Said, once returned to public life,
He needn't make breakfast for his wife.

'Go back into the world of telly?'
Our hero growled. 'Not on your nellie.
Compared with smoothing over, say,
The ruffled Men of Yesterday
It was a life of perfect heaven
Trying to smooth Aneurin Bevan.
I've done my duty in that trade :
I watched the programmes of Lew Grade;
I sat with Bakewell through the night;
I met the Festival of Light;
Heard about frequencies from Redmond
And read the judgements of Sir Edmund;
Suffered Frost's playing to the gallery
And dealt with a notorious salary.'

He paused and with his usual calm
Rested his hand on Eden's arm
And gently shook his snowy tuft
And said 'In other words, get stuffed.'

So, as the glum-faced delegation
Shivered on some Hertford station,
It was agreed the CCC
Without our hero could not be.
In consequence, the IBA
Was left to go its curious way
And the Beeb's charter was renewed;
Alf Garnett continued to be rude;
Governors with dictionaries went
On puzzling what *The Listener* meant;
George Howard dined the office cleaners;
Ken Russell made a film called – 'Venus';
Ambitious men intrigued and stabbed;
And others wrote and spoke and blabbed.
In short, that mighty heart was still
Beating from Bush to Pebble Mill :
The heart its wise physician came
To love – for whom heart felt the same.

At the conclusion of the board meeting the following morning Henry Dunleath did an even better job than at the dinner
when he staggered in with a case of claret, the governors' personal parting gift. Tom Jackson made a kindly little speech and
hands were shaken. The Board of Management gave a farewell
cocktail party, to which they kindly invited those of the executives who had been closest to me over the years. Generous letters
came in from the Minister, from governors and from executives.
Colin Shaw, my adviser and friend over two years, gave me a
book with an inscription I shall always cherish, 'In gratitude
and with affection'.

The next morning, the 14th, the name of my successor, Sir
Michael Swann, was announced. I regard him as an excellent
choice. Courageous as well as determined, he gave a press conference on the day of his appointment and subsequently ap-

peared on *Midweek*. He took some terrifying risks for, in BBC circles, an incautious sentence can dog its author for a long, long time. But he did not supply any hostages to fortune. Curran was delighted at the choice.

On the last day of the year, I gave a party which in previous years I had given just before Christmas, to those of the staff – personal assistants, secretaries, programme correspondence and duty office staff, my admirable chauffeur, Geoff Carpenter, the two helpful and thoughtful head waitresses, Mrs Smith and Mrs Reynolds, Mr Tomlinson, the kindly major-domo of Broadcasting House, and others – who contributed so much to my work and comfort over the years. Finally, just before I departed for home, a few special friends, John Crawley, George Campey, Desmond Taylor, Colin Shaw, Hazel Fenton and Roland Fox, by an artful device, inveigled my wife and myself to Desmond's office to give us a really final drink and to present me with a bottle of malt whisky, encased in a box on which was plastered a selection of the liveliest press comments on my appointment. Then they came to the door of Broadcasting House where Mrs Fenton's assistants, Linda and Lesley, were also waiting to wave us a final farewell. Fortified, and a little touched by this unexpected ceremony, away we sped for home.

31

Retrospect

When, at the age of fifty-eight, I left the Macmillan government I assumed that, after the next general election when I
should not be standing, my public life would be over and that,
with reasonable luck, the rest of my working days would be
spent in interesting work, away from the public gaze. I had
been in the heat of the kitchen for a long time. Membership of
the boards of Laportes and of the Abbey National Building
Society, and the independent chairmanship of a Whitley Council, were an excellent beginning.

Then, unexpectedly, came the chair of the ITA and a life
peerage, followed even more unexpectedly by the chair of the
governors of the BBC – nearly ten years' work in all. I have
recorded my main personal impressions of the events of these
lively years – aided in the BBC phase by a diary – without pre-
tending that I alone was responsible for those events. The years
at the ITA were more serene than those at the BBC if only
because the former was supervising and transmitting television
and employing 800 people, while the BBC was programme-
making in radio, television and radio overseas and employing
some 25,000 people.

When I arrived at Brompton Road, Independent Television
was still reeling from the Pilkington blows. It had just begun to
recover its pride in itself, to rebuild its morale and to consider
what should be done to ensure that never again would it be so
misunderstood, indeed so maligned. For all its faults, it was far
better than Pilkington had asserted and its successes needed to

be made more evident to the public. The Authority had to be clearly seen for what it was, a body which was distinct from the programme companies and which because of its different role would from time to time be at odds with the companies. Some, though by no means all, principals and executives of companies needed jolting into a more serious attitude and a fresh awareness of their responsibilities as people in broadcasting. Not least, the Authority needed to exercise the powers imposed on it by the Act, and to be seen to be doing it.

The Authority tackled these problems in the ways which I have described. The necessary decisions were reached by the Authority as a whole. If ever I was a 'strong chairman' – as is sometimes asserted – it was not in seeking to impose my own views but in striving to get decisions reached when decisions were necessary.

There is, however, one charge to which I plead guilty. I did strive during my four years in the chair to strengthen the role of the Authority. I believed that it should fulfil the responsibilities and exercise the powers conferred on it by law, even if it meant invading somewhat the area of responsibility which over the years – following the precedent of the BBC – had been assumed by the director-general. And, as I later discovered, the news of this invasion was wafted along to Broadcasting House and Hugh Greene.

Looking back over my time at the BBC I think I reacted too vigorously and for too long to the early hostility. After all, a feeling of resentment (if not what Greene called 'a sense of outrage') was natural and inevitable. Lusty, acting chairman since Lord Normanbrook's death, no doubt had the kindest intentions in offering to mediate between Greene and me and to take the chair at my first meeting so that he could show me how 'they did things at the BBC'. If I had consulted him more during the five months we were together on the board before his retirement I might have been spared some of the remarks he has made since about my style of chairmanship.

For years I had greatly admired Greene's achievements and, from what I knew of him, I believed we could work well together, once the temperature had fallen. Indeed, I thought we had worked well together when I read the final paragraph of his letter of resignation from the office of director-general, 'I should like to say how much I have come to enjoy our personal association in recent months. I think, if I may say so, that the BBC is in good hands, both at Board level and at Board of Management level.'

No less important to me in my early years at Portland Place was the attitude of some governors, who had become accustomed to the domination of Greene and accepted it as the way of BBC life. If I had any idea of strengthening the role of the governors at this stage it soon became obvious that I should not carry the whole board with me. Three years later, the position changed.

I became convinced that it was necessary to strengthen the role of the governors, particularly in their capacity as trustees of the public. In law, the governors are the BBC, but this does not and should not mean that governors should pose as professionals and intervene in the skilled work of programme-making. They were amateurs representing a public of amateurs, the public at large. They should deal with policies and principles and overall finance and not become involved in detailed decisions which only professionals can make. They should make the senior appointments. They were not managers. These were the basic principles which I accepted and within which I believed the governors should work. But they were not operating in the BBC as I found it.

History was largely responsible. The first governors of the BBC found already installed in office that remarkable and dominant character, John Reith, who, as he put it, always functioned best when decision rested solely with him. Reith clashed with his first chairman, Lord Clarendon, and openly rejoiced at his departure. Whitley, who followed Clarendon, was a man who accepted the dominance of Reith. When asked by Reith to define the functions of the governors, Whitley included in his document some words devised by Reith, saying of the governors that 'with the director-general, they discuss and decide upon major matters of policy and finance, but they leave the execution of that policy in all its branches to the director-general'.

Then came Lord Simon of Wythenshawe, who challenged the Whitley definition of the governors' functions. He said that 'in conjunction with Reith's overpowering personality and prestige, its effect has been to confine the activities of the Governors (other than the Chairman) to reading papers and attending board meetings' and that 'no other chief official of any public concern has the "de facto" power comparable to that of the Director-General of the BBC'. The Beveridge Committee, to whom Simon put his arguments, modified the Whitley doctrine, maintaining that the governors' function resembled that of a minister, 'that is, bringing outside opinion to bear upon all the activities of the permanent staff, causing change where change is necessary, and preventing broadcasting from falling in any way into the hands of a bureaucracy which is not controlled'.

Of Sir Arthur ffordes' view of the role of governors, I have no direct knowledge for, to the best of my recollection, I met him but twice, once when I was a minister and once when I paid a courtesy call on him by appointment, soon after I went to Brompton Road. Incidentally, he kept me waiting for twenty minutes and, when I was admitted to his office, seemed astonished that I should have called.

Then came Lord Normanbrook's comprehensive definition of the functions of the governors in which he stated that 'within the BBC the ultimate level of decision, even executive decision on matters of first importance, lies in the Board of Governors, or, in a matter of urgency, the Chairman acting under the authority delegated to him by the Board'. Lord Normanbrook and I (as chairman of ITA) began to meet privately together every other month and the subject of the functions of the governors and of the Authority frequently arose. It was in these candid talks that I got the clear impression that he was less than satisfied with the control which was, in reality, being exercised by the board.

I unhesitatingly accepted the Normanbrook definition of the board's role, stemming as it did from the Beveridge recommendation. But my predecessor had found, when he had exercised his authority in 1965 by deciding that an invitation to Mr Ian Smith to appear on a programme should not be renewed, that the reaction to his decision both inside and outside the BBC was critical. It was, for example, argued against him in one of the weeklies that his actions would disturb the understanding necessary for maintaining morale, 'that the Director-General is in command, showing a sensitivity to the mood of the Governors but independent of them, in the view of BBC staff'. To these critics the Whitley doctrine still prevailed as if Beveridge had never happened. Lord Normanbrook's comment was crisp : 'I am not concerned to argue whether that decision was wrong. I am only concerned with my right to make it.'

I accepted the Normanbrook, not the Whitley theme or the 'director-general in command' interpretation of it. The ultimate responsibility for what the BBC does rests on the Board of Governors, in fact as in law, just as the ultimate responsibility for what a government department does rests on ministerial shoulders. The minister is the amateur and his department consists of professionals. So within the BBC. It is the mode of applying this principle which presents the real problems, not the basic principle itself. The governors represent the outside world to a complex organization of professionals.

Broadcasting is something quite different from building houses or roads or schools or mining coal or transmitting electricity. It demands not only a wide range of professional skills but a capacity for instant decision and an atmosphere of intellectual freedom. None of this need be inconsistent with the fact that the governors are the ultimate authority. They are the trustees for the national interest, taking, as Lord Normanbrook put it, 'the final decisions on all major matters of management and on all matters of controversy which may arouse strong feeling in Parliament or among large sections of public opinion'.

In my first two years there was but marginal strengthening of the role of the governors, because only a minority of governors wanted it. The Reith tradition of the board's unimportance had lasted too long and, although my predecessor had redefined the functions in terms which I wholly accepted, redefinition was one thing and application was another. Only when the composition of the board changed was substantial progress really possible.

But the objectives were clear. The board should decide the larger issues of policy and finance, management questions coming to it when the director-general sought the board's view. The board should make the senior appointments – perhaps its most important function – and approve the command structure at its higher levels. It should be generally responsible for major exchanges with government and outside bodies. It should not intervene in the programme-making process or, save in exceptional circumstances, see or hear programmes before transmission. It should be kept informed of proposed major programme policy developments, of major expressions of public and political opinion and of the advice of advisory bodies. Before reaching decisions within its scope, the board should give the director-general and any senior colleagues he may select opportunity to put views fully and frankly. Once decisions are reached, the responsibility of their translation into action rests on the director-general.

The argument that unless the director-general is seen to be the commander-in-chief it is difficult for him to enjoy the loyalty of the staff is plausible but not wholly convincing. I do not believe that the assumption by the Board of Governors of its proper responsibilities, as Normanbrook defined them, involves an improper invasion of the scope of the director-general, or damages his image as a commanding figure in the organization. These things depend on him, on his personality, his leadership and his capacity. He participates in all the board's discussions, offering any advice he wishes, and no board would fail to give the fullest weight to his views. Indeed, in most cases his views are likely to be accepted. Whether or not they are accepted, it will be his responsibility to see the board's decisions carried out. There are vast areas of management and programme-making which belong wholly to him as chief officer and editor-in-chief. Both the influence and the power of an able chief executive are immense, as the permanent secretary of every government department – and every minister – knows.

When I was chief officer in the British Medical Association, I did not lose in standing or satisfaction in my job because my masters made the main policy decisions. Nor was my permanent secretary at the Ministry of Housing in any way inhibited because the main policy decisions were made by ministers. The system works well elsewhere and I see no reason why in an appropriate form it should not work at the BBC.

There is a significant problem but it is of a different kind. Can a governing body which is responsible for overall policy, finance, senior appointments and the like be, at one and the same time, representative of the public? Is not conflict between the two roles inevitable? Is it not necessary for those who are to be successful trustees for the public to stand back from the controlling role, or, better still, be entirely separate from the body controlling the broadcasting service?

This argument is used both by those who would keep the board in a purely decorative advisory role and by those who argue for an external viewers' council. To the advocates of an advisory role I reply that the argument would be valid only if the board, despite its amateur status, intervened in the professional day-to-day work of making programmes. My reply to advocates of a viewers' council is this: to separate those who criticize from those who bear responsibility is to create other and more formidable problems.

Linked with the issue of the functions of the board is that of the relationship between the chairman of the board and the director-general. I went to the BBC with a reputation as an 'interventionist' chairman who had diminished the role of the director-general at the ITA. If that means that I sought a strengthening of the authority of the ITA, even at the expense of some diminution in responsibilities of its chief officer, then that reputation was justified.

Similarly, if it is interventionist to work for a more powerful (or to be more accurate less impotent) Board of Governors, then an interventionist chairman I was at Portland Place. But if the adjective 'interventionist' is taken to mean that I assumed some of the management responsibilities of the director-general, the word does not fit the facts.

I was an active chairman. Providence did not construct me for a decorative role and I do not fit easily into the role of stooge. I like to know what is going on in any organization with which I am associated even in a non-executive role and to know personally the people who run it. I confess I worked hard. For most of my time in the chair, I was an active chairman of a chemical company and a director of a building society. I set aside four mornings a week for BBC work, staying on in the afternoon when other duties allowed and the work load required it. I read all the letters addressed to me by name : to some I drafted replies though to most I replied on the basis of drafts prepared within the organization. I saw the director-general every morning on which we were both in the office and the secretary at least once a day. Both men raised any points they liked with me and I often had a point on which I sought their advice.

With the director-general's general agreement I sometimes saw other senior executives, often at his request – for example, the director of personnel on some important problem in his discussions with the unions, the head of publicity on, say, a controversy raging in the press, a managing director on some policy point which was troubling him or me.

Then there were fortnightly board meetings, committee meetings, an occasional visitor or deputation. I went around the country a good deal visiting centres in Glasgow, Cardiff, Belfast, Newcastle, Leeds and Bristol, as well as in London, meeting all the staff who were available. I visited every one of the twenty local radio stations. I attended meetings of National Broadcasting Councils, meetings of chairmen of Regional Committees and, of course, meetings of the General Advisory Council. There was much to see and there were many to meet.

What I did not do, and could not have done, was to intervene in management, although management questions were sometimes put to me. The commonest phrases I used at my daily meetings with Curran were 'That's your business' and 'That's management, decide it yourself'. Our relations were friendly and frank and we both enjoyed our daily exchanges.

I urged him again and again to be more visible, to give more speeches of general interest, to establish closer personal relations with some ministers – something he did most effectively. Those ministers who saw him frequently, like Fred Peart and Willie Whitelaw, both liked and admired him. I asked Mr Wilson to see him privately and he did; I asked Mr Heath to do the same, and he did not. Curran had been brilliant in the back room and he had now to be seen more and more in the front room, something which, like other intellectuals, he did not find easy. Indeed he did not find the exercise of authority or the making of decisions easy. I know that he felt that the simplicity of my name and the publicity to which over the years I had been exposed, made his emergence as an authoritative figure more difficult. Only the passage of time can demonstrate whether in this view he was right. I do not think he was.

One of the curses of our time is the custom in the press of taking in each other's washing. A carelessly inaccurate label is lightly attached to an event or a man and there it stays. My modest bedroom and bathroom were a penthouse, according to a pressman who had never seen them, and that they remained. I was an executive chairman and that I had to remain, whatever the facts. Hill had done this and not done that, whereas it was the Board of Governors who had reached the decision – or the director-general – without any initiative of mine. Many a time I read in the press of something Hill had done or ordered or refused to do, when in fact the first I heard anything of the matter was in the press.

I do not believe I am a dominant or domineering chairman. At the BBC as at the ITA I rarely opened a discussion with an expression of my views. I voted infrequently and I never used a second or casting vote. I saw my job as that of a referee whose responsibility it was to see that everyone had his or her say and, whenever possible, to secure a decision when a decision was needed.

My shortcomings were of a different kind. In my early days, I tended to invite the board to decide by vote too often because it seemed that an over-reliance on the consensus method made it possible for a minority to frustrate a majority. I was slow to realize that ex-politicians are apt to be automatically regarded as tough, astute, worldly wise, even cunning. Occasionally I was brusque at the end of long and tiring meetings. I was reluctant to decide matters on behalf of the board, between meetings, preferring to consult my colleagues on matters I was authorized to decide between meetings.

They were fascinating and exciting years at the BBC. I did not need reminding that the independence of the BBC was its most precious asset, that its output had no equal anywhere else in the world. I found it as natural as it was necessary to work to preserve its independence at all costs.

As a former politician, I had learned a wrinkle or two and I thought I understood the techniques of political pressures and the ways to counter them. I believed that a sufficiency of income was something more than a means of meeting the costs of good programmes and that, because the size of the licence fee was determined by governments, it was in itself a factor in maintaining the intellectual freedom of writers and producers and sustaining the Corporation's independence.

I was soon to learn, by direct experience, of the amazing range and quality of talents to be found in the BBC's ranks, of the high standard of managerial efficiency and, above all, its belief in public service as a basis of broadcasting. I enjoyed immensely the association with some really remarkable men and women, so varied and so versatile – and so articulate. Charles Curran's wide intellectual range, Huw Wheldon's boisterous and creative vigour and captivating eloquence, Ian Trethowan's logical mind and strength of leadership, David Attenborough's personal charm and phenomenal versatility, Howard Newby's strength of mind and character so modestly concealed, Jimmy Redmond's confidence and competence, and Maurice Tinniswood's mixture of steely determination and negotiating skill. These are but some of the impressions I retain.

Frank Gillard, John Crawley, George Campey and Desmond Taylor have a special place in my memory as able, forthright and understanding friends, so candid in their advice to me and so stalwart when the heat was greatest. Tony Whitby and Colin Shaw gave me sustained help and unfailing loyalty as secretaries of the Corporation. So I could go on to praise and thank others like Paul Fox, Robin Scott and Douglas Muggeridge, all of them first-class men, and many others, including that remarkable woman whom I admired from afar, for our paths rarely crossed, Joanna Spicer.

Of the governors during my stint in the chair, the successive vice-chairmen, John Fulton and Bridget Plowden, stand out in my memory, in their completely different ways, for the strength they gave to the board and the advice, the loyalty and the friendship they gave to me. John Fulton brought to the board discussions, as to our private talks, a deep understanding of the philosophy of public service broadcasting, a quick and penetrating mind, and an unusual willingness to listen to views he could not accept. Bridget Plowden brought, not only her experience over a wide field of human affairs, including education, but a charm of personality associated with a courage and candour of utterance which stimulated without offending. She knew her mind and spoke it. I cannot praise too highly the value of her advice to me, not least in the many tough spots in which we found ourselves.

Then there was Tom Jackson, shrewd, wise and remarkably well-informed, who can carry even heavier responsibilities than those which have yet come his way; Molly Green, a great team-worker, keen, articulate and an inveterate traveller to BBC out-posts; Henry Dunleath, gaily stimulating, intensely musical, with a love of the sparkling phrase to present a serious point; Glanmor Williams, courteous, thoughtful, utterly devoted to the BBC (and who never quite accepted me); Ralph Murray, steely-minded, devastatingly logical yet never minding when his logic did not prevail; Robert Bellinger, direct, straight, never hesitating to make his point, however unpopular; Paul Wilson, with his silent commonsense; Bobby Allen, calm, cogent and sparing of words; Roy Fuller, lawyer and poet, ideally equipped for governorship by practical experience and cultural interests; George Howard, with questing mind and a thirst for detail; Tony Morgan, the whiz-kid who sought to understand the young and trendy; Tegai Hughes, who would rather lose an argument than sacrifice a principle; and Janet Avonside, a bonny fighter for Scotland, who did not always realize when she had won.

If my years at the BBC had their troubles, the years ahead will be no less troubled, for a troubled country means a troubled BBC. The last five years have brought vast changes in the mood of our country, even the awakening of a new kind of society. Gone are the days of a serene and settled mood and a wide area of consensus in our national life. Authority is challenged and not only by students. Unions are more militant. In the larger organizations there is a widespread demand from below for more and more participation in the making of decisions. The division between the generations is deeper and the division in attitudes towards religion, ethics, aesthetics and sex more apparent. There is public disenchantment with politics and politicians, with broadcasters being constantly blamed for the disenchantment.

A BBC which has to do its work in such a disturbed, uncertain and divided society, expressing its many moods and providing a platform for its many contenders, is on a 'hiding to nothing'. It just cannot win for it is too inviting a national target. It can only please some by offending others. But if it is to retain its credibility it must reflect the real troubles and divisions of the world around it, so becoming the messenger who is blamed for the message. In a world of such conflict, the BBC is on the rack. My trials, I suspect, have been small compared with those which await my successors.

Now for half-retirement, with the building society movement and the deputy chairmanship of Abbey National as my main interest, with more frequent attendance at the House of Lords and with other and less demanding activities (like fishing) to fill in the gaps. Many men fear the retirement for which they have not prepared themselves, for many are the frightening tales told them of active men unready for retirement and unaccustomed to unimportance who have slithered into a vegetable existence and an early grave. 'Keep working' is the text of these gloomy prophets. I hope, when full retirement comes, to prove these prophets wrong. It is surely possible and pleasant to do damn-all in one's dotage with dignity and delight and, given the chance, I propose to try.

Index